Arthur Holmes, Charles Bigg

Catena Classicorum

Arthur Holmes, Charles Bigg

Catena Classicorum

ISBN/EAN: 9783741180583

Manufactured in Europe, USA, Canada, Australia, Japa

Cover: Foto ©Andreas Hilbeck / pixelio.de

Manufactured and distributed by brebook publishing software (www.brebook.com)

Arthur Holmes, Charles Bigg

Catena Classicorum

CATENA CLASSICORUM

EDITED BY

THE REV.
ARTHUR HOLMES M.A.
FELLOW AND LECTURER OF CLARE COLLEGE CAMBRIDGE
CLASSICAL LECTURER OF ST. JOHN'S COLLEGE AND OF EMMANUEL

AND

THE REV.
CHARLES BIGG M.A.
LATE SENIOR STUDENT AND TUTOR OF CHRIST CHURCH OXFORD
SECOND CLASSICAL MASTER OF CHELTENHAM COLLEGE

RIVINGTONS
 ... ... *Waterloo Place*
 ... ... *High Street*
 ... ... *Trinity Street*

DEMOSTHENIS
ORATIONES PUBLICAE

EDITED BY

G. H. HESLOP M.A.

LATE FELLOW AND ASSISTANT TUTOR OF QUEEN'S COLLEGE OXFORD
HEAD MASTER OF ST. BEES

THE PHILIPPICS

RIVINGTONS
London, Oxford, and Cambridge
1868

PREFACE.

As the plan of this edition seems sufficiently indicated by the general character of the series of which it forms a part, a few words of explanation will suffice by way of preface. To the three genuine speeches of Demosthenes contained in this Part of Vol. I. the Fourth Philippic has been added for the sake of completeness, and in compliance with the example set by many editors. The text is that of Bekker's stereotyped edition, published in 1854 by B. Tauchnitz, which has been implicitly followed, except in some few instances where reasons have been assigned for the changes made. In other speeches, where matter purely critical will be more in place than in the present volume, it will probably be necessary to depart from Bekker's text more frequently, as I cannot but think that his deference to the unsupported authority of MS. S has been carried to an extent which seriously impairs the value of his last recension. In the mean time changes of the text have been sparingly made, and the readings of the best MSS. and conjectures of critics noticed only where they were likely to be interesting.

It only remains for me to acknowledge my obligations to the editions of Sauppe, Westermann, Franke, and Redhautz, which I have had before me throughout; and especially to Mr. Shilleto's edition of the *De Falsâ Legatione*. The numerous references in the notes will suffice to show how much this edition owes to that admirable work. The abbreviations used in referring to Grammars and Editions are not likely to present any difficulty. It is only necessary to say, that by 'Bekk. st.' is meant Bekker's stereotyped edition; and by 'Bekker,' the edition of 1824 contained in Bekker's 'Oratores Attici.'

March, 1868.

ΔΗΜΟΣΘΕΝΟΥΣ

ΚΑΤΑ ΦΙΛΙΠΠΟΥ Α.

ΥΠΟΘΕΣΙΣ. Κακῶς ἐν τῷ πολέμῳ τῷ πρὸς Φίλιππον οἱ Ἀθηναῖοι φερόμενοι συνεληλύθασιν εἰς ἐκκλησίαν ἀθυμοῦντες. ὁ τοίνυν ῥήτωρ τὴν τε ἀθυμίαν πειρᾶται παύειν, λέγων οὐδὲν εἶναι θαυμαστὸν εἰ ῥᾳθυμοῦντες κεκράτηνται, καὶ εἰσηγεῖται πῶς ἂν ἄριστα τῷ πολέμῳ προσενεχθεῖεν. κελεύει δὲ δύο δυνάμεις παρασκευάσασθαι, μίαν μὲν μείζω, πολιτικήν, ἥτις οἴκοι μένουσα πρὸς τὰς κατὰ καιρὸν χρείας ἕτοιμος ὑπάρξει, ἑτέραν δὲ ἐλάττω, ξένων ὄντων τῶν στρατευομένων, παραμεμιγμένων δὲ (πολιτῶν). ταύτην κελεύει τὴν δύναμιν μὴ Ἀθήνησι μένειν μηδὲ ἐκ τῆς πόλεως ποιεῖσθαι τὰς βοηθείας, ἀλλὰ περὶ τὴν Μακεδονίαν ἀναστρέφεσθαι πολεμοῦσαν ἀδιαλείπτως, ἵνα μὴ τοὺς ἐτησίας πνέοντας ἐπιτηρήσας ὁ Φίλιππος ἢ καὶ τὸν χειμῶνα, ἡνίκα Ἀθήνηθεν εἰς Μακεδονίαν πλεῖν οὐ δυνατόν, ἐπιχειρῇ τοῖς πράγμασι καὶ παρὰ τὴν ἀπουσίαν τὴν τῶν Ἀθηναίων ἁπάντων κρατῇ, ἀλλ' ἐγγὺς ἡ πρὸς αὐτὸν ἀντιταξομένη δύναμις ὑπάρχῃ.

1. Εἰ μὲν περὶ καινοῦ τινὸς πράγματος προυτίθετο, ὦ ἄνδρες Ἀθηναῖοι, λέγειν, ἐπισχὼν ἂν ἕως οἱ πλεῖστοι τῶν

ARGUMENT.—ἐν τῷ π.] i. e. the war about Amphipolis. Their losses in the war are given in l. 9, &c.

ἀθυμοῦντες] Cf. § 2.

After παραμεμιγμένων δὶ Bekk. st. has πολιτῶν in brackets. Dind. reads παραμεμιγμένων δὲ καὶ πολιτῶν, and omits καὶ ταύτην and τὴν δύναμιν.

τὰς βοηθείας] Cf. § 32, where βοηθείαις, "militibus subitariis," are opposed to παρασκευῇ συνεχεῖ.

τοὺς ἐτησίας] These were northwest winds, which blew every year about the dog-days (Arist. *Probl.* 26. 2, οἱ μὲν ἐτησίαι βορέαι καθεστηκότες τοῦ ἀέρος πνέουσι (θέρους γὰρ πνέουσι), οἱ δὲ νότοι ἦρος), breaking the heat of the summer (Sen.

Quaest. Nat. 8. 10, " Etesiarum flatus aestatem frangit "). Philip availed himself of them, as they were strong enough to prevent the Athenians from sailing to the north. 4. 31.

τὸν χειμῶνα] § 31.

παρὰ] "through," § 11. For an analysis of the speech, see Grote, 11. 434. Thirl. 5. 297.

§ 1. προυτίθετο] Isocr. 8. 15 has the fuller expression παρεληλύθα γὰρ ... ἀποφανούμενος ἃ τυγχάνω γιγνώσκων ... περὶ ὧν οἱ πρυτάνεις προτιθέασι. Cf. Schöm. *Ass. of the Ath.* c. 11. But the people and the city are also said προτιθέναι λόγον, Ps. Dem. 25. 9; 18. 236, and Dissen. in l. We have also the passive construction

εἰωθότων γνώμην ἀπεφήναντο, εἰ μὲν ἤρεσκέ τί μοι τῶν ὑπὸ τούτων ῥηθέντων, ἡσυχίαν ἂν ἦγον, εἰ δὲ μή, τότ' ἂν αὐτὸς ἐπειρώμην ἃ γιγνώσκω λέγειν· ἐπειδὴ δὲ περὶ ὧν πολλάκις εἰρήκασιν οὗτοι πρότερον συμβαίνει καὶ νυνὶ σκοπεῖν, ἡγοῦμαι καὶ πρῶτος ἀναστὰς εἰκότως ἂν συγγνώμης τυγχάνειν. εἰ γὰρ ἐκ τοῦ παρεληλυθότος χρόνου τὰ δέοντα οὗτοι συνεβούλευσαν, οὐδὲν ἂν ὑμᾶς νῦν ἔδει βουλεύεσθαι.

2. Πρῶτον μὲν οὖν οὐκ ἀθυμητέον, ὦ ἄνδρες Ἀθηναῖοι, τοῖς παροῦσι πράγμασιν, οὐδ' εἰ πάνυ φαύλως ἔχειν δοκεῖ. ὃ γάρ ἐστι χείριστον αὐτῶν ἐκ τοῦ παρεληλυθότος χρόνου, τοῦτο πρὸς τὰ μέλλοντα βέλτιστον ὑπάρχει. τί οὖν ἐστὶ τοῦτο; ὅτι οὐδέν, ὦ ἄνδρες Ἀθηναῖοι, τῶν δεόντων ποιούντων ὑμῶν κακῶς τὰ πράγματα ἔχει, ἐπεί τοι εἰ πάνθ' ἃ

in 3. 18. As the subject of debate had already been laid before the assembly, it has been thought that the imperfect could not have been used by the orator. Dind. feels the difficulty so strongly that he proposes in his notes to read προυτέθειτο. But the passage quoted from Isocrates shows that the objection is without ground, and that the present or imperfect could be used with propriety by any speaker till the debate was concluded. "had the subject just proposed for debate been any new one, I should have waited..." In ἐπισχὼν ἄν, ἄν of course belongs to ἦγον.

ἕως...ἀπεφήναντο] "till..had (should have) addressed you." West., who thinks that ἄν affects ἀπεφήναντο, is clearly wrong. Cf. Don. p. 581.

τῶν εἰωθότων] sc. γν. ἀποφήνασθαι. Cf. Schöm. p. 111, Engl. Tr. Cf. Isocr. 6. 2, εἰ μέν τις τῶν εἰθισμένων ἐν ὑμῖν ἀγορεύειν ἀξίως ἦν τῆς πόλεως εἰρηκώς, πολλὴν ἂν ἡσυχίαν ἦγον, νῦν δ' ὁρῶν... and the parody of this locus communis in Arist. Eccl. 151.

γνώμην in this phrase is regularly used without the article, as in 18. 189; al.

ἡ. ἂν ἦγον] "I had remained silent."

περὶ ὧν] Bekk. and Dind. West. and Sauppe follow S in reading ὑπέρ, referring to ὑπὲρ τούτων 2. 3.

ἀναστάς) (the people who sat: 18. 191 ; 6. 3, ἡμεῖς οἱ παριόντες ... ὑμεῖς οἱ καθήμενοι, "our hearers."

ἐκ τοῦ π. χ.] "a superiore inde tempore." "Usu factum est, ut obscurata initii cogitatione saepe nihil nisi tempus significet quo quid eveniat; sic ἐκ νυκτός significant 'noctu,' ἐξ ἡμέρας 'interdiu.'" Sauppe. 18. 26, ἐκ παντὸς τοῦ χρόνου. Cf. 2. 12, πρότωθεν. "had advised proper measures in time past, there would have been no need for us to be deliberating now."

§ 2. οὖν] 1. 3.

ἀθ.... πράγμασιν] Madv. 44.

ἃ ... αὐτῶν] 1. 4. "that feature of them," "that which is the worst in them as regards the past." In 9. 5 we have τὸ χ. ἐν τοῖς παρεληλυθόσι. The argument is similar to that in 1. 4: cf. also 9. 5.

ποιούντων ... πραττόντων] The sense is, "your affairs are in a bad state because you do nothing that is

ΚΑΤΑ ΦΙΛΙΠΠΟΥ Α.

προσῆκε πραττόντων οὕτως εἶχεν, οὐδ᾽ ἂν ἐλπὶς ἦν αὐτὰ βελτίω γενέσθαι. 3. ἔπειτα ἐνθυμητέον καὶ παρ᾽ ἄλλων ἀκούουσι καὶ τοῖς εἰδόσω αὐτοῖς ἀναμιμνησκομένοις, ἡλίκην ποτ᾽ ἐχόντων δύναμιν Λακεδαιμονίων, ἐξ οὗ χρόνος οὐ πολύς, ὡς καλῶς καὶ προσηκόντως οὐδὲν ἀνάξιον ὑμεῖς ἐπράξατε τῆς πόλεως, ἀλλ᾽ ὑπεμείνατε ὑπὲρ τῶν δικαίων τὸν πρὸς ἐκείνους πόλεμον. τίνος οὖν ἕνεκα ταῦτα λέγω; ἵν᾽ εἰδῆτε, ὦ ἄνδρες Ἀθηναῖοι, καὶ θεάσησθε ὅτι οὐδὲν οὔτε φυλαττομένοις ὑμῖν ἐστὶ φοβερὸν οὔτ᾽, ἂν ὀλιγωρῆτε, τοιοῦτον οἷον ἂν ὑμεῖς βούλοισθε, παραδείγμασι χρώμενοι

needful; were it otherwise, if you performed every duty and they were in this state notwithstanding, there could be no possible hope of their amendment." The aor. inf. without ἂν after ἐλπίς, as in 1. 14. Bacon, as is well known, employs this passage in his *Novum Org.* 1, Aphor. 94.

§ 3. ἔπειτα] without δέ after πρῶτον μέν, as in § 34; 6. 3, &c.

ἐνθυμητέον] sc. ὑμῖν. "Deinde considerare vos oportet, et ab aliis audientes, et qui ipsi nostis [the older members of the assembly] in memoriam revocantes." Schäf. Cf. Thuc. i. 42, ἂν ἐνθυμηθέντες καὶ νεώτερός τις παρὰ πρεσβυτέρων αὐτὰ μαθών: Isocr. 5. 43; Lyc. § 93, τίς γὰρ οὐ μέμνηται τῶν πρεσβυτέρων ἢ τῶν νεωτέρων οὐκ ἀκήκοε; and so frequently.

ἡλίκην ... ὡς] "what a mighty power ... it is not long ago, and yet how nobly." Such multiplication of interrogatives in the same sentence is common: inf. § 36; 19. 63; 21. 143, ᾧ τινῶν εὐεργεσιῶν ὑπαρχουσῶν ... τῶς ἐχρῆσανθ᾽ ὑμῶν οἱ πρόγονοι; 33. 107; Soph. *Aj.* 1185. Don. p. 382.

ἐξ οὗ χ. οὐ πολύς] Isocr. 5. 47 uses the same expression in speaking of the power of Sparta at the time alluded to by Dem., οὗτοι ἄρχοντες τῶν Ἑ. ἐξ οὗ χρόνος οὐ πολὺς καὶ κατὰ γῆν καὶ κατὰ θάλατταν: Thuc. 1. 6, οὐ πολὺς χρόνος ἐπειδή

Ib. ad fin. οὐ πολλ᾽ ἔτη ἐπειδή. Cf. Lob. Soph. *Aj.* 600. ἔστι, which Schäfer supplies, never appears, I think, in these phrases, which seem to have been used parenthetically as adverbial expressions.

προσηκόντως] because it was the privilege of Athens, as the orators told them, to be the champion of the oppressed and defender of the liberties of the rest of the Greeks. Cf. 6. 8; 10. 11; 9. 45; 15. 23, ὑμᾶς ... δόξαν ἔχοντας τοῦ σώζειν τοὺς ἀτυχοῦντας δεῖ: ib. 30, ἐὰν ὑπολήφθητε κοινοὶ προστάται τῆς πάντων ἐλευθερίας εἶναι: 16. 15; al. Arist. *Rhet.* i. 9. 31, καὶ ὅσα κατὰ τὸ προσῆκον οἷον, εἰ ἄξια τῶν προγόνων, καὶ τῶν προϋπηργμένων. This war is mentioned also in 2. 24.

τῶν δικαίων] Cf. 2. 24, where the words τῶν Ἑλληνικῶν are added. They are read here by some MSS., and inserted in the text by Dind. and Redh. According to Bekker's reading the meaning is general, "in the cause of right and justice," and the words cannot, in the absence of some defining phrase, be translated "the rights of G.," however much this may be implied.

φυλαττομένοις = ἂν φυλάττησθε.

ἂν .. βούλοισθε] Bekk. st.; Bekk. ἂν βούλησθε, and so Redh. and Fr. The optative is required by the sense, which is "as you would wish," "nothing goes as you would like to see it."

τῇ τότε ῥώμῃ τῶν Λακεδαιμονίων, ἧς ἐκρατεῖτε ἐκ τοῦ προσέχειν τοῖς πράγμασι τὸν νοῦν, καὶ τῇ νῦν ὕβρει τούτου, δι' ἣν ταραττόμεθα ἐκ τοῦ μηδὲν φροντίζειν ὧν ἐχρῆν. 4. εἰ δέ τις ὑμῶν, ὦ ἄνδρες Ἀθηναῖοι, δυσπολέμητον οἴεται τὸν Φίλιππον εἶναι, σκοπῶν τό τε πλῆθος τῆς ὑπαρχούσης αὐτῷ δυνάμεως καὶ τὸ τὰ χωρία πάντα ἀπολωλέναι τῇ πόλει, ὀρθῶς μὲν οἴεται, λογισάσθω μέντοι τοῦθ', ὅτι εἴχομέν ποτε ἡμεῖς, ὦ ἄνδρες Ἀθηναῖοι, Πύδναν καὶ Ποτίδαιαν καὶ Μεθώνην καὶ πάντα τὸν τόπον τοῦτον οἰκεῖον κύκλῳ, καὶ πολλὰ τῶν μετ' ἐκείνου νῦν ὄντων ἐθνῶν αὐτονομούμενα καὶ ἐλεύθερα ὑπῆρχε καὶ μᾶλλον ἡμῖν ἐβούλετ' ἔχειν οἰκείως ἢ 'κείνῳ. 5. εἰ τοίνυν ὁ Φίλιππος τότε ταύτην ἔσχε τὴν γνώμην, ὡς χαλεπὸν πολεμεῖν ἐστιν Ἀθηναίοις ἔχουσι τοσαῦτα ἐπιτειχίσματα τῆς αὑτοῦ χώρας ἔρημον

τῇ τότε ῥ.] "the strength... at that time." So τῇ νῦν ὕβρει: 23. 13.4. τὴν ἤδη χάριν. Thuc. 2. 64. τῷ ἤδη προθύμῳ.

τούτου] the word here does not express contempt, as Stallb., Pl. *Crito*, p. 65 A, seems to suppose. Krüger, correctly I think, remarks, "omnino οὗτος et ὅδι nunquam nisi nomine addito sic videntur usurpata esse." Cf. 3. 12.

§ 4. εἰ δέ τις] With the mode of argument comp. 2. 22; 8. 48. For the position of εἶναι, 8. 33; 9. 31; 20. 92, ἀλλὰ νεώτεροι οἱ νόμοι... τῶν ψηφισμάτων αὐτῶν ἡμῖν εἰσίν.

πλῆθος] "at the magnitude of the power (Grote, 11. 410) now at his command (his existing power) and the loss by our state of..."

χωρία] Pydna, &c.

μέντοι] after μέν, as 3. 2; 4. 4; al.

τὸν τ. τοῦτον] defined by Pydna &c., "that we (emphatic) once held ... all that region as our own (1. 18) round about." Isocr. 15. 107 says that Timotheus took some towns (he mentions Torone and Potidæa among others), ὧν ληφθεισῶν ἅμα ὁ τόπος ὁ περιέχων οἰκείους

ἠναγκάσθη τῇ πόλει γενέσθαι.

πολλά] 1. 12, 13, 23.

μετ' ἐκείνου] "on his side:" inf. 8; Thuc. 3. 56; 6. 88.

αὐτ. καὶ ἐλ.] see n. to 1. 23.

ἢ 'κείνῳ] Bekk. His note is "'κεῖνοι S, quae est perpetua hujus pronominis in bonis libris vel elisio vel crasis; ceteri ἐκείνῳ." He now reads ἢ 'κείνῳ, as also in 8. 15; ἢ 'κείνους, 9. 11; ἃ 'κεῖνοι, 9. 41; ἢ 'κεῖνοι, 18. 178; but ἢ ἐκείνῳ, 2. 22, and ὁ ἐκεῖνων, 15. 27. Dind. in these passages has ἢ 'κείνῳ, &c.; in 9. 41, ἐκεῖνοι: in l. 27 he has ἢ 'κεῖ where Bekk. reads ἢ ἐκεῖ. I have followed Dind. in rejecting the Ionic form.

§ 5. ἔσχε τὴν γν.] "got the idea," "been possessed with the idea."

ἐστίν] Madv. 130 b.

ἐπιτειχίσματα] i. e. Pydna, &c. Cf. Thuc. i. 143 with Arnold's note. χώρας is in the gen. as depending on the whole word, not on the preposition. Madv. 48 r. Dem. 15. 12, τῆς αὐτῆς (Artemisia) ἀρχῆς ἐπιτείχισμα. Ar. Rhet. 3, c. 3, καὶ ὡς Ἀλκιδάμας τὴν φιλοσοφίαν ἐ. τῶν νόμων.

—7.]   ΚΑΤΑ ΦΙΛΙΠΠΟΥ Α.   5

ὄντα συμμάχων, οὐδὲν ἂν ὧν νυνὶ πεποίηκεν ἔπραξεν, οὐδὲ τοσαύτην ἐκτήσατο δύναμιν. ἀλλ᾽ εἶδεν, ὦ ἄνδρες Ἀθηναῖοι, τοῦτο καλῶς ἐκεῖνος, ὅτι ταῦτα μέν ἐστιν ἅπαντα τὰ χωρία ἆθλα τοῦ πολέμου κείμενα ἐν μέσῳ, φύσει δ᾽ ὑπάρχει τοῖς παροῦσι τὰ τῶν ἀπόντων καὶ τοῖς ἐθέλουσι πονεῖν καὶ κινδυνεύειν τὰ τῶν ἀμελούντων. 6. καὶ γάρ τοι ταύτῃ χρησάμενος τῇ γνώμῃ πάντα κατέστραπται καὶ ἔχει, τὰ μὲν ὡς ἂν ἑλών τις ἔχοι πολέμῳ, τὰ δὲ σύμμαχα καὶ φίλα ποιησάμενος· καὶ γὰρ συμμαχεῖν καὶ προσέχειν τὸν νοῦν τούτοις ἐθέλουσιν ἅπαντες οὓς ἂν ὁρῶσι παρεσκευασμένους καὶ πράττειν ἐθέλοντας ἃ χρή. ἂν τοίνυν, ὦ ἄνδρες Ἀθηναῖοι, καὶ ὑμεῖς ἐπὶ τῆς τοιαύτης ἐθελήσητε γενέσθαι γνώμης νῦν. 7. ἐπειδήπερ οὐ πρότερον, καὶ ἕκαστος ὑμῶν, οὗ δεῖ καὶ δύναιτ᾽ ἂν παρασχεῖν αὑτὸν χρήσιμον τῇ πόλει, πᾶσαν ἀφεὶς τὴν εἰρωνείαν ἕτοιμος πράττειν ὑπάρξῃ, ὁ μὲν

πεποίηκεν ἔπραξεν] "notabilis copulatio verborum, non vere synonymorum, sed hic pro synonymis positorum." Schäf. I believe this to be as unfounded as his remark about θέλω and βούλομαι referred to on l. 1. An examination of the passages where the verbs are found together will show that there is no necessity in any to depart from the usual distinction. Cf. supr. 2; infr. 20; 9. 5; 8. 2; 9. 17; 18. 62, τί προσῆκον ἦν ἑλέσθαι πράττειν (what particular measures) καὶ ποιεῖν (general policy) τὴν πόλιν; 19. 102, ὅτι πράξει ταῦτα καὶ ποιήσει, "execute and do these things." Here we may translate "nothing (emphasized by ἂν as l. 1) of all that he has accomplished would he have attempted."

For εἶδεν Cobet, Nov. Lect. p. 222, proposes ᾔδειν, which West. adopts. But cf. 6. 8, εἶδε τοῦτο ὀρθῶς ὅτι (where West. also reads εἶδε); 19. 139; 23. 156, where again West. has εἶδε. "but he saw this well," though we doubt not.

κείμενα ἐν μ.] "offered to competition," a common metaphor.

Ps. Dem. 7. 31; Xen. An. 3. 1. 21.

ὑπάρχει] "belong to." "Sensus est: τοῦ ἐφ᾽ ἅπασι παρόντος (2. 23) τῷ στρατεύματι (1. 4) φ. ὑπάρχει τὰ τῶν ἀπηρτημένων καὶ ταῖς παρασκευαῖς καὶ ταῖς γνώμαις (infr. 12)." Krüger.

§ 6. χρ. τῇ γ.] "by acting on this principle."

τὰ μὲν] "some as conquests, others attached to him as friends and allies," i. e. the Thessalians and Olynthians.

In ὡς ἄν, ἂν of course goes with the verb. Cf. 1. 7.

καὶ προσ.... ἅπαντες] an hexameter line; cf. 1. 5.

ἐπὶ ... γενέσθαι] "adopt the same principle." εἶναι ἐπί, on the other hand, of a principle adopted and acted upon. 21. 113, τὴν γνώμην ... ἐφ᾽ ἧς νῦν ἐστέ: ib. 199, ἐπὶ ὑπερηφανίας εἶναι: inf. § 9. Jelf, 633. 3 f.

§ 7. ἐπειδήπερ] note to 3. 33. "now, since you did not before."

παρασχεῖν .. χρ.] "make himself useful."

τὴν εἰρωνείαν] infr. 37. "εἰρωνεία

χρήματ' ἔχων εἰσφέρειν, ὁ δ' ἐν ἡλικίᾳ στρατεύεσθαι,— συνελόντι δ' ἁπλῶς ἦν ὑμῶν αὐτῶν ἐθελήσητε γενέσθαι καὶ παύσησθε αὐτὸς μὲν οὐδὲν ἕκαστος ποιήσειν ἐλπίζων, τὸν δὲ πλησίον πάνθ' ὑπὲρ αὐτοῦ πράξειν, καὶ τὰ ὑμέτερ' αὐτῶν κομιεῖσθε, ἂν θεὸς ἐθέλῃ, καὶ τὰ κατερρᾳθυμημένα πάλιν ἀναλήψεσθε, κἀκεῖνον τιμωρήσεσθε. 8. μὴ γὰρ ὡς θεῷ νομίζετ' ἐκείνῳ τὰ παρόντα πεπηγέναι πράγματα ἀθάνατα, ἀλλὰ καὶ μισεῖ τις ἐκεῖνον καὶ δέδιεν, ὦ ἄνδρες Ἀθηναῖοι, καὶ φθονεῖ, καὶ τῶν πάνυ νῦν δοκούντων οἰκείως ἔχειν καὶ ἅπανθ' ὅσα περ καὶ ἐν ἄλλοις τισὶν ἀνθρώποις ἔνι, ταῦτα κἂν τοῖς μετ' ἐκείνου χρὴ νομίζειν ἐνεῖναι. κατέπτηχε μέντοι πάντα ταῦτα νῦν, οὐκ ἔχοντ' ἀποστροφὴν διὰ τὴν ὑμετέραν βραδυτῆτα καὶ ῥᾳθυμίαν, ἣν

τὸ ἐναντίον ἐστι τῇ ἀλαζονείᾳ ὅταν δυνάμενός τις ποιῆσαι φάσκῃ μὴ δύνασθαι· ἀλαζὼν γάρ ἐστιν ὁ ἐπὶ πλέον ἑαυτοῦ κομπάζων καὶ αὔξων, εἴρων δ' ἐπὶ τὸ ἧττον ἄγων καὶ μείων." Bekk. Anecd. 143. 20 (quoted by Sauppe). Arist. Eth. Nic. 2. 7. 11. "and each of you giving up all evasion, hold himself ready."

ὁ δ' ἂν ᾖλ.] 1. 18.
σ. δ' ἁπλῶς] Madv. 38 c. Ps. Dem. 11. 16, συνελόντι φράσαι. Hyper. Fun. Or. § 110, συνελόντι δ' εἰπεῖν. "and in a word plainly."
ὑμῶν . . γ.] 2. 30 ; here explained by what follows.
αὐτός] Madv. 160. Cobet, Λ'ον. L. p. 237. "each of you expecting to do nothing himself . . . will perform all duties for him." 14. 15, quoted on 2. 25. Cf. 9. 7+
κομιεῖσθε] "will recover," 2. 28. Isocr. (8. 5) complains of those who inspired the people with such hopes, ὡς καὶ τὰς κτήσεις τὰς ἐν ταῖς πόλεσι κομιούμεθα καὶ τὴν δύναμιν ἀναληψόμεθα . . ."
ἐθέλῃ] Dind. and others θέλῃ. Cf. 2. 20.
πάλιν ἀναλ.] an apparent pleonasm often found. Thuc. 4. 75, ἀναλαμβάνουσι τὸ χωρίον πάλιν. Ps. Dem. 11. 11. Redh. calls at-

tention to the antithesis in κατερρᾳθυμημένα and ἀναλήψεσθε.
§ 8. **ἀθάνατα**] proleptic: "that his present power is secured to him as a god in everlasting possession."
ἀλλά] "no ! there are that both hate . . ." For the matter of fact see 1. 21 ; 2. 15; 8. 41. For τις comp. Aesch. Choeph. 59. Bekk. now follows S in omitting αὐτῷ, which he had after ἔχειν: and with the same MSS. omits ὑμῖν after συνοίσειν in § 51. Dind. retains αὐτῷ.
ὅσα περ καὶ . . . κἄν] The young student should notice the double καὶ required by the "prope constans Graecorum usus" (Heind. Phaed. 64 c). Cf. 21. 1 ; Thuc. 1. 83 ; al. "and all the feelings there are in any other men (fear, hatred, the love of freedom, 1. 23) we must suppose . . ."
π. ταῦτα] "alle diese Völkerschaften." Cf. 1. 22, ταῦτα ; Thuc. 1. 18. 5 ; Eth. Nic. 8. 8. 3. And so in reference to classes of men, 18. 318 ; and Xen. Oecon. 6. 13 (quoted by Schäf.), ζωγράφους ἀγαθούς . . . καὶ τὰ ἄλλα τὰ τοιαῦτα.
ἀποστροφήν] ἀντὶ τοῦ καταφυγήν. Harpocr. Thuc. 8. 75, ἀποστροφὴν σωτηρίας. Cf. 8. 41.

—10.] ΚΑΤΑ ΦΙΛΙΠΠΟΥ Λ. 7

ἀποθέσθαι φημὶ δεῖν ἤδη. 9. ὁρᾶτε γὰρ, ὦ ἄνδρες Ἀθηναῖοι, τὸ πρᾶγμα, οἷ προελήλυθεν ἀσελγείας ἄνθρωπος, ὃς οὐδ᾽ αἵρεσιν ὑμῖν δίδωσι τοῦ πράττειν ἢ ἄγειν ἡσυχίαν, ἀλλ᾽ ἀπειλεῖ καὶ λόγους ὑπερηφάνους, ὥς φασι, λέγει, καὶ οὐχ οἷός ἐστιν ἔχων ἃ κατέστραπται μένειν ἐπὶ τούτων, ἀλλ᾽ ἀεί τι προσπεριβάλλεται καὶ κύκλῳ πανταχῇ μέλλοντας ἡμᾶς καὶ καθημένους περιστοιχίζεται. 10. πότ᾽ οὖν, ὦ ἄνδρες Ἀθηναῖοι, πότε ἃ χρὴ πράξετε; ἐπειδὰν τί γένηται; ἐπειδὰν νὴ Δί᾽ ἀνάγκη ᾖ. νῦν δὲ τί χρὴ τὰ γιγνόμενα ἡγεῖσθαι; ἐγὼ μὲν γὰρ οἴομαι τοῖς ἐλευθέροις μεγίστην ἀνάγκην τὴν ὑπὲρ τῶν πραγμάτων αἰσχύνην εἶναι. ἢ βούλεσθε, εἰπέ μοι, περιιόντες αὐτῶν πυνθάνεσθαι "λέγεταί τι καινόν;" γένοιτο γὰρ ἄν τι καινότερον ἢ Μακεδὼν ἀνὴρ Ἀθηναίους καταπολεμῶν καὶ τὰ τῶν Ἑλλήνων διοικῶν;

ἤδη] 1. 2. Cf. 2. 26.
§ 9. ἀσελγείας] in its usual sense of insolence or violence towards others. Hence it is joined with ὕβρις (21. 1) and ἐμότης (21. 88).
οἷός ἐστιν] "and incapable of resting in the possession of... he is ever trying to compass something more, and is throwing his net about us on every side while we dally and sit still."
μένειν ἐπί] 8. 14, 47; 24. 86, ἐπέμεινεν ἐπὶ τοῦ κακουργήματος. Cf. what he says of P. in 1. 14.
περιστοιχίζεται continues the metaphor from hunting, κατὰ γὰρ τὰς ἐκδρομὰς τῶν θηρίων ὀρθὰ ξύλα ἱστᾶσιν ἃ καλοῦσι στοίχους ἢ στάχους, κατατεταννύντες αὐτῶν δίκτυα ἵν᾽ ἐὰν αὐτοὺς ἐκφύγῃ τὰ θηρία εἰς τὰ δίκτυα ἐμπέσῃ. Harp. Cf. 6. 27.
§ 10. πότ᾽... ποτέ] 1. 19.
ἐπειδὰν τί γ.] Madv. 198. Don. p. 383. Lob. Aj. 77.
νὴ Δί᾽] "I suppose:" very common in Dem. after ὅταν, ἵνα, &c. in giving, with a touch of irony, answers to such questions as that here. 8. 50.
ἀνάγκη ᾖ] Bekk. st. from S; ἀνάγκη τις ᾖ, Bekk.
τί.. τὰ γ.] Madv. 97, note.

Dem. 9. 16, "but in what light ought we to regard what is taking place now" if not as such a case of necessity, so that the time you are waiting for is come?
ἐγὼ μὲν γάρ] Cf. 3. 8. "[I ask you] for 1;" "for my part I." With this section comp. 8. 51.
εἰπέ μοι, without reference to the number of persons addressed; so 8. 74. Arist. Ach. 319. εἰπέ μοι, τί φειδόμεσθα; so φέρε 8. 34. S has ὅρα used in the same way in 20. 21, and 55.
περιιόντες] Cf. § 48. Bekk., συνθανόμενοι [κατὰ τὴν ἀγοράν]. The words in brackets he now omits as a gloss from the margin.
αὐτῶν] "of one another:" 9. 21. Herm. Trach. 451. Don. New Crat. § 174.
γένοιτο γάρ] "why can there be any greater news than a M. (contemptuously, 3. 16; 9. 31) .. and controlling the affairs of Greece?" γάρ often introduces in this way a question expressive of surprise, impatience, and the like, as nam in Latin, "why," "pray," "I should like to know:" 9. 68. Virg. Georg. 4. 445, "nam quis te juvenum..."

"τέθνηκε Φίλιππος;" οὐ μὰ Δί'. 11. "ἀλλ' ἀσθενεῖ;" τί δ' ὑμῖν διαφέρει; καὶ γὰρ ἂν οὗτός τι πάθῃ, ταχέως ὑμεῖς ἕτερον Φίλιππον ποιήσετε, ἄνπερ οὕτω προσέχητε τοῖς πράγμασι τὸν νοῦν· οὐδὲ γὰρ οὗτος παρὰ τὴν αὑτοῦ ῥώμην τοσοῦτον ἐπηύξηται ὅσον παρὰ τὴν ἡμετέραν ἀμέλειαν. καίτοι καὶ τοῦτο. 12. εἴ τι πάθοι καὶ τὰ τῆς τύχης ἡμῖν, ἥπερ ἀεὶ βέλτιον ἢ ἡμεῖς ἡμῶν αὐτῶν ἐπιμελούμεθα, καὶ τοῦτ' ἐξεργάσαιτο, ἴσθ' ὅτι πλησίον μὲν ὄντες, ἅπασιν ἂν τοῖς πράγμασι τεταραγμένοις ἐπιστάντες ὅπως βούλεσθε διοικήσαισθε, ὡς δὲ νῦν ἔχετε, οὐδὲ διδόντων τῶν καιρῶν Ἀμφίπολιν δέξασθαι δύναισθ' ἄν, ἀπηρτημένοι καὶ ταῖς παρασκευαῖς καὶ ταῖς γνώμαις.

13. Ὡς μὲν οὖν δεῖ τὰ προσήκοντα ποιεῖν ἐθέλοντας ὑπάρχειν ἅπαντας ἑτοίμως, ὡς ἐγνωκότων ὑμῶν καὶ πεπεισ-

§ 11. ἀσθενεῖ] 1. 23; 3. 5, which passage explains why they took so lively an interest in the news of Philip's sickness.

οὗτος] "for even should any thing happen to this Philip (cf. the next section) . . ."

οὕτω] "in this way," "in the way you are doing."

παρά] "through." Arn. on Thuc. i. 141, παρὰ τὴν αὑτοῦ ἀμέλειαν, says, "this is exactly expressed in vulgar English, 'all along of his own neglect.'" It is surprising that he should have thought this sense of παρά unusual. Cf. 9. 2; 18. 232; 19. 42; 21. 96; Lys. 3. 4, παρὰ τὴν ἡλικίαν: al. Madv. 75. 1 f. Buttm. Ind. Mid. s. v.

καίτοι καὶ τ.] the same phrase occurs 18. 133: cf. 19. 314, καὶ γὰρ ἂδ τοῦτο: 21. 167. "there is this also."

§ 12. τὰ τῆς τ.] "the favour of F." Cf. § 45. Bekk. st. omits ὑπάρξαι, which he read after ἡμῖν from "mrg. S." Dind. retains ὑπάρξαι, and encloses καὶ τοῦτ' ἐξεργάσαιτο in brackets.

ἐπιμελούμεθα is sufficiently supported by Thuc. i. 82, against Cobet's proposal to read ἐπιμελεῖται. This special favour of Τύχη, which obviated the ill effects of their δυσβουλία, is often alluded to. Eupolis, Πόλεις, fr. 7, ἃ πόλις, πόλις, ὡς εὐτυχὴς εἶ μᾶλλον, ἢ καλῶς φρονεῖς: Arist. Aud. 583; Eccl. 476: cf. 2, 22.

καὶ τοῦτ'] i.e. the death of P. to crown her other favours: 1. 7.

ἐπιστάντες must not be taken with ἄν, as West. proposes. Cf. 1. 1, ἀκούσαντες. "If you were on the spot, coming as you would upon (you would come upon) the general confusion (which would follow his death), and manage . . at your pleasure." With ἐπιστάντες comp. 6. 5.

διδόντων] "offered you."

ἀπηρτημένοι)(πλησίον ὄντες. "far away from the spot with both .." In 18. 59 we have the active ἀπαρτᾶν τὸν λόγον τῆς γραφῆς: Ps. D. 10. 1, ταῖς γνώμαις ὑμῶν ἀφιστήκατε τῶν πραγμάτων.

§ 13. ἐθ. ὑπάρχειν not quite = ἐθέλειν: ὑπάρχω does not lose in this resolution with the participle its proper force of "to be ready beforehand." "presuming then (Madv. 181) that you are con-

ΚΑΤΑ ΦΙΛΙΠΠΟΤ Α.

μένων, παύομαι λέγων· τὸν δὲ τρόπον τῆς παρασκευῆς ἣν ἀπαλλάξαι ἂν τῶν τοιούτων πραγμάτων ὑμᾶς οἴομαι, καὶ τὸ πλῆθος ὅσον, καὶ πόρους οὕστινας χρημάτων, καὶ τἄλλα ὡς ἄν μοι βέλτιστα καὶ τάχιστα δοκεῖ παρασκευασθῆναι, καὶ δὴ πειράσομαι λέγειν, δεηθεὶς ὑμῶν, ὦ ἄνδρες Ἀθηναῖοι, τοσοῦτον. 14. ἐπειδὰν ἅπαντα ἀκούσητε, κρίνατε, μὴ πρότερον προλαμβάνετε· μηδ' ἂν ἐξ ἀρχῆς δοκῶ τινὶ καινὴν παρασκευὴν λέγειν, ἀναβάλλειν με τὰ πράγματα ἡγείσθω. οὐ γὰρ οἱ ταχὺ καὶ τήμερον εἰπόντες μάλιστα εἰς δέον λέγουσιν (οὐ γὰρ ἂν τά γε ἤδη γεγενημένα τῇ νυνὶ βοηθείᾳ κωλῦσαι δυνηθείημεν), 15. ἀλλ' ὃς ἂν δείξῃ τίς πορισθεῖσα παρασκευὴ καὶ πόση καὶ πόθεν διαμεῖναι δυνήσεται ἕως ἂν ἢ διαλυσώμεθα πεισθέντες τὸν πόλεμον ἢ περιγενώμεθα τῶν ἐχθρῶν· οὕτω γὰρ οὐκέτι

vinced .. that there ought to exist a readiness on the part of all ..:" cf. 3. 7; 18. 95, ὑπάρχειν .. εἰδότας, "know already;" 21. 41, ἐγνωσμένʼ ὑπάρχῃ παρ' ὑμῖν.

ἀπαλλάξαι ἄν] Madv. 173. Cf. 6. 10, ἄν .. προσθεῖναι; 9. 1, οὐκ ἂν ἡγοῦμαι δύνασθαι. After ὅσον and οὕστινας we must understand ἄν. ἄν οἴομαι, "its strength and the supplies of money, and how the other requisites might, I think, be best and most expeditiously got ready, I will at once .."

καὶ δή] 20. 65. Herm. Vig. p. 817.

§ 14. κρίνατε .. προλ.] i.e. "form your judgment when you have heard all I have to say—don't be prejudging as I go on." Madv. 141.

μή] Bekk. with S, and so Dind. Vulg. καὶ μή. The passages quoted by Sauppe show that both modes of expression are common. 18. 287, ἐμὲ ἐχειροτόνησαν καὶ οὐχ ὑμᾶς; 21. 74, ὕβρει καὶ οὐκ οἴνῳ: 20, to 141; 21. 182, δι' ἔνδειαν οὐ δι' ὕβριν: ib. 183; 5. 16; 19. 94; infr. § 26: cf. 1. 22.

πρότερον προλ.] for the apparent pleonasm cf. Thuc. 1. 23, προέγραψα πρῶτον: 6. 57, πρότερον .. προτιμωρήσασθαι; 8. 66, πρότερον .. προύπικτο.

καινήν] "Talem (novum dicit) qualem Athenienses hucusque non instruxerant, aptum ad illum atque parem rebus cum successu gerendis." Schäf. Rather it was καινήν, as being one that διαμεῖναι δυνήσεται, and ἣ συνεχῶς πολεμήσει, § 19, as opposed to the hasty βοήθειαι usually recommended.

λέγειν] "propose," "recommend."

ἀναβάλλειν] "that I am putting off," "delaying our operations." 8. 52, λόγους ἐξ ὧν ἀναβάλλουσι .. ὑμᾶς, "put you off," "amuse you." More commonly in the middle, of those who put things off on their own account : infr. 38; 3. 9 al.

μ. εἰς δέον] "most to the purpose;" 3. 28; infr. 40.

τῇ νυνὶ β.] supr. 5, τῇ νῦν ὕβρει.

§ 15. ἀλλ' ὅς] "but he who can show what, and how large, and from what source provided, must be the force that will be able to keep the field." He had already used nearly the same words in 14. 2.

πεισθέντες] "on our own terms."

οὕτω contains the condition. Madv. 135 b.

ΔΗΜΟΣΘΕΝΟΥΣ [4. 16

τοῦ λοιποῦ πάσχοιμεν ἂν κακῶς. οἶμαι τοίνυν ἐγὼ ταῦτα λέγειν ἔχειν, μὴ κωλύων εἴ τις ἄλλος ἐπαγγέλλεταί τι. ἡ μὲν οὖν ὑπόσχεσις οὕτω μεγάλη, τὸ δὲ πρᾶγμα ἤδη τὸν ἔλεγχον δώσει· κριταὶ δ' ὑμεῖς ἔσεσθε.

16. Πρῶτον μὲν τοίνυν, ὦ ἄνδρες Ἀθηναῖοι, τριήρεις πεντήκοντα παρασκευάσασθαί φημι δεῖν, εἶτ' αὐτοὺς οὕτω τὰς γνώμας ἔχειν ὡς, ἐάν τι δέῃ, πλευστέον εἰς ταύτας αὐτοῖς ἐμβᾶσιν. πρὸς δὲ τούτοις τοῖς ἡμίσεσι τῶν ἱππέων ἱππαγωγοὺς τριήρεις καὶ πλοῖα ἱκανὰ εὐτρεπίσαι κελεύω. 17. ταῦτα μὲν οἶμαι δεῖν ὑπάρχειν ἐπὶ τὰς ἐξαίφνης ταύτας ἀπὸ τῆς οἰκείας χώρας αὐτοῦ στρατείας εἰς Πύλας καὶ Χερρόνησον καὶ Ὄλυνθον καὶ ὅποι βούλεται· δεῖ γὰρ ἐκείνῳ τοῦτο ἐν τῇ γνώμῃ παραστῆναι, ὡς ὑμεῖς ἐκ τῆς ἀμελείας

τοῦ λοιποῦ] Don. § 452 ; Madv. 66 a, r. 1.
μὴ κ.] "without offering opposition." Thuc. 2. 83, ἐνάξοντο εὔπλουν τῶν νεῶν ὅτι μέγιστον οἷοί τ' ἦσαν μὴ διδόντες διέκπλουν.
τὸ δὲ πρ.] "but the performance shall at once give the means of testing it."
§ 16. τριήρ. πεντ.] a small number, relatively to the strength of their fleet which consisted at this time of at least 300 triremes. Cf. 14. 18. Böckh, Publ. Econ. bk. 3, c. 21.
οὕτω .. ὡς] "be prepared, should circumstances require it, to embark on board them ourselves, and sail."
πλευστέον] sc. ἐν. 14. 14, οὕτω διακεῖσθαι τὰς γνώμας ὡς ἕκαστον ἐλπόντα προθύμως ὅ τι ἂν δέῃ ποιήσοντα. Madv. 181, r. 2 ; Lob. Aj. 281.
τοῖς ἡ.] Madv. 50 a, r. 3. In 14. 13 Dem. gives 1000 as the number of the Athenian cavalry: ὅστις ὁρῶν ὑμῖν χιλίους μὲν ἱππέας .. At the beginning of the Peloponnesian War they had, including ἱπποτοξόται, 1200. Thuc. 2. 13 ; Arist. Eq. 225. Böckh, Publ. Econ. p. 263. Engl. Tr.
ἱ. τριήρεις] "Vide ne τριήρεις ex antecedentibus irrepserit. Inf. 21, καὶ ἱππαγωγοὺς τούτοις .. Nisi forte al l. τριήρεις oppositae fuerunt ταῖς ταχείαις, de quibus § 22." Schäf. The latter is the true view. Inscriptions published by Böckh (De Re Navali Ath. pp. 74, 403) show that Trierarchs were appointed to them as to the regular war vessels: Τριήραρχοι Σπίνθαροι Μυησιείδου Φυλάσιοι, Τριήρης ἱππαγὸς Καλλιστώ, Λυσικλέους ἔργον. Cf. Thuc. 2. 56.
πλοῖα] τὰ φέροντα τὰ ἐπιτήδεια καὶ ὑπηρετικά. Schol. "auxiliary vessels." In Thuc. 6. 30 the πλοῖα which accompanied the expedition to Sicily are distinguished from the σιταγωγοὶ ὁλκάδες : cf. Thuc. 2. 83 ; 6. 44.
§ 17. ὑπάρχειν] "be ready."
ἐξ .. στρατείας] Grote, 11. 447.
Πύλας] 18. 32 ; Grote, ib. p. 414.
παραστῆναι] Bekk. and Dind. "the thought ought to present itself to him in his mind;" "he ought to be impressed with the belief that .." West. and Redh. read παραστῆσαι, from S, "you ought to make this suggest itself to him .." Cf. 3. 1.
ἐκ] "rousing out of."
τῆς ἀ... τῆς ἔγαν] For the re-

—19.] ΚΑΤΑ ΦΙΛΙΠΠΟΥ Α. 11

ταύτης τῆς ἄγαν, ὥσπερ εἰς Εὔβοιαν καὶ πρότερόν ποτέ φασιν εἰς Ἁλίαρτον καὶ τὰ τελευταῖα πρώην εἰς Πύλας, ἴσως ἂν ὁρμήσαιτε. 18. οὔτοι παντελῶς οὐδ᾽ εἰ μὴ ποιήσαιτ᾽ ἂν τοῦτο, ὡς ἔγωγέ φημι δεῖν, εὐκαταφρόνητόν ἐστιν, ἵν᾽ ἡ διὰ τὸν φόβον εἰδὼς εὐτρεπεῖς ὑμᾶς (εἴσεται γὰρ ἀκριβῶς· εἰσὶ γάρ, εἰσὶν οἱ πάντ᾽ ἐξαγγέλλοντες ἐκείνῳ παρ᾽ ἡμῶν αὐτῶν πλείους τοῦ δέοντος) ἡσυχίαν ἔχῃ, ἢ παριδὼν ταῦτα ἀφύλακτος ληφθῇ, μηδενὸς ὄντος ἐμποδὼν πλεῖν ἐπὶ τὴν ἐκείνου χώραν ὑμῖν, ἂν ἐνδῷ καιρόν. 19. ταῦτα μέν ἐστιν ἃ πᾶσι δεδόχθαι φημὶ δεῖν καὶ παρεσκευάσθαι προσήκειν οἶμαι· πρὸς δὲ τούτοις δύναμίν τινα,

pected art. cf. 2. 16, ταῖς στρ. ταύταις ταῖς ἄνω κάτω. Madv. 9 α. With τῆς ἄγαν cm. supr. τὰς ἐξαίφνης .. αἱ λίαν, 6. 21; 19. 272.
ὥσπερ] sc. ὁρμήσατε, "as you did to E.," 1. 8: cf. 8. 74.
φασιν] the antithesis to ἀκούω, 3. 21.
'Ἁλίαρτον] 18. 32. Grote, 9.408.
τὰ τελ. πρώην] "lastly the other day," inf. 24. Lys. 6. 12, τὸ τελ. νυνί: Dem. 19. 200, τὰ τελ. δ᾽ ἔναγχος.

§ 18. οὐδ᾽ εἰ μὴ π. ἄν] "even supposing you should not do this . ." 24. 154, οὐδὲ σπέρμα δεῖ καταβάλλειν .. οὐδ᾽ εἰ μή να ἂν ἐκφύοι .. In this construction the opt. with ἄν included in the clause introduced by εἰ is the apodosis to a condition commonly suppressed. In 20. 62 it is expressed, οὐκοῦν αἰσχρὸν εἰ μέλλοντες μὲν εὖ πάσχειν συκοφάντην ἂν ταῦτα λέγοντα ἡγοῖσθε, ἐπὶ δὲ τῷ ἀφελέσθαι .. ἀκούεσθε: μέλλοντες being the protasis to ἂν ἡγοῖσθε, and in Antiph. 6. 29, δεινὸν εἰ οἱ αὐτοὶ μάρτυρες τούτους μὲν ἂν μαρτυροῦντες πιστοὶ ἦσαν, ἐμοὶ δὲ μαρτυροῦντες ἄπιστοι ἔσονται. Here an εἰ τύχοι or the like might be supplied. Cf. Jelf, 860. 1; Don. § 507, and the admirable note of Mr. Shil. on De F. Leg. § 190.
εὐτρεπεῖς] "participium requiro," Schäf.; but cf. 2. 1; 18.

10, εἰ γὰρ ἴστε με τοιοῦτος· 19. 87, πρὸς Πορθμῷ .. ἀκούοντες δύναμιν Φίλιππου καὶ ξένους: 20. 13, ἐπ᾽ ἄλλων .. ἴδοι τις ἂν τοιούτον, where Cobet would insert ὂν: al.
εἰσὶ .. εἰσὶν] 1. 19. "for there are, there are, I repeat, persons from among ourselves (inf. § 27) more than there ought to be, who report every thing to him." We can hardly suppose that there was as yet any Macedonian party. The expressions used by Dem. in 2. 4, &c. only refer to the character of the policy of those to whom he refers, and do not mean to imply that they were in Philip's pay. The allusion here is no doubt more particularly to the actors Neoptolemus and Aristodemus (5. 6; 19. 12). The Athenians, when they heard the words οἱ ἐξαγγέλλοντες, would have no doubt as to the persons meant.
μηδενὸς] neuter: "there being nothing to hinder."
ἐνδῷ κ.] "should he give you . ." Thuc. 2. 87, οὐκ ἐνδώσομεν πρόφασιν.

§ 19. δεδόχθαι .. π.] "at once determined upon . ." Madv. 171. r. 1; Don. p. 409. 8. 3, συμφώνως καὶ βεβουλεῦσθαι καὶ παρεσκευάσθαι: 14. 17, οὕτω συντετάχθαι φημὶ δεῖν: 18. 78; Soph. El. 1338.
For πρὸς δὲ τούτοις F S have πρὸ δὲ τούτων, which is adopted by

ΔΗΜΟΣΘΕΝΟΥΣ [4. 20

ὦ ἄνδρες Ἀθηναῖοι, φημὶ προχειρίσασθαι δεῖν ὑμᾶς, ἢ συνεχῶς πολεμήσει καὶ κακῶς ἐκεῖνον ποιήσει. μή μοι μυρίους μηδὲ δισμυρίους ξένους, μηδὲ τὰς ἐπιστολιμαίους ταύτας δυνάμεις, ἀλλ' ἢ τῆς πόλεως ἔσται, κἂν ὑμεῖς ἕνα κἂν πλείους κἂν τὸν δεῖνα κἂν ὁντινοῦν χειροτονήσητε στρατηγόν, τούτῳ πείσεται καὶ ἀκολουθήσει. 20. καὶ τροφὴν ταύτῃ πορίσαι κελεύω. ἔσται δ' αὕτη τίς ἡ δύναμις καὶ πόση, καὶ πόθεν τὴν τροφὴν ἕξει, καὶ πῶς ταῦτ' ἐθελήσει ποιεῖν; ἐγὼ φράσω, καθ' ἕκαστον τούτων διεξιὼν χωρίς. ξένους μὲν λέγω — καὶ ὅπως μὴ ποιήσετε ὃ πολλάκις ὑμᾶς ἔβλαψεν πάντ' ἐλάττω νομίζοντες εἶναι τοῦ δέοντος, καὶ τὰ μέγιστ' ἐν τοῖς ψηφίσμασιν αἰρούμενοι, ἐπὶ τῷ πράττειν οὐδὲ τὰ μικρὰ ποιεῖτε ἀλλὰ τὰ μικρὰ ποιήσαντες καὶ πορίσαντες τούτοις προστίθετε, ἂν ἐλάττω φανῆται. 21. λέγω δὴ τοὺς πάντας στρατιώτας δισχιλίους, τούτων δὲ

Dind. and Sauppe. Cf. inf. § 22, τί πρὸς τούτοις, which, together with the import of the previous sentence, is conclusive in favour of Bekker's reading.

§ with the fut. ind. as 1. 3.

μή μοι] Madv. 32. Ar. *Nub.* 84; *Acharn.* 345, μή μοι πρόφασιν, "none of your 10,000 mercenaries;" the accusative depending on the verb involved in μή μοι.

ἐπιστολιμαίους] as we say "on paper." The meaning is made clear by § 30.

ταύτας] i. e. of which you are so fond, "of yours:" sup. § 17.

τῆς π. ἔσται] "but one which will belong to the state" (inf. 27; Ps. Dem. 25. 25, τῶν πονηροτάτων . . ἡ πόλις γίγνεται: Soph. *Ant.* 737); whereas the mercenaries went off upon expeditions of their own: inf. 24; 2. 28.

Before the first μέν, "and whether," West. and Fr., following II. Wolf and Schäf., unnecessarily insert καί: "and whether you elect one or more, or this or that man (2. 31), or any one whatever as general, will . ."

§ 20. ἔσται δ'] "what kind of a force this shall be" (sup. § 13, τὸν . . τρόπον), τίς being here equivalent to ποία τις.

ταῦτ'] referring to ἡ τῆς π. ἔσται and τούτῳ to ἀκολουθήσει.

καθ' ἕκαστον] "discussing each of these points separately," the gen. τούτων depending on καθ' ἕκαστον, regarded as one word: cf. 2. 24; 9. 22, καθ' ἕνα . . τῶν Ἑλλήνων.

ξένους μέν] the sentence, interrupted by καὶ ὅπως, is commenced afresh by λέγω δή at the beginning of § 21.

καὶ ὅπως μή] "and beware of doing . ." Madv. 124, r. 1; 8. 38; affirmatively 19. 94, καὶ ὅπως, ὅσπερ ἐρωτῶσι προθύμως, οὕτω καὶ ποιεῖν ἐθελήσουσιν.

τοῦ δ.] "the occasion."

τὰ μέγιστ'] 3. 14. "the strongest measures in your decrees, when it comes to the execution you do not perform even the least . . :" cf. 3. 4, 5, 15; inf. §§ 36, 37.

ἐλάττω] "inadequate," "insufficient."

§ 21. τοὺς πάντας] "I recommend then . . in all." Madv. 11, r. 4.

στρατιώτας] here "foot-sol-

ΚΑΤΑ ΦΙΛΙΠΠΟΥ Α.

Ἀθηναίους φημὶ δεῖν εἶναι πεντακοσίους, ἐξ ἧς ἂν τινος ὑμῖν ἡλικίας καλῶς ἔχειν δοκῇ, χρόνον τακτὸν στρατευομένους, μὴ μακρὸν τοῦτον, ἀλλ' ὅσον ἂν δοκῇ καλῶς ἔχειν, ἐκ διαδοχῆς ἀλλήλοις· τοὺς δ' ἄλλους ξένους εἶναι κελεύω. καὶ μετὰ τούτων ἱππέας διακοσίους, καὶ τούτων πεντήκοντα Ἀθηναίους τοὐλάχιστον, ὥσπερ τοὺς πεζούς, τὸν αὐτὸν τρόπον στρατευομένους· καὶ ἱππαγωγοὺς τούτοις. 22. εἶεν· τί πρὸς τούτοις ἔτι; ταχείας τριήρεις δέκα· δεῖ γάρ, ἔχοντος ἐκείνου ναυτικόν, καὶ ταχειῶν τριήρων ἡμῖν, ὅπως ἀσφαλῶς ἡ δύναμις πλέῃ. πόθεν δὴ τούτοις ἡ τροφὴ γενήσεται; ἐγὼ καὶ τοῦτο φράσω καὶ δείξω, ἐπειδάν, διότι τηλικαύτην ἀποχρῆν οἶμαι τὴν δύναμιν καὶ πολίτας τοὺς στρατευομένους εἶναι κελεύω, διδάξω.

diers:" cf. §§ 28, 33, where στρ. are opposed to ξένοι.

ἐξ ἧς ἂν τινος .. ἡλ.] i. e. from whatever age, down to the περίπολοι or any intermediate year. We have the reverse mode of reckoning in 3. 4. Aristotle (ap. Harpocr. p. 170, Bekk.) says, χρῶνται δέ (the Athenians) τοῖς ἐπωνύμοις καὶ πρὸς τὰς στρατείας καὶ ὅταν ἡλικίαν ἐκπέμπωσι προγράφουσιν ἀπὸ τίνος ἄρχοντος ἐπωνύμου μέχρι τίνος δεῖ στρατεύεσθαι, which clearly explains this passage. Hence the expression in Aesch. 3. 168, τὰς ἄλλας τὰς ἐκ διαδοχῆς ἐξόδους τὰς ἐν τοῖς ἐπωνύμοις ἐξήλθον: cf. Schöm. Ant. Jur. Gr. p. 251. "of whatever age you may think advisable."

ἀλλήλοις] depending on ἐκ διαδοχῆς, Jelf, 593. 2: "relieving each other." Cf. the passage just quoted from Aesch. Dem. 21. 164. In 2. 31 we have κατὰ μέρος.

τοὐλάχιστον] Madv. 14 a, r. 3.

ὥσπερ . . . τὸν αὐτόν] 1. 15. In many of the passages where ὥσπερ is found after ὁ αὐτός, critics have wished to substitute ὅσπερ. But we find καθάπερ also after ὁ αὐτός, which proves, as Bremi remarks (App. Crit. p. 93. 15), that such change would be wrong. 23. 41, τοῖς αὐτοῖς ἐπιχίσθω καθάπερ ἂν τὸν Ἀθηναῖον καταντείνῃ, though he had just before said τὴν αὐτὴν δίκην δίδωσιν ἥπερ ἂν . . : cf. Heind. on Pl. Phaed. 86 A, τῷ αὐτῷ λόγῳ ὥσπερ σύ .. On the navy of Philip see Grote, 11. 424; on the dat. τούτοις, 1. 22.

τοὺς πεζούς] the case being, as often after ὥσπερ, &c., assimilated to that to which ὥσπερ, &c., refer. Thuc. 1. 69, ὥσπερ ἐκεῖνοι: 6. 65, ὥσπερ καὶ ἡμᾶς.

§ 22. τηλικαύτην] "of such amount," the context in each case determining whether the amount is great or small; here of course the latter. As only part of the expedition was to consist of Athenian citizens, Dobree and Halm propose to read συστρατευομένους: Spengel conj. τοῖς στρατευομένοις παρεῖναι (as in the next section πολ. δὲ παρεῖναι). West. takes εἶναι as = παρεῖναι, which is impossible. But the ordinary reading does not seem to present any insuperable difficulty if we suppose the article to refer to those mentioned in τακτὸν χρόνον στρατευομένους and τὸν αὐτὸν χρ. στρ. ι "why I think a force of such amount is sufficient, and recommend that those serving (as I have said) should be citizens," πολίτας being emphatic by position.

23. Τοσαύτην μὲν, ὦ ἄνδρες Ἀθηναῖοι, διὰ ταῦτα, ὅτι οὐκ ἔνι νῦν ἡμῖν πορίσασθαι δύναμιν τὴν ἐκείνῳ παραταξομένην, ἀλλὰ λῃστεύειν ἀνάγκη καὶ τούτῳ τῷ τρόπῳ τοῦ πολέμου χρῆσθαι τὴν πρώτην· οὔ τοίνυν ὑπέρογκον αὐτὴν (οὐ γὰρ ἔστι μισθὸς οὐδὲ τροφή) οὐδὲ παντελῶς ταπεινὴν εἶναι δεῖ· πολίτας δὲ παρεῖναι καὶ συμπλεῖν διὰ ταῦτα κελεύω, ὅτι καὶ πρότερόν ποτ᾽ ἀκούω ξενικὸν τρέφειν ἐν Κορίνθῳ τὴν πόλιν, οὗ Πολύστρατος ἡγεῖτο καὶ Ἰφικράτης καὶ Χαβρίας καὶ ἄλλοι τινές, καὶ αὐτοὺς ὑμᾶς συστρατεύεσθαι· 24. καὶ οἶδα ἀκούων ὅτι Λακεδαιμονίους παραταττόμενοι μεθ᾽ ὑμῶν ἐνίκων οὗτοι οἱ ξένοι καὶ ὑμεῖς μετ᾽ ἐκείνων. ἐξ οὗ δ᾽ αὐτὰ καθ᾽ αὑτὰ τὰ ξενικὰ ὑμῖν στρατεύεται, τοὺς φίλους νικᾷ καὶ τοὺς συμμάχους, οἱ δ᾽ ἐχθροὶ μείζους τοῦ δέοντος γεγόνασιν. καὶ παρακύψαντα ἐπὶ τὸν τῆς πόλεως πόλεμον, πρὸς Ἀρτάβαζον καὶ παν-

So that the meaning will simply be, "why I recommend that there should be a body of citizens in the force sent out."

§ 23. Τοσαύτην μέν] "a force of such strength (ἀποχρῶν οἴμαι) because."

ἔνι] 2. 4.

νῦν] emphatic.

παραταξομένην] "to meet him in the field." 9. 49; 16. 10, ἐκινδυνεύσατε καὶ παρετάξασθε: 18. 208; Thuc. 5. 4.

λῃστεύειν] of guerilla warfare. Thuc. 4. 41, λῃστείας καὶ τοιούτου πολέμου. Comp. Livy, 3. 61 fin.; 29. 6, "latrocinils magis quam justo bello—gerebatur res."

τὴν πρώτην] 3. 2.

ἀκούω] 3. 71. On the pres. inf. Madv. 171 b, r. 2.

ἐν Κορίνθῳ] Thirl. 4, c. 36; Grote, 9. 454 sq.

§ 24. οἶδα ἀκούων] 3. 3. "I have heard."

μεθ᾽ ὑμῶν] "fighting by your side and you by theirs." K.

ἐνίκων] "pluries," Fr. Though the orator may mean to be understood so here, the imperfect is regularly used in reference to single victories. Thuc. 1. 13 ad fin.; 1. 49; Andoc. 1. 107, μαχεσάμενοι τε ἐνίκων, i. e. in the battle of Marathon. Madv. 110 a, r. 2. Dem. refers in particular, no doubt, to the famous exploit of Iphicrates in cutting off the Spartan Mora. Thirl. 4. 423; Grote, 9. 482.

ἐξ οὗ .. στρ.] Madv. 110 a, r.

νικᾷ] "they have been gaining victories over," not your enemies, but "your friends." On the increasing employment of mercenaries and soldiers of fortune at this period see Grote, 11. 390; Thirl 5. 210. We find bitter complaints in the orators of their excesses: cf. the passages quoted by Grote, ib. p. 312; also Isocr. 4. 115; 8. 44. Dem. here and in 8, 9 sq. points out with justice that this was in a great degree owing to their not providing them with pay.

δ᾽] "while your enemies."

παρακ. ἐπί] "after a hasty glance at:" cf. the illustrations in L. and S.

πρὸς Ἀρτάβαζον] as Chares, 2. 28.

—26.] ΚΑΤΑ ΦΙΛΙΠΠΟΥ Α. 15

ταχοῖ μᾶλλον οἴχεται πλέοντα, ὁ δὲ στρατηγὸς ἀκολουθεῖ, εἰκότως· οὐ γὰρ ἔστιν ἄρχειν μὴ διδόντα μισθόν. 25. τί οὖν κελεύω; τὰς προφάσεις ἀφελεῖν καὶ τοῦ στρατηγοῦ καὶ τῶν στρατιωτῶν, μισθὸν πορίσαντας καὶ στρατιώτας οἰκείους ὥσπερ ἐπόπτας τῶν στρατηγουμένων παρακαταστήσαντας, ἐπεὶ νῦν γε γέλως ἔσθ᾽ ὡς χρώμεθα τοῖς πράγμασιν. εἰ γὰρ ἔροιτό τις ὑμᾶς, εἰρήνην ἄγετε, ὦ ἄνδρες Ἀθηναῖοι; μὰ Δί᾽ οὐχ ἡμεῖς γε, εἴποιτ᾽ ἄν, ἀλλὰ Φιλίππῳ πολεμοῦμεν. 26. οὐκ ἐχειροτονεῖτε δὲ ἐξ ὑμῶν αὐτῶν δέκα ταξιάρχους καὶ στρατηγοὺς καὶ φυλάρχους καὶ ἱππάρχους δύο; τί οὖν οὗτοι ποιοῦσιν; πλὴν ἑνὸς ἀνδρός, ὃν ἂν ἐκπέμψητε ἐπὶ τὸν πόλεμον, οἱ λοιποὶ τὰς πομπὰς πέμπουσιν ὑμῖν μετὰ τῶν ἱεροποιῶν· ὥσπερ γὰρ οἱ πλάττοντες τοὺς πηλίνους, εἰς τὴν ἀγορὰν χειροτονεῖτε τοὺς

μὴ διδόντα] "if he does not find them pay."

§ 25. τὰς προφάσεις] 2. 27.

τοῦ στρ.] "of the conduct of the officers in command;" cf. 1. 28; inf. 47.

παρακαταστήσαντας] "attaching to them." Ps. Dem. 49. 25. ἀλλ᾽ οὐκ ἂν παρακαταστήσαντά τινα τῶν οἰκείων φυλάττειν, "would not have set .."

γέλως] the predicate, as in 1. 3; 19. 72, ἔστι δὲ ταῦτα γέλως. "for the way in which we are now managing the thing is a mockery," "perfectly ridiculous."

μὰ Δί᾽] "no, indeed, you would say, we are at war with Philip."

§ 26. ἐχειροτονεῖτε, κ.τ.λ.] "Suspicor scribendum .. καὶ χειροτονεῖτε .. Ipsum imperfectum ἐχειροτονεῖτε, cui hic locus non est, movet vitii suspicionem." Schäf. The ordinary reading is beyond suspicion. "but did you not keep electing (during the whole time you have been at war) from among yourselves .."

ἐνὸς ἀνδρός.] Gr. and R. Ant. 2. v.; Schöm. Ant. Jur. Gr. p. 251 sq.

μετὰ τῶν ἱ.] "assist the sacrificers to conduct your processions for you," instead of being on service, as they ought to be if you are really at war with P.: cf. 21. 171. It was part of the duty of the hipparch, according to Xen. Hipparch. 3, § 1, to take care ὅπως τὰς πομπὰς ἐν ταῖς ἑορταῖς ἀξιοθεάτους ποιήσει, ἔτι δὲ καὶ τἆλλα ὅσα ἐπιδεικνύναι δεῖ τῇ πόλει ὅπως ἢ δυνατὸν κάλλιστα ἐπιδείξαι, τά τε ἐν Ἀκαδημίᾳ καὶ τὰ ἐν Λυκείῳ καὶ τὰ Φαληροῖ καὶ τὰ ἐν τῷ ἱπποδρόμῳ. On the Ἱεροποιοί, Aristotle, ap. Etymol. Mag. 468. 56, says, Κληρωτοὶ ἄρχοντές εἰσι δέκα τὸν ἀριθμόν, οἱ τά τε μαντεύματα ἱεροθυτοῦσι, κἂν τι καλλιερῆσαι δέῃ, καλλιεροῦσι μετὰ τῶν μάντεων καὶ θυσίας τὰς νομιζομένας ἐπιτελοῦσι καὶ τὰς πεντετηρίδας ἁπάσας διοικοῦσι πλὴν τῶν Παναθηναίων.

τοὺς πηλίνους] "like those who model the clay figures (i. e. of generals, &c.);" see Bekker's Charicles, p. 183, Engl. Tr. εἰς τὴν ἀγ. belongs also to οἱ πλάττοντες: cf. Cob. Nov. Lect. p. 94. Why Dem., after saying that the generals helped to conduct the processions, adds that they were elected for the agora, is explained by the remark of C. O. Müller, quoted by Sauppe, "Fori

ΔΗΜΟΣΘΕΝΟΥΣ [4. 27

ταξιάρχους καὶ τοὺς φυλάρχους, οὐκ ἐπὶ τὸν πόλεμον. 27. οὐ γὰρ ἐχρῆν, ὦ ἄνδρες Ἀθηναῖοι, ταξιάρχους παρ' ὑμῶν, ἵππαρχον παρ' ὑμῶν, ἄρχοντας οἰκείους εἶναι, ἵν' ἦν ὡς ἀληθῶς τῆς πόλεως ἡ δύναμις; ἀλλ' εἰς μὲν Λῆμνον τὸν παρ' ὑμῶν ἵππαρχον δεῖ πλεῖν, τῶν δ' ὑπὲρ τῶν τῆς πόλεως κτημάτων ἀγωνιζομένων Μενέλαον ἱππαρχεῖν; καὶ οὐ τὸν ἄνδρα μεμφόμενος ταῦτα λέγω, ἀλλ' ὑφ' ὑμῶν ἔδει κεχειροτονημένον εἶναι τοῦτον, ὅστις ἂν ᾖ.

28. Ἴσως δὲ ταῦτα μὲν ὀρθῶς ἡγεῖσθε λέγεσθαι, τὸ δὲ τῶν χρημάτων, πόσα καὶ πόθεν ἔσται, μάλιστα ποθεῖτε ἀκοῦ-

Atheniensis is suit situs, ut nullam pompam vel theoriam .. ex interiore urbe missam non oportuerit per forum duci."
§ 27. γάρ] sup. § 10.
παρ' ὑμῶν] "from among yourselves."
ἄρχοντας] closing the enumeration—"in short, officers of your own:" 1. 13, τάνδ'.
ἵν' ἦν] Madv. 131 δ, r. 3. So frequently after ἐχρῆν, οὐκ ἐχρῆν, and similar expressions. Eur. *Hipp.* 641, 929; Pl. *Prot.* 335 c. After questions such as in Lys. 1. 42, εἰ προσδεῖν, οὐκ ἂν δοκῶ .. τοῖς φίλοις παραγγεῖλαι, ἵν' ὡς ἀσφαλέστατα .. εἰσίειν: 7. 17; after ἐβουλόμην ἄν, Lys. 3. 31, 44; 4. 3, &c. "that so the force might be.."
εἰς .. Λῆμνον] From a lately-discovered frag. of Hyperides we learn that one of the two hipparchs was sent every year to Lemnos, for the purpose, as we may conclude from this passage, of taking part in some procession of the Cleruchs, or other sacred solemnity, rather than for the discharge of military duty.
τὸν παρ' ὑ.)(Menelaus, a foreigner. Lyc. § 105, τοὺς παρ' ὑμῶν ἡγεμόνας: Pl. *Soph.* 242 D, τὸ δὲ παρ' ὑμῶν 'Ελεατικὸν ἔθνος: Dein. 1. 56, τὸν παρ' αὐτῶν ἀποστερήσαντα τὸ ναῦλον τὸν πορθμέα, "that member of their body."
Later writers went so far as to say

ἡ παρ' αὐτῶν χώρα, ὁ παρ' ἡμῶν πατήρ, &c. The Menelaus here spoken of is supposed to have been Philip's half-brother Amyntas' son by his wife Gygaea, as we learn from Justin, 7, c. 4. He and his brother Arrhidaeus are said to have fallen into the hands of Philip when he took Olynthus, and to have been put to death by him.
τῶν .. κτημάτων] Perhaps the Chersonese is meant: cf. 19. 78, where it is spoken of as τῶν ἰδίων τι κτημάτων of Athens. Philip had just before this time been extending his dominion in Thrace, and carrying his aggressions to the immediate neighbourhood of the Chersonese. Grote, 11. 428.
καὶ οὐ .. μ.] Cf. 3. 36.
κεχειροτονημένον] "Ab Atheniensibus non poterat χειροτονεῖσθαι nisi esset Athenensis; M. ut peregrinus et ξεναγὸς non fuit κεχειροτονημένος: cf. § 33, ὁ κύριος καταστὰς ὑφ' ὑμῶν." Schäf. The meaning then is, "the officer fighting in defence of your possessions ought to have been an Athenian."
§ 28. τὸ . . . τῶν χρημάτων] depending upon ἀκοῦσαι: "about the supplies, what their amount should be, and where they are to come from," how they are to be raised: supr. 13, πόρον οὕστινας χρ., the third part of his promised exposition.

ΚΑΤΑ ΦΙΛΙΠΠΟΥ Α.

σαι. τοῦτο δὴ καὶ περαίνω. χρήματα τοίνυν, ἔστι μὲν ἡ τροφή, σιτηρέσιον μόνον τῇ δυνάμει ταύτῃ, τάλαντα ἐνενήκοντα καὶ μικρόν τι πρός, δέκα μὲν ναυσὶ ταχείαις τετταράκοντα τάλαντα, εἴκοσιν εἰς τὴν ναῦν μναῖ τοῦ μηνὸς ἑκάστου, στρατιώταις δὲ δισχιλίοις τοσαῦθ᾽ ἕτερα, ἵνα δέκα τοῦ μηνὸς ὁ στρατιώτης δραχμὰς σιτηρέσιον λαμβάνῃ, τοῖς δ᾽ ἱππεῦσι διακοσίοις οὖσιν, ἐὰν τριάκοντα δραχμὰς ἕκαστος λαμβάνῃ τοῦ μηνός, δώδεκα τάλαντα. 29. εἰ δέ τις οἴεται μικρὰν ἀφορμὴν εἶναι σιτηρέσιον τοῖς στρατευομένοις ὑπάρχειν, οὐκ ὀρθῶς ἔγνωκεν· ἐγὼ γὰρ οἶδα σαφῶς ὅτι, τοῦτ᾽ ἂν γένηται, προσποριεῖ τὰ λοιπὰ αὐτὸ τὸ στράτευμα ἀπὸ τοῦ πολέμου, οὐδένα τῶν Ἑλλήνων ἀδικοῦν οὐδὲ τῶν συμμάχων, ὥστ᾽ ἔχειν μισθὸν ἐντελῆ. ἐγὼ συμπλέων ἐθελοντὴς πάσχειν ὁτιοῦν ἕτοιμος, ἐὰν μὴ ταῦθ᾽ οὕτως ἔχῃ. πόθεν οὖν ὁ πόρος τῶν χρημάτων ἃ παρ᾽ ὑμῶν κελεύω γενέσθαι; τοῦτ᾽ ἤδη λέξω.

τοῦτο δή] "I proceed then to despatch this point also."

χρήματα is put absolutely, as it were a heading to the sentence which follows: "as to supplies, then, the cost of maintenance, mere ration-money .. comes to."

πρός] "over." 22. 60, καὶ μικρόν τι πρός. Heind. *Gorg.* 55.

εἰς τὴν ναῦν] "to each ship:" inf. ὁ στρατιώτης and τοῦ μηνός. On the pay of the Athenian army and navy cf. Böckh, *Publ. Econ.* bk. 2, c. 22.

τοσαῦθ᾽ ἕτερα] "as much more:" cf. Böckh, ib. bk. 2, c. 11 ad fin. note.

§ 29. ἀφορμὴν εἶναι] Bekk. st. from F S. Bekk., ἀφορμήν. L. and S., who translate "inducement," have mistaken the meaning of the passage, which is, "If any of you thinks that finding the men ration-money only to begin with is a small start, and insufficient provision, he is wrong."

τοῦτ᾽] i. e. σιτηρέσιον ὑπάρχειν: emphatic. Cf. 5. 16, εἰς τὴν οἰκείαν εἴ τις ἐμβάλοι: 9. 44, τῶν Ἀθηναίων δικαίων εἰ μὴ μεθέξει: 23. 42, οὕτως ἂν ἄρα τοῦτο γένηται.

προσποριεῖ] "will provide what else is required from the war" (i. e. not for itself, which would require the middle, but so that you will not have to provide it: cf. ποριώσιν, 2. 16). The meaning is the same as in Thuc. 1. 11, ὅσον ἤλπιζον αὐτόθεν πολεμοῦντα βιοτεύσειν. We are reminded of Arist. *Rhet.* 3. 2. 10, καὶ οἱ μὲν λῃσταὶ αὐτοὺς "ποριστὰς" καλοῦσι νῦν. Böckh remarks on this passage, in his *Publ. Econ.* bk. 2, c. 22, "this proposal is worthy of remark, as having no parallel in any Grecian author; it is the outline of a plan for embodying a military force to maintain itself at free quarters, and at the same time to form a permanent standing army; though its continuance was indeed limited to the duration of war."

ἕτοιμος is very frequently used without εἰμί, as here. Ps. Dem. 10. 4 al.

πόθεν] sc. ἔσται.

παρ᾽ ὑ...γ.] "to be provided by you."

λέξω] strictly, "I will recite." The way in which he proposed to

ΔΗΜΟΣΘΕΝΟΥΣ   [4. 30

ΠΟΡΟΥ ΑΠΟΔΕΙΞΙΣ.

30. Ἃ μὲν ἡμεῖς, ὦ ἄνδρες Ἀθηναῖοι, δεδυνήμεθα εὑρεῖν, ταῦτά ἐστιν ἐπειδὰν δ' ἐπιχειροτονῆτε τὰς γνώμας, ἃ ἂν ὑμῖν ἀρέσκῃ χειροτονήσατε, ἵνα μὴ μόνον ἐν τοῖς ψηφίσμασι καὶ ἐν ταῖς ἐπιστολαῖς πολεμῆτε Φιλίππῳ, ἀλλὰ καὶ τοῖς ἔργοις.

31. Δοκεῖτε δέ μοι πολὺ βέλτιον ἂν περὶ τοῦ πολέμου καὶ ὅλης τῆς παρασκευῆς βουλεύσασθαι, εἰ τὸν τόπον, ὦ ἄνδρες

raise the money required, he had worked out in a written scheme, which he now reads to the assembly.

§ 30. *Ἃ μὲν .. ταῦτα*] according to Dionysius (*Ep.* 1 ad Ammon. c. 10) this was the commencement of a new speech. He says, ἔπειτα (after the archonship of Theophilus, *Ol.* 108. 1) Θεμιστοκλῆς ἐφ' οὗ τὴν ἐπιστήν τῶν κατὰ Φιλίππου δημηγοριῶν ἀπήγγειλε Δημοσθένης περὶ τῆς φυλακῆς τῶν νησιωτῶν καὶ τῶν ἐν Ἑλλησπόντῳ πόλεων, .. ἧς ἐστιν ἀρχή, Ἃ μὲν ἡμεῖς .. The student may consult on this point Grote, 11. 431, note, and A. Schäf. 2, p. 64. It is sufficient here to say that ταῦτ' ἐστίν must, as Petrenz observes, refer to what has gone before, as in 1. 19; 2. 18 al., which would be unintelligible on this hypothesis; and the references in the latter part of the speech to the former are too distinct to admit of our regarding it as the beginning of a distinct oration. Comp. § 32 with 19; 33, ἐπὶ τῷ π. μένειν, with § 24; § 43 sq. with 19 sq., &c.

ἡμεῖς] As Dem. never uses the plural in speaking of himself, we may conjecture that ἡμεῖς means his political friends, from among whom he had risen, or with whom he was known to act. Others have thought of the Poristae, the Boule, &c. The reader may take his choice. No doubt this was explained in the Πόρου Ἀπόδειξις.

ἃ ἂν ὑμῖν ἀρέσκῃ χειροτονήσατε] Bekk. Schäfer proposed ἐπειδὰν δὲ χειροτονήσητε τὰς γν... ἃ ποιήσατε, a violent and improbable change. Sauppe reads ἂν ὑμῶν ἀρέσκῃ, χειροτονήσετε, quoting in support 9. 70, and 14. 14, and this reading Dind. and West. adopt. If Bekker's reading is retained, we must translate, "this is what we have been able to devise: when you come to vote on the resolutions (mine and others that may be proposed, sup. 15), vote whatever you approve (whether mine or another) that .."
ἐν ταῖς ἐπ.] sup. §§ 19, 20; inf. 45. West. appositely quotes Livy 31. 44, "Athenienses quidem literis verbisque quibus solis valent bellum adversus Philippum gerunt."

§ 31. ἂν .. β.] Madv. 173. In some passages of this kind errors have crept in through ἂν being withdrawn from the infinitive, as in Isocr. 1. 12, ἐγώ σοι πειράσομαι συντόμως ὑποθέσθαι δι' ὧν ἂν μοι δοκοίης .. πρὸς ἀρετὴν ἐπιδοῦναι. Arist. *Vesp.* 1404, εἰ νὴ Δί' ἀντὶ τῆς κακῆς γλώττης τοῦδ' πυροὺς τρίαιο σωφροσύν' ἂν μοι δοκοῖς, which Cobet (*Nov. Lect.* p. 362) has well corrected by substituting the indic. δοκεῖς. So in 19. 4 the vulg. had ὡς δή μοι δοκοῖτ' ἂν .. γνῶναι .. τοῦθ' ὑμῖν λέξω.

τὸν τόπον] "the (geographical) position." 23. 182, ὅσπερ ἡ Χαλκὶς τῷ τόπῳ τῆς Εὐβοίας πρὸς τῆς Βοιωτίας κεῖται; ib. ἣν ἂν ἔχει

ΚΑΤΑ ΦΙΛΙΠΠΟΥ Α.

Ἀθηναῖοι, τῆς χώρας, πρὸς ἣν πολεμεῖτε, ἐνθυμηθείητε, καὶ λογίσαισθε ὅτι τοῖς πνεύμασι καὶ ταῖς ὥραις τοῦ ἔτους τὰ πολλὰ προλαμβάνων διαπράττεται Φίλιππος καὶ φυλάξας τοὺς ἐτησίας ἢ τὸν χειμῶνα ἐπιχειρεῖ, ἡνίκ' ἂν ἡμεῖς μὴ δυναίμεθα ἐκεῖσε ἀφικέσθαι. 32. δεῖ τοίνυν ταῦτ' ἐνθυμουμένους μὴ βοηθείαις πολεμεῖν (ὑστεριοῦμεν γὰρ ἁπάντων) ἀλλὰ παρασκευῇ συνεχεῖ καὶ δυνάμει. ὑπάρχει δ' ὑμῖν χειμαδίῳ μὲν χρῆσθαι τῇ δυνάμει Λήμνῳ καὶ Θάσῳ καὶ Σκιάθῳ καὶ ταῖς ἐν τούτῳ τῷ τόπῳ νήσοις, ἐν αἷς καὶ λιμένες καὶ σῖτος καὶ ἃ χρὴ στρατεύματι πάνθ' ὑπάρχει· τὴν δ' ὥραν τοῦ ἔτους, ὅτε καὶ πρὸς τῇ γῇ γενέσθαι ῥᾴδιον καὶ τὸ τῶν πνευμάτων ἀσφαλές, πρὸς αὐτῇ τῇ χώρᾳ καὶ πρὸς τοῖς τῶν ἐμπορίων στόμασι ῥᾳδίως ἔσται.

τόπον ὅστις οἷον ὑμῶν .. Cic. *ad Fam.* 1. 7. 6 (quoted by Sauppe), "eam esse naturam et regionem provinciae tuae;" *Pro Arch.* § 21; Dem. 18. 145.

τοῖς πνεύμασι] explained by φυλάξας τοὺς ἐτησίας: "by the winds and seasons gets the start of us, and accomplishes most of his designs, and watches for the monsoon to commence them."

τοὺς ἐτησίας] note to Arg.: cf. 8. 14. 17. Grote, 5, p. 297, note.

τὸν χ.] 2. 23. We have an instance of this in the siege of Heraeum Teichos, 3. 4. Navigation was suspended in the winter. Vegetius, 4. 39, "Ex die tertio Iduum Novembris usque in diem sextum Iduum Martiarum maria clauduntur." Comp. the remarkable passage in Andoc. 1. 137, where he argues that if the gods had looked upon him as the impious person he was represented by his enemies to be, they would surely have punished him when he ventured across the sea in winter: τίς γὰρ αἰθυιῶν μείζων ἀνθρώποις ἢ χειμῶνος ὥρᾳ πλεῖν τὴν θάλατταν; With φυλάξας cf. Thuc. 2. 2. 3. So τηρῶ, Thuc. 4. 26. 4.

ἡνίκ' ἂν ... μὴ δ.] i. e. in his opinion, "when he thinks we .."

Xen. *Oecon.* c. 11. 14, ἀνίστασθαι μὲν ἐξ εὐνῆς εἴθισμαι ἡνίκ' ἂν ἔτι ἔνδον καταλαμβάνοιμι, εἴ τινα δεόμενοι ἰδεῖν τυγχάνοιμι.

§ 32. βοηθείαις] "subitariis militibus" }(παρασκευῇ συνεχεῖ καὶ δυνάμει: cf. 8. 47.

ἁπάντων] "for every thing:" as they were on the occasions mentioned below in § 35.

συνεχεῖ] "standing," "permanent," such as he recommends in §§ 15, 19.

χειμαδίῳ] "as a winter station for the force." δυνάμει as ἔθνει, 1. 22.

ταῖς .. νήσοις] i. e. Halonnesus, Peparethus, &c.

ἃ χρή] sc. ὑπάρχειν, "every thing required by." 1. 27, ἡ ἀνάγκη στρατοπέδῳ.

τὴν .. ὥραν] "during the season." Madv. 30.

τὸ τῶν πν.] "there is no danger from the winds." Inf. 45, τὸ τῶν θεῶν .. τὸ τῆς τύχης.

πρὸς . . . β. ἔσται] "immo ἔσεσθε," Bekk., which Dind. now adopts: "You will easily learn the time of the year when .." This conj. had already been made by H. Wolf. Surely there is no need for any change. During the winter the force will be stationed at one of

ΔΗΜΟΣΘΕΝΟΥΣ [4. 33

33. Ἃ μὲν οὖν χρήσεται καὶ πότε τῇ δυνάμει, παρὰ τὸν καιρὸν ὁ τούτων κύριος καταστὰς ἐφ' ὑμῶν βουλεύσεται· ἃ δ' ὑπάρξαι δεῖ παρ' ὑμῶν, ταῦτ' ἐστὶν ἃ ἐγὼ γέγραφα. ἂν ταῦτα, ὦ ἄνδρες Ἀθηναῖοι, πορίσητε τὰ χρήματα πρῶτον ἃ λέγω, εἶτα καὶ τἆλλα παρασκευάσαντες, τοὺς στρατιώτας, τὰς τριήρεις, τοὺς ἱππέας, ἐντελῆ πᾶσαν τὴν δύναμιν νόμῳ κατακλείσητε ἐπὶ τῷ πολέμῳ μένειν, τῶν μὲν χρημάτων αὐτοὶ ταμίαι καὶ πορισταὶ γιγνόμενοι, τῶν δὲ πράξεων παρὰ τοῦ στρατηγοῦ τὸν λόγον ζητοῦντες, παύσεσθ' ἀεὶ περὶ τῶν αὐτῶν βουλευόμενοι καὶ πλέον οὐδὲν ποιοῦντες. 34. καὶ ἔτι πρὸς τούτῳ πρῶτον μέν, ὦ ἄνδρες Ἀθηναῖοι, τὸν μέγιστον τῶν ἐκείνου πόρων ἀφαιρήσεσθε. ἔστι δ' οὗτος τίς; ἀπὸ τῶν ὑμετέρων ὑμῖν πολεμεῖ συμμάχων, ἄγων καὶ φέρων τοὺς

the neighbouring Islands—"during the season of the year when it is both easy to stand in to the shore .. it will easily operate close to his country and the entrances of his seaports," to land troops to carry out the system of λῃστεία recommended in § 23, and to interfere with commerce.

§ 33. Ἅ... χρ.] Madv. 27 a, r. 2: cf. 3. 6, "how then, and when he... the officer put by you in command of." On the position of the participle, 3. 3.

παρὰ τὸν κ.) "alongside of," "at the moment of," "according to circumstances." 18. 239, εἴπερ ἐνεδέχετο παρὰ τοὺς παρόντας καιρούς.

ἃ.. ὑπ. δεῖ] "what you must find to begin with."

γέγραφα] i. e. in the Πόρου Ἀπόδειξις he had just read to them."

ἐντελῆ] proleptic—"in short the whole force complete."

ἐπὶ .. μένειν] "to remain for the war," "in the field," so that it may be συνεχής. 21. 176, μένειν ἐπὶ τῇ καταχειροτονίᾳ.

[ζητοῦντες] "while you seek an account (the account he should of course render [τόν]) .. of his conduct." Cobet (Nov. L. p. 275) proposes ἀπαιτοῦντες, which is

adopted by Dind. and West. No doubt ἀπαιτεῖν is the proper word in this case, and ζητοῦντες is not supported by the passages quoted by Redh., 19. 109, ἐγὼ δ' ἐκείνους τοὺς λόγους ἐζήτουν παρὰ τούτου, and Aesch. 3. 22, ἀνεύθυνον καὶ ἀνεξέταστον καὶ ἀζήτητον οὐδέν ἐστι τῶν ἐν τῇ πόλει. It shows the reckless haste with which so-called emendations are made, that West. proposes to alter ἐζήτουν into ἀπῄτουν in 19. 109 just referred to, where it is used in the perfectly legitimate sense, "I should have looked for such language as this from him."

§ 34. ἀπό] Cf. 1. 22. "he carries on the war against us by means of what he gets from," "from the resources of.." Madv. 39, r.

ἄγων καὶ φέρων] a standing expression for hostile plundering, as the Lat. "ferre et agere" (Livy 23. 3, "res sociorum ante oculos suos ferri agique videret"). 9. 52; 23. 61, τίνα γὰρ οἴσει ἢ ἄξει βίᾳ ἀδίκως Χαρίδημος; from which and similar passages we see that ἄγειν καὶ φ. had become a phrase in which the original difference between the verbs had become merged in a general signification.

—35.] ΚΑΤΑ ΦΙΛΙΠΠΟΥ Α. 21

πλέοντας τὴν θάλατταν. ἔπειτα τί πρὸς τούτῳ; τοῦ πάσχειν αὐτοὶ κακῶς ἔξω γενήσεσθε, οὐχ ὥσπερ τὸν παρελθόντα χρόνον εἰς Λῆμνον καὶ Ἴμβρον ἐμβαλὼν αἰχμαλώτους πολίτας ὑμετέρους ᾤχετ' ἔχων, πρὸς τῷ Γεραιστῷ τὰ πλοῖα συλλαβὼν ἀμύθητα χρήματ' ἐξέλεξε, τὰ τελευταῖα εἰς Μαραθῶνα ἀπέβη καὶ τὴν ἱερὰν ἀπὸ τῆς χώρας ᾤχετ' ἔχων τριήρη, ὑμεῖς δ' οὔτε ταῦτα ἠδύνασθε κωλύειν οὔτ' εἰς τοὺς χρόνους οὓς ἂν προθῆσθε βοηθεῖν.

35. καίτοι τί δή ποτε, ὦ ἄνδρες Ἀθηναῖοι, νομίζετε τὴν μὲν τῶν Παναθηναίων ἑορτὴν καὶ τὴν τῶν Διονυσίων ἀεὶ τοῦ καθήκοντος χρόνου γίγνεσθαι, ἄν τε δεινοὶ λάχωσιν ἄν τε ἰδιῶται οἱ τούτων ἑκατέρων ἐπιμελούμενοι, εἰς ἃ τοσαῦτ' ἀναλίσκεται χρήματα ὅσα οὐδ' εἰς ἕνα τῶν ἀποστόλων, καὶ τοσοῦτον ὄχλον καὶ παρασκευὴν ὅσην οὐκ οἶδ' εἴ τι τῶν

τοὺς πλ. τὴν θάλ.] "their traders," "their commerce." Compare the illustrative passage in 32, §§ 4, 5, and Lys. *c. Andoc.* 19, ναυκληρίᾳ ἐπιθέμενος ἕπλει τὴν θάλατταν. On the acc. after πλεῖν, Madv. 22 *b*.

ἔξω] "out of the reach of," as in *Prom.* 271, πημάτων ἔξω, and similar phrases.

οὐχ ὥσπερ . . ᾤχετ'] Arist. *Eq.* 780, οὐ φροντίζει σκληρῶς σε καθήμενον οὕτως, οὐχ ὥσπερ ἐγὼ ῥαψάμενός σοι τουτὶ φέρω, "not like me who," "whereas I." Pl. *Gorg.* 522 A, Βιρῆν ἀναγκάζων οὐχ ὥσπερ ἐγὼ . . ἰώχουσ, where see Heind. *Prot.* 341 A ; *Symp.* 179 Ε, 189 C; Dem. 21. 218; Eur. *Bacch.* 928, "not like as in time past, when he made a descent upon . ."

πολίτας] settled there as Cleruchs. In reference to this period Aesch. says, 2. 72, Φίλιππος ... πρὸς ἡμᾶς ἠγωνίζετο ... ἤδη περὶ Λήμνου καὶ Ἴμβρου τῶν ἡμετέρων κτημάτων. Böckh, *Publ. Ec.* bk. 3, c. 18.

πρὸς τῷ Γ.] where the corn-ships from the Euxine used to touch. Grote, 10, p. 176; Thirl. 5. 38. On the orthography of the word see

L. Dind., Xen. *Hell.* 3. 4. 4.

ἐξέλεξε] "levied." Thuc. 8. 44; Dem. 19. 293. Also with an acc. of the person like πράττω : Aesch. 3. 35, τέλη τοὺς καταπλέοντας ἐξέλεξαν. On this section see Grote, 11. 424 sq.

εἰς τοὺς χ.] "at the times." Cf. 2. 20, εἰς μακρόν : 18. 151 ; al. So *ad* in Latin, Cic. *ad Att.* 12. 46, "utrum illuc nunc veniam, an ad decem annos," "ten years hence." *Tusc. D.* 1, § 82, "fit etiam ad punctum temporis ;" al.

§ 35. τοῦ κ. χ.] "at the proper time." Madv. 66. *Oed. Tyr.* 75.

ἄν τε] "whether persons of experience, or the reverse, have been chosen by lot to . . ."

ἰδιῶται) (the ordinary person, ἰδιώτης is the adept, "the expert."

οἱ . . . ἐπιμ.] Madv. 180 *b*, r. 1.

τοσαῦτ' ... ὅσα] "larger sums of money than upon any one whatever of your armaments."

καὶ (ἃ)] "and which are solemnized (on ἔχω cf. 2. 3) with a greater attendance and magnificence than I should suppose any in the world."

οὐκ οἶδ' εἰ] Don. §.538.

ΔΗΜΟΣΘΕΝΟΥΣ [4. 36

ἁπάντων ἔχει, τοὺς δ' ἀποστόλους πάντας ὑμῖν ὑστερίζειν τῶν καιρῶν, τὸν εἰς Μεθώνην, τὸν εἰς Παγασάς, τὸν εἰς Ποτίδαιαν; 36. ὅτι ἐκεῖνα μὲν ἅπαντα νόμῳ τέτακται, καὶ πρόοιδεν ἕκαστος ὑμῶν ἐκ πολλοῦ τίς χορηγὸς ἢ γυμνασίαρχος τῆς φυλῆς, πότε καὶ παρὰ τοῦ καὶ τί λαβόντα τί δεῖ ποιεῖν, οὐδὲν ἀνεξέταστον οὐδ' ἀόριστον ἐν τούτοις ἠμέληται, ἐν δὲ τοῖς περὶ τοῦ πολέμου καὶ τῇ τούτου παρασκευῇ ἄτακτα ἀδιόρθωτα ἀόριστα ἅπαντα. τοιγαροῦν ἅμα ἀκηκόαμέν τι καὶ τριηράρχους καθίσταμεν καὶ τούτοις ἀντιδόσεις ποιούμεθα καὶ περὶ χρημάτων πόρου σκοποῦμεν, καὶ μετὰ ταῦτα ἐμβαίνειν τοὺς μετοίκους ἔδοξε καὶ τοὺς χωρὶς οἰκοῦντας, εἶτ' αὐτοὺς πάλιν ἀντεμβιβάζειν, 37. εἶτ' ἐν ὅσῳ ταῦτα μέλλεται, προαπόλωλε τὸ ἐφ' ὃ ἂν ἐκπλέωμεν τὸν

ὑστερίζειν] 1. 9; sup. 32.
§ 36. ἐκ πολλοῦ] "long before." Thuc. 1. 68; Dem. 9. 51, ὡς ἐκ πλείστου.
τῆς φ.] "his tribe."
τί καὶ] cf. § 3. "when and from whom and what he is to receive, and what do."
ἀν... ἠμέληται] "has carelessly been left undetermined," the adj. being proleptic.
περὶ τοῦ π.] "pertaining to war" —generally, not that in which they were engaged.
ἄτακτα, κ.τ.λ.] with the asyndeton here comp. 9. 40, ἄχρηστα, ἄπρακτα, ἀνόητα.
ἅμα... καὶ] "as soon as we have ... we;" 18. 33; 19. 34; 23. 209, καὶ ἅμα δεῖ τι ποιεῖν καὶ πόθεν οὐκ ἔχετε. Comp. what is said in 8. 11, ἡμεῖς δ' ἐπειδὰν πυθώμεθά τι γιγνόμενον τηνικαῦτα θορυβούμεθα καὶ παρασκευαζόμεθα. On the exchanges of property cf. Gr. and R. Ant. s. v.; Böckh, Publ. Ec. bk. 4, c. 16. The forty-second speech, which is on a case of Ἀντιδόσεις, will repay perusal.
περὶ χρ. π.] "about ways and means."
τοὺς μετοίκους] Böckh, ibid. bk. 2, c. 21; Gr. and R. Ant. s. v.
ἔδοξε] the empirical aorist, expressing what took place in the several instances involved in ἅμα ἀκηκόαμεν... Cf. 2. 10, ἤνθησεν. "It is resolved."
τοὺς χ. οἰκοῦντας] "the outdwellers," "by whom we must understand with the grammarians freedmen, or else persons who, though still slaves, lived apart from their masters, and supported themselves by their own labour." Böckh, l. c. Ps. Dem. (47. 72) says of a freedwoman, ᾤχετο γὰρ.. ἐλευθέρα καὶ χωρὶς ᾤκει καὶ ἄνδρα ἔσχεν.
εἶτ' αὐτοὺς π. ἀντεμβιβάζειν] Bekk., "put ourselves on board," a strange expression, which can hardly be right. West. reads εἶτ' αὐτοὺς πάλιν, εἶτ' ἀντεμβιβάζειν, from S. Dind. omits the second εἶτ' and encloses ἀντεμβιβάζειν in brackets, understanding ἐμβαίνειν with αὐτοὺς πάλιν. If we read as West., ἐκείνους cannot be dispensed with.

§ 37. μέλλεται] here used passively, as in Xen. An. 3. 1. 47, ὡς μὴ μέλλοιτο... τὰ δέοντα: Thuc. 5. 111, ὑμῶν τὰ μὲν ἰσχυρότατα ἐλπιζόμενα μέλλεται. Comp. Oed. Col. 1618, τἀνὰ σου βραδύνεται. "so whilst these delays are taking place, the objects, whatever they may be, of our expedition are already lost."

γὰρ τοῦ πράττειν χρόνον εἰς τὸ παρασκευάζεσθαι ἀναλίσκομεν, οἱ δὲ τῶν πραγμάτων καιροὶ οὐ μένουσι τὴν ἡμετέραν βραδυτῆτα καὶ εἰρωνείαν. ἃς δὲ τὸν μεταξὺ χρόνον δυνάμεις οἰόμεθ' ἡμῖν ὑπάρχειν, οὐδὲν οἷαί τε οὖσαι ποιεῖν ἐπ' αὐτῶν τῶν καιρῶν ἐξελέγχονται. ὃ δ' εἰς τοῦθ' ὕβρεως ἐλήλυθεν ὥστ' ἐπιστέλλειν Εὐβοεῦσιν ἤδη τοιαύτας ἐπιστολάς.

ΕΠΙΣΤΟΛΑΙ.

38. Τούτων, ὦ ἄνδρες Ἀθηναῖοι, τῶν ἀνεγνωσμένων ἀληθῆ μέν ἐστι τὰ πολλά, ὡς οὐκ ἔδει, οὐ μὴν ἀλλ' ἴσως οὐχ ἡδέα ἀκούειν. ἀλλ' εἰ μέν, ὅσα ἄν τις ὑπερβῇ τῷ λόγῳ ἵνα μὴ λυπήσῃ, καὶ τὰ πράγματα ὑπερβήσεται, δεῖ πρὸς ἡδονὴν δημηγορεῖν· εἰ δ' ἡ τῶν λόγων χάρις, ἂν ᾖ μὴ προσήκουσα, ἔργῳ ζημία γίγνεται, αἰσχρόν ἐστιν, ὦ ἄνδρες Ἀθηναῖοι, φενακίζειν ἑαυτούς, 39. καὶ ἅπαντ' ἀναβαλλομένους ἃ ἂν ᾖ δυσχερῆ πάντων ὑστερίζειν τῶν ἔργων, καὶ μηδὲ τοῦτο δύνασθαι μαθεῖν, ὅτι δεῖ τοὺς ὀρθῶς πολέμῳ χρωμένους οὐκ

οἱ... καιροί] comp. with Dobree, Thuc. i. 142, τοῦ δὲ πολέμου καιροὶ οὐ μενετοί. Livy 31. 48, "non exspectare belli tempora moras ac dilationes imperatorum."
εἰρωνείαν] sup. § 7.
τὸν μ. χρόνον] i. e. till we can send a larger force.
οἷαί τε...ἐξ.] "are proved when the opportunities actually come..."
ἐπ'] as in 2. 1. Madv. 73. 3 d. For the participle, Madv. 178 a. 2. 8; 6. 2.
εἰς τοῦθ' ὕ.] 3. 3.
ἐπιστολάς] ὁ σκοπὸς τῆς ἐπιστολῆς ἐστιν οὗτος· Ὁ Φ. ἐπέστειλεν Εὐβοεῦσι συμβουλεύων μὴ δεῖν ἐλπίζειν ἐπὶ τὴν Ἀθηναίων συμμαχίαν, οἱ οὐδὲ αὑτοὺς δύνανται σάζειν. Schol.
§ 38. μέν... οὐ μὴν ἀλλ'] 1. 16.
ὡς οὐκ ἔδει] "unhappily."
εἰ μέν] the sense of the passage seems clear: "much of what has been said, though unhappily true, is for all that not pleasant to hear. Still it is idle to shut our eyes to the stern facts of the case. If by passing over an unpleasant reality in a speech we could make it cease to be a reality, it would be proper and necessary to study your pleasure, and only say what is agreeable. But as this cannot be, it is a shame for us to go on deceiving ourselves." If this is right, τις is the nom. to ὑπερβήσεται, not τὰ πράγματα as West. and Redh. say. τὰ πρ. therefore are "the realities," i. e. those matters as they exist as facts.
πρὸς ἡδονήν] 3. 3. Cf. 9. 4.
εἰ δ'] "but if agreeableness of speech when it is out of place proves a harm in action, it is a shame..."
ἑαυτούς] "ourselves:" sup. § 10.
§ 39. χρωμένους] "deal with," "conduct war properly, ought not to be attendants on circumstances, but be themselves in advance of them." Sall. Jug. c. 1, "neque regerentur magis quam regerent ca-

ἀκολουθεῖν τοῖς πράγμασιν ἀλλ' αὐτοὺς ἔμπροσθεν εἶναι τῶν πραγμάτων, καὶ τὸν αὐτὸν τρόπον ὥσπερ τῶν στρατευμάτων ἀξιώσειέν τις ἂν τὸν στρατηγὸν ἡγεῖσθαι, οὕτω καὶ τῶν πραγμάτων τοὺς βουλευομένους, ἵν' ἃ ἂν ἐκείνοις δοκῇ, ταῦτα πράττηται καὶ μὴ τὰ συμβάντα ἀναγκάζωνται διώκειν. 40. ὑμεῖς δέ, ὦ ἄνδρες Ἀθηναῖοι, πλείστην δύναμιν ἁπάντων ἔχοντες, τριήρεις ὁπλίτας ἱππέας, χρημάτων πρόσοδον, τούτων μὲν μέχρι τῆς τήμερον ἡμέρας οὐδενὶ πώποτε εἰς δέον τι κέχρησθε, οὐδὲν δ' ἀπολείπετε, ὥσπερ οἱ βάρβαροι πυκτεύουσιν, οὕτω πολεμεῖν Φιλίππῳ. καὶ γὰρ ἐκείνων ὁ πληγεὶς ἀεὶ τῆς πληγῆς ἔχεται, κἂν ἑτέρωσε πατάξῃς, ἐκεῖσέ εἰσιν αἱ χεῖρες· προβάλλεσθαι δ' ἢ βλέπειν ἐναντίον οὔτ' οἶδεν οὔτ' ἐθέλει. 41. καὶ ὑμεῖς, ἐὰν ἐν Χερρονήσῳ πύθησθε Φίλιππον, ἐκεῖσε βοηθεῖν ψηφίζεσθε, ἐὰν ἐν Πύλαις, ἐκεῖσε,

sus." Hor. 1 Epp. 1. 19. In 24. 95, ταῖς ἐξύτησι δυναίμεθα καὶ τοῖς τοῦ πολέμου καιροῖς ἀκολονθεῖν, the meaning seems rather to be "keep pace with..." οὐκ, which belongs to δεῖ, here attaches itself, as very commonly, to the infinitive. Cf. Eur. *Hipp.* 507, 645; al.

τὸν αὐτὸν ... ὥσπερ ... οὕτω καὶ (δεῖ)] l. 15. "and that in the same way as one would expect a general (Madv. 6) to lead his troops, ought men of counsel (those who do not act at random, but thoughtfully) to guide circumstances..."

τὰ σ. ... διώκειν] "to follow events." Ps. Dem. 10. 21, τὸ συμβαῖνον ἀεὶ διώκετε. Redh. quotes Livy 9. 18, "reges ... trahunt consiliis cuncta, non sequuntur;" and Cic. *pro Balbo* 4. 9, "cum etiam casus eventusque rerum non duces sed comites ejus consiliorum fuerint."

§ 40. πλείστην δ. ἁπάντων] cf. 24. 216, ἔσθ' ὅτι πωλοῦσι τὴν πόλιν μεγίστην εἶναι: οὐ τριήρεις ὅσας οὐδεμία πόλις Ἑλληνίς (which determines the sense of ἁπάντων here: cf. 1. 19) κέκτηται: οὐχ ὁπλίτας: οὐχὶ ἱππέας: οὐ προσόδους: οὐ τόπους: οὐ λιμένας; Cf. 6. 12; 14. 13.

μ. τῆς τ. ἡ.] "up to the present day." 9. 28.

εἰς δέον τι] supr. 14; 3. 28.

οὐδὲν .. ἀπολείπετε, ὥσπερ] Bekk. st. and Dind. from S. Bekk., οὐδὲν δὲ δ' ἀπολείπεσθε· "Ὥσπερ δὲ ..." οὐδέν is due to Dobree. "Nihil reliqui facitis quin ut barbari luctantur, ita ...," Sauppe, who quotes Pl. *Phaed.* p. 69 b, ἂν δὴ καὶ ἔγωγε ... οὐδὲν ἀπολίπον ... γενέσθαι. Cf. 9. 32.

ὥσπερ .... οὕτω] "exactly," "just as the b. box."

τῆς π. ἔχεται] "always feels for the blow;" lays hold, as it were, of it. His hands, instead of being employed in vigorous retaliation, are feeling the part hit.

ἐκεῖσέ εἰσιν] "so sind die Hände dorthin," "thither go his hands" to feel the part struck, as just said. Madv. 79 a. Herod. 1. 32, ὁ μὲν ἀπόστολος ἐς τὴν Μίλητον ἦν.

προβάλλεσθαι = to put out the hands for defence, "to guard." Hence the expression 19. 27, τὴν προαίρεσιν ... ὡς προβεβλημένην, "how guarded."

§ 41. καὶ ὑμεῖς] "so you!" l. 11.

πύθησθε] sc. ὄντα; sup. 18.

—43.] ΚΑΤΑ ΦΙΛΙΠΠΟΥ Α. 25

ἐὰν ἀλλοθί που, συμπαραθεῖτε ἄνω κάτω, καὶ στρατηγεῖσθε
μὲν ὑπ' ἐκείνου, βεβούλευσθε δ' οὐδὲν αὐτοὶ συμφέρον περὶ
τοῦ πολέμου, οὐδὲ πρὸ τῶν πραγμάτων προορᾶτε οὐδέν, πρὶν
ἂν ἢ γεγενημένον ἢ γιγνόμενόν τι πύθησθε. ταῦτα δ' ἴσως
πρότερον μὲν ἐνῆν· νῦν δὲ ἐπ' αὐτὴν ἥκει τὴν ἀκμήν, ὥστ'
οὐκέτ' ἐγχωρεῖ. 42. δοκεῖ δέ μοι θεῶν τις, ὦ ἄνδρες
Ἀθηναῖοι, τοῖς γιγνομένοις ὑπὲρ τῆς πόλεως αἰσχυνόμενος
τὴν φιλοπραγμοσύνην ταύτην ἐμβαλεῖν Φιλίππῳ. εἰ γὰρ
ἔχων ἃ κατέστραπται καὶ προείληφεν ἡσυχίαν ἔχειν ἤθελε
καὶ μηδὲν ἔπραττεν ἔτι, ἀποχρῆν ἐνίοις ὑμῶν ἄν μοι δοκεῖ,
ἐξ ὧν αἰσχύνην καὶ ἀνανδρίαν καὶ πάντα τὰ αἴσχιστα
ὠφληκότες ἂν ἦμεν δημοσίᾳ· νῦν δ' ἐπιχειρῶν ἀεί τινι καὶ
τοῦ πλείονος ὀρεγόμενος ἴσως ἂν ἐκκαλέσαιθ' ὑμᾶς, εἴπερ μὴ
παντάπασιν ἀπεγνώκατε. 43. θαυμάζω δ' ἔγωγε εἰ μηδεὶς
ὑμῶν μήτ' ἐνθυμεῖται μήτ' ὀργίζεται, ὁρῶν, ὦ ἄνδρες Ἀθηναῖοι,
τὴν μὲν ἀρχὴν τοῦ πολέμου γεγενημένην περὶ τοῦ τιμωρήσασθαι Φίλιππον, τὴν δὲ τελευτὴν οὖσαν ἤδη ὑπὲρ τοῦ μὴ
παθεῖν κακῶς ὑπὸ Φιλίππου. ἀλλὰ μὴν ὅτι γε οὐ στήσεται,
δῆλον, εἰ μή τις κωλύσει. εἶτα τοῦτ' ἀναμενοῦμεν, καὶ

ἄνω κάτω] 2. 16.
στρατηγεῖσθε] "you are com-
manded..." he determines all
your movements; you have no
plan of your own.
πρὸ τῶν πρ.] emphatic; "nor
before events take place do you
foresee any thing." The clause πρὶν
ἂν... is explanatory of πρὸ τῶν
πραγμάτων, "till you hear that
something has happened or is happening." Cf. 5. 2; Ps. Dem. 10.
21, 29.
ἐνῆν] Bekk. from S; ἦν ποιεῖν
F; cet. ἐνῆν ποιεῖν.
ἥκει] impersonal: "matters have
come to the very crisis." Madv.
7 a, 4.
ἐγχωρεῖ] sc. ταῦτα, as in Pl. Soph.
246 D (quoted by Sauppe), εἰ δὲ
τοῦτο μὴ ἐγχωρεῖ, λόγῳ τοιῷμιν.
§ 42. τοῖς γ.] "for what is taking
place." Madv. 41, r.
ἔχων] "in possession of:" § 9.

ἔπραττεν] "were trying to effect," "were attempting."
ἀποχρῆν... δοκεῖ] "would be
content with a state of things which
would bring upon us as a people
the imputation of cowardice and
the deepest disgrace."
With ἀνανδρίαν comp. Thuc. 1.
35, ἀρετή, "a character for virtue;"
κακία, Thuc. 3. 61.
ὀρεγόμενος] "reaching out after,"
"grasping after more." New Crat.
§ 477. Thuc. 4. 17, ἀεὶ γὰρ τοῦ
πλείονος ἐλπίδι ὀρεγόμενοι Thuc.
lb. c. 22. 2; c. 92.
ἀπεγνώκατε] 3. 33. "if, that
is, you have not altogether given up
in despair."
§ 43. ἀρχήν] Grote, 11. 427.
ὑπέρ] "to save ourselves from:"
1. 5.
στήσεται] i. e. Philip, "that
he certainly will not stop."
εἶτα] 1. 24.

26   ΔΗΜΟΣΘΕΝΟΥΣ   [4. 44

τριήρεις κενὰς καὶ τὰς παρὰ τοῦ δεινὸς ἐλπίδας ἐὰν ἀποστείλητε, πάντ' ἔχειν οἴεσθε καλῶς; 44. οὐκ ἐμβησόμεθα; οὐκ ἔξιμεν αὐτοὶ μέρει γέ τινι στρατιωτῶν οἰκείων νῦν, εἰ καὶ μὴ πρότερον; οὐκ ἐπὶ τὴν ἐκείνου πλευσόμεθα; ποῖ οὖν προσορμιούμεθα, ἤρετό τις. εὑρήσει τὰ σαθρά, ὦ ἄνδρες Ἀθηναῖοι, τῶν ἐκείνου πραγμάτων αὐτὸς ὁ πόλεμος, ἂν ἐπιχειρῶμεν· ἂν μέντοι καθώμεθα οἴκοι, λοιδορουμένων ἀκούοντες καὶ αἰτιωμένων ἀλλήλους τῶν λεγόντων, οὐδέποτ' οὐδὲν ἡμῖν μὴ γένηται τῶν δεόντων. 45. ὅποι μὲν γὰρ ἄν, οἶμαι, μέρος τι τῆς πόλεως συναποσταλῇ, κἂν μὴ πᾶσα, καὶ τὸ τῶν θεῶν εὐμενὲς καὶ τὸ τῆς τύχης συναγωνίζεται· ὅποι δ' ἂν στρατηγὸν καὶ ψήφισμα κενὸν καὶ τὰς ἀπὸ τοῦ βήματος ἐλπίδας ἐκπέμψητε, οὐδὲν ὑμῖν τῶν δεόντων γίγνεται, ἀλλ' οἱ μὲν ἐχθροὶ καταγελῶσιν, οἱ δὲ σύμμαχοι τεθνᾶσι τῷ δέει τοὺς τοιούτους ἀποστόλους.

κενάς] 3. 5.
παρὰ τοῦ δ.] "from this person or that." infr. 45, τὰς ἀπὸ τοῦ βήματος ἐλπίδας.
§ 44. νῦν, κ.τ.λ.] supr. 7. "now though we did not before."
πλευσόμεθα] Bekk. st. ; πλευσούμεθα, Bekk. Cf. L. Dind. on Xen. An. 5. 1. 10.
ἤρετό τις] The question is rhetorically put, as if actually heard by the orator. "I heard some one ask." Cobet (Hyper. Fun. Or. p. 33) says, "quum has verborum faces civibus admoveret Dem. non potuit languidum illud et iners ἤρετό τις apponere;" and accordingly he omits the words. Others, if I mistake not, will look upon the expression discarded by Cobet as, in a rhetorical point of view, particularly effective.
τὰ σ. ... τῶν . . . πρ.] Cf. 2. 14, 21; supr. 8; Tac. Hist. 2. 77 (quoted by Sauppe), "Aperiet et recludet contecta et tumescentia victricium partium vulnera ipsum bellum." "The war itself will find out the unsound parts of his power."
καθώμεθα] 2. 23.

οὐδέποτ' οὐδὲν ... μὴ γ.] Madv. 124, r. 3 ; Don. § 546. 6. 24 ; 9. 75 ; al. Dind., Sauppe, and others have rightly omitted the οὐ which Bekk. has before μή. Bekker's reading can neither be justified nor explained. Some few similar examples are found in the ordinary editions, but they have very properly been corrected. "There is no chance of our ever having any thing done that should be done," "any good achieved."
§ 45. τὸ τῶν θ. ... τὸ τῆς τ.] "both heaven is favourable and fortune favours us." Τύχη is similarly represented as an independent power co-ordinate with the gods in Phoen. 1209, καλῶς τὰ τῶν θεῶν καὶ τὰ τῆς τύχης ἔχει : cf. 2, 2.
ψ. κενόν] §§ 19, 30.
τεθνᾶσι . . θ. τοὺς . . ἀ.] "are dead for fear of," "stand in mortal fear of,"—the acc. being governed by τεθ. τῷ δέει, as = μάλα δεδίασι. Cf. Mr. Shill. de F. Leg. § 81 ; Madv. 22 b, note. Cf. Bacch. 1287, λέγ', ὡς τὸ μέλλον καρδία πήδημ' ἔχει.

ΚΑΤΑ ΦΙΛΙΠΠΟΥ Α.

46. οὐ γὰρ ἔστιν, οὐκ ἔστιν ἕνα ἄνδρα δυνηθῆναί ποτε ταῦθ᾽ ὑμῖν πρᾶξαι πάνθ᾽ ὅσα βούλεσθε· ὑποσχέσθαι μέντοι καὶ φῆσαι καὶ τὸν δεῖνα αἰτιάσασθαι καὶ τὸν δεῖνα ἔστιν. τὰ δὲ πράγματα ἐκ τούτων ἀπόλωλεν· ὅταν γὰρ ἡγῆται μὲν ὁ στρατηγὸς ἀθλίων ἀπομίσθων ξένων, οἱ δ᾽ ὑπὲρ ὧν ἂν ἐκεῖνος πράξῃ πρὸς ὑμᾶς ψευδόμενοι ῥᾳδίως ἐνθάδ᾽ ὦσιν, ὑμεῖς δ᾽ ἐξ ὧν ἀκούσητε ὅ τι ἂν τύχητε ψηφίζησθε, τί καὶ χρὴ προσδοκᾶν;

47. Πῶς οὖν ταῦτα παύσεται; ὅταν ὑμεῖς, ὦ ἄνδρες Ἀθηναῖοι, τοὺς αὐτοὺς ἀποδείξητε στρατιώτας καὶ μάρτυρας τῶν στρατηγουμένων καὶ δικαστὰς οἴκαδ᾽ ἐλθόντας τῶν εὐθυνῶν, ὥστε μὴ ἀκούειν μόνον ὑμᾶς τὰ ὑμέτερ᾽ αὐτῶν, ἀλλὰ καὶ παρόντας ὁρᾶν. νῦν δ᾽ εἰς τοῦθ᾽ ἥκει τὰ πράγματα αἰσχύνης ὥστε τῶν στρατηγῶν ἕκαστος δὶς καὶ τρὶς κρίνεται παρ᾽ ὑμῖν περὶ θανάτου, πρὸς δὲ τοὺς ἐχθροὺς οὐδεὶς οὐδὲ ἅπαξ αὐτῶν

---

§ 46. ἕνα ἄνδρα] i. e. a general sent out with an empty decree and hopes from the platform (Thuc. 3. 38, τὰ μὲν μέλλοντα ἔργα ἀπὸ τῶν εὖ εἰπόντων σκοποῦντες ὡς δυνατὰ γίγνεσθαι), but without troops. "It is impossible, impossible, I repeat, that one man should be able..."

ὑ... καὶ φ.] "to promise however and make assertions... is possible." The promises of Chares passed into a proverb: Zenob. 2. 13, αἱ Χάρητος ὑποσχέσεις... ἐπὶ τῶν προχείρως ἐπαγγελλομένων πολλά.

ἀπομίσθων] on the want of pay cf. 2. 28.

οἱ δ᾽.. ἔστιν] "and there are here persons who without scruple tell you lies about.." West. is wrong, I think, in taking ῥᾳδίως with ἔστιν —"ungehindert ihr Wesen treiben," and so Mr. K., "here are persons easily found." Much of the eighth speech is a commentary on this passage: e. g. § 19 sq.

ἐξ ὧν] "from what." 21. 102, ἐκ τῶν εἰρημένων καταψηφίζεσθαι: ib. 159, κρίνειν ἐκ τούτων.

ὅ τι ἂν... τί] "at random:"

1. 3; 24. 157, οὐ γὰρ ἀτυχῶς, οὐδ᾽ ὡς ἔτυχεν... ἀλλ᾽ ἐσκεμμένως καὶ αὐτὸ τοῦτο πράττοντες.

τί καὶ χρὴ π.] The force of καὶ may be best expressed by an emphasis—"what *are* we to expect?" "what *can* we expect?"

§ 47. Πῶς] "parum accurate interrogatio orditur a particula πῶς, quasi sequatur ὅταν." Schäf. Comp. 25. 68 (quoted by Fr.), ὁ δ᾽ ἀναιδὴς ἐκ τίνος ὀνομάσθη τῶν ἄλλων ἢ ὅταν .. τολμᾷ, and the precisely similar passage in Pr. Dem. 13. 15, ἀλλὰ πῶς καταλύσεις;... ὅταν ὑμεῖς., "they will cease as soon as.."

τῶν στρ.] Cf. § 25, and for μάρτυρας cf. ib., ὥσπερ ἐνόντας.

τῶν εὐθυνῶν] i. e. of the generals.

κρίνεται... περὶ θ.] "is tried before you for his life." On this subject cf. 2. 25 and 29; Aesch. 2. 71, ἐν τοῖς ἀγῶσι .. τοῖς Χάρητος. Dem. 19. 332. Allusion is made in 23. 104 to the trial of Autocles for having caused the ruin of Miltoscythes; of Cephisodotus, ib. 167; of Callisthenes, Aesch. 2. 71. Comp. Dem. 19. 180.

ἀγωνίσασθαι περὶ θανάτου τολμᾷ, ἀλλὰ τὸν τῶν ἀνδραποδιστῶν καὶ λωποδυτῶν θάνατον μᾶλλον αἱροῦνται τοῦ προσήκοντος κακούργου μὲν γάρ ἐστι κριθέντ' ἀποθανεῖν, στρατηγοῦ δὲ μαχόμενον τοῖς πολεμίοις. 48. ὑμῶν δ' οἱ μὲν περιιόντες μετὰ Λακεδαιμονίων φασὶ Φίλιππον πράττειν τὴν Θηβαίων κατάλυσιν καὶ τὰς πολιτείας διασπᾶν, οἱ δ' ὡς πρέσβεις πέπομφεν ὡς βασιλέα, οἱ δ' ἐν Ἰλλυριοῖς πόλεις τειχίζειν, οἱ δὲ λόγους πλάττοντες ἕκαστος περιερχόμεθα. 49. ἐγὼ δ' οἶμαι μέν, ὦ ἄνδρες Ἀθηναῖοι, νὴ τοὺς θεοὺς ἐκεῖνον μεθύειν τῷ μεγέθει τῶν πεπραγμένων καὶ πολλὰ τοιαῦτα ὀνειροπολεῖν ἐν τῇ γνώμῃ, τήν τ' ἐρημίαν τῶν κωλυσόντων ὁρῶντα καὶ τοῖς πεπραγμένοις ἐπηρμένον, οὐ μέντοι γε μὰ Δί' οὕτω προαιρεῖσθαι πράττειν ὥστε τοὺς ἀνοητοτάτους τῶν παρ' ἡμῖν εἰδέναι τί μέλλει ποιεῖν ἐκεῖνος· ἀνοητότατοι γάρ εἰσιν οἱ λογοποιοῦντες. 50. ἀλλ' ἐὰν ἀφέντες

περὶ θ.] "to the risk of his life."
τὸν .. ἀνδρ. καὶ λ.] The kind of death meant is clear from Lys. 13. 68, τὸν δὲ τρίτον .. λωποδυτὴν ἀπήγαγε, καὶ ὁμεῖς κρίναντες .. καὶ κατεγνόντες αὐτοῦ θάνατον ἀπετυμπανίσαι ἀκέλετε.
τοῦ πρ.] "that which becomes them," a soldier's death. Dobr. and Cobet condemn the sentence κακούργου ... πολεμίοις as a gloss.
§ 48. περιιόντες] in the Agora: § 10; 6. 14; 18. 158.
τὴν Θηβαίων κατάλυσιν] "concerting the humiliation of Thebes," by the re-establishment of Orchomenos, Thespiae, and Plataea. Dem. 16. 4 sq. is the best commentary on this passage: cf. Grote, 11. 405.
τὰς π. δ., depending on πράττειν —"and the breaking up of the free states," and their dispersion into villages, especially Megalopolis: Dem. l. c. Cf. 15. 20, τὰς πολιτείας καταλύοντας. The Spartans treated Mantinea in this way after the Peloponnesian War, B.C. 385: Xen. Hell. 5. 2. 7. Pl. Symp. p. 193 A. A people so treated were said to be διῳκισμένοι κατὰ κώμας:

Xen. l. c.; Dem. 19. 81. Cf. Cobet, Nov. Lect. p. 288. For the constr. here cf. 32. 8, μὴ καταπλεῖν Ἀθηνάζε τὸ πλοῖον ἔπραττε, quoted by Sauppe.
πρ. .. ὡς βασιλέα] A. Schäf. (2. 31), referring to the letter from Darius to Alexander (ap. Arrian. Anab. 2. 14. 2), is disposed to think that this was not the mere gossip Dem. represents it to be.
οἱ δ'] "others—in short, we go about each inventing stories."
§ 49. ἐγὼ δ'] "but for my part, though before heaven I believe he is intoxicated with the greatness of his achievements, and dreams many such things in his imagination, ... still I most certainly do not think that he intends to act in such a way as to let .. know what he is going to do." With μεθύειν .. comp. Hor. 1 Carm. 37. 10, "Fortunâque dulci ebria;" Pl. Rep. 562 D, ὅταν .. δημοκρατουμένη πόλις ἐλευθερίας διψήσασα ... ἀκράτου αὐτῆς μεθυσθῇ.
ἄνευ .. τῷ γ.] the "quidlibet impotens sperare" of Horace, l. c.
τὴν . ἐρημίαν] Cf. 3. 27.
ἀνοητότατοι .. λ.] Dobree and

ΚΑΤΑ ΦΙΛΙΠΠΟΥ Α.

ταῦτ' ἐκεῖνο εἰδῶμεν, ὅτι ἐχθρὸς ἄνθρωπος καὶ τὰ ἡμέτερα ἡμᾶς ἀποστερεῖ καὶ χρόνον πολὺν ὕβρικε, καὶ ἅπανθ' ὅσα πώποτ' ἠλπίσαμέν τινα πράξειν ὑπὲρ ἡμῶν καθ' ἡμῶν εὕρηται, καὶ τὰ λοιπὰ ἐν αὐτοῖς ἡμῖν ἐστί, κἂν μὴ νῦν ἐθέλωμεν ἐκεῖ πολεμεῖν αὐτῷ, ἐνθάδ' ἴσως ἀναγκασθησόμεθα τοῦτο ποιεῖν, ἂν ταῦτα εἰδῶμεν, καὶ τὰ δέοντα ἐσόμεθα ἐγνωκότες καὶ λόγων ματαίων ἀπηλλαγμένοι· οὐ γὰρ ἄττα ποτ' ἔσται δεῖ σκοπεῖν, ἀλλ' ὅτι φαῦλ', ἂν μὴ προσέχητε τοῖς πράγμασι τὸν νοῦν καὶ τὰ προσήκοντα ποιεῖν ἐθέλητ', εὖ εἰδέναι.

51. Ἐγὼ μὲν οὖν οὔτ' ἄλλοτε πώποτε πρὸς χάριν εἱλόμην λέγειν, ὅ τι ἂν μὴ καὶ συνοίσειν πεπεισμένος ὦ, νῦν τε ἃ γιγνώσκω πάνθ' ἁπλῶς, οὐδὲν ὑποστειλάμενος, πεπαρρησίασμαι. ἐβουλόμην δ' ἄν, ὥσπερ ὅτι ὑμῖν συμ-

Cobet follow Lambinus in branding this sentence as a gloss. Theophr. *Char.* 7, ἡ λογοποιία ἐστὶ ψευδῶν λόγων καὶ πράξεων ὧν βούλεται ὁ λογοποιῶν. Such persons are frequently spoken of by the orators: Dein. 1. 35, κατασκευάζων λογοποιοὺς: ib. 32, περιιὼν κατὰ τὴν ἀγορὰν ἐλογοποίει: Dem. 24. 15; Andoc. 1. 54. Cf. Thuc. 6. 38.

§ 50. ἄνθρωπος] Libri ἄνθρωπος: cf. 1. 3.

τινα] West., understanding Philip only to be meant, takes τινα with ὅσα, as ὅσα ἔνια in 27. 23, where however the words are in juxtaposition. It seems better to understand it generally, as an argument why they should depend on their own exertions; "and in every instance in which we ever hoped that any one (Philip among the rest—2. 6) would act in our interest, he has been found to act against us.." With εὕρηται we must therefore sc. πρᾶξαι. Schäf. compares 25. 7, ἃ μηδεὶς μὲν ἂν αὐτὸς πεποιηκέναι φήσειεν, ἐν δὲ ταῖς ψήφοις εὑρεθήσεται (sc. πεποιηκώς).

ἐν . . ἡμῖν] "and that the future depends on ourselves." Soph. *Phil.*

963; *Oed. Col.* 247.

ἐνθάδ'] an alternative put before them also in 1. 15, 25, al.

ἂν ταῦτα] "if I say.."

ἐσόμεθα ἐγν.] The ful. ex., as in 1. 14, "we shall have come to a right determination and have done with idle talk."

σκοπεῖν . . . εὖ ἰδέναι] "speculate what the future will be,.. but feel convinced that."

§ 51. Ἐγὼ μέν] "as I never on any previous occasion sought your favour by saying what I am not convinced will also be for your interest, so now I have spoken out my whole mind honestly and without reservation." εἴην would have referred directly to the occasions on which he had addressed them in the speeches numbered 14, 15, 16, and 23. The conj. represents his abiding determination on all occasions to say only that which he believed to be for their good: cf. 2. 24.

ἁπλῶς, οὐδὲν ὑ.] Cf. 1. 16; Isocr. 8. 41, οὐδὲν ὑποστειλάμενος ἀλλ' ἀνειμένως τοὺς λόγους μέλλω ποιεῖσθαι.

ἐβ. . . ἄν] Madv. 118 b, r. 2. "I could have wished, knowing

ΚΑΤΑ ΦΙΛΙΠΠΟΥ Α.

φέρει τὰ βέλτιστα ἀκούειν οἶδα, οὕτως εἰδέναι συνοίσον καὶ τῷ τὰ βέλτιστα εἰπόντι· πολλῷ γὰρ ἂν ἥδιον εἶπον. νῦν δ᾽ ἐπ᾽ ἀδήλοις οὖσι τοῖς ἀπὸ τούτων ἐμαυτῷ γενησομένοις, ὅμως ἐπὶ τῷ συνοίσειν, ἐὰν πράξητε, ταῦτα πεπεῖσθαι λέγειν αἱροῦμαι. νικῴη δ᾽ ὅ τι πᾶσιν ὑμῖν μέλλει συνοίσειν.

that it is to your advantage to hear good advice, I were equally certain that it will be to the advantage of the giver of it." Isocr. 8. 36, *ἐβουλόμην δ᾽ ἄν, ὥσπερ πρόχειρόν ἐστιν ἐπαινεῖσθαι τὴν ἀρετήν, οὕτω προσῆκον εἶναι*.. Lyc. § 3. After *συνοίσον* Sauppe and West. understand *τὸ τὰ β. εἰπεῖν*. I prefer to take it absolutely (Madv. 178 a, and r. 2). For the apprehension here expressed cf. 2. 21 and 32; 1. 16.

γάρ] referring to the suppressed protasis—"I should then." 1. 1, *οὐ γὰρ μόνον*: Thuc. 3. 42, *ἐλάχιστα γὰρ ἂν πεισθείησαν*: al. West. from S reads *εἶχον* for *εἶπον*.

ἐπ᾽ ἀδήλοις] "as it is, though uncertain what the result of these counsels will be to myself, still in the conviction that . . ." So Eur. *Ion* 228, *ἐπὶ δ᾽ ἀσφάκτοις μήλοισι*, "with unslaughtered sheep." Dem. 21. 30, *ἐπ᾽ ἀδήλοις . . . τοῖς ἀδικήσουσιν* . . .

νικῴη] Thuc. 2. 12, *ἣν Περικλέους γνώμη πρότερον νενικηκυῖα*: ib. 54. 3. Mr. Shill. *De F. Leg.* § 48.

συνοίσειν] Cf. the conclusions of speeches 3 and 9; Arist. *Rht.* 1. 3, *τέλος δὲ . . τῷ μὲν συμβουλεύοντι τὸ συμφέρον καὶ βλαβερόν*.

ΚΑΤΑ ΦΙΛΙΠΠΟΥ Β.

ΥΠΟΘΕΣΙΣ. Παραινεῖ διὰ τούτου τοῦ λόγου τοῖς Ἀθηναίοις ὁ ῥήτωρ πολέμου ὑποπτεύειν τὸν Φίλιππον καὶ τῇ εἰρήνῃ μὴ πάνυ πιστεύειν, ἀλλ' ἐγείρεσθαι καὶ προσέχειν τὸν νοῦν τοῖς πράγμασι καὶ εὐτρεπίζεσθαι πρὸς πόλεμον· ἐπιβουλεύειν γὰρ αἰτιᾶται καὶ τοῖς Ἀθηναίοις καὶ πᾶσι τοῖς Ἕλλησι τὸν Φίλιππον, καὶ τοῦτο αὐτοῦ καταμαρτυρεῖν τὰς πράξεις φησίν. ἐπαγγέλλεται δὲ καὶ ἀποκρίσεις δώσειν πρός τινας πρέσβεις ἥκοντας, ἀπορούντων τῶν Ἀθηναίων ὅ τι ποτὲ ἀποκρίνασθαι δεῖ. πόθεν δὲ οὗτοι καὶ περὶ τίνων ἥκουσιν, ἐν τῷ λόγῳ μὲν οὐ δηλοῦται, ἐκ δὲ τῶν Φιλιππικῶν ἱστοριῶν μαθεῖν δυνατόν. κατὰ γὰρ τοῦτον τὸν καιρὸν ἔπεμψε πρέσβεις ὁ Φίλιππος πρὸς Ἀθηναίους, αἰτιώμενος ὅτι διαβάλλουσιν αὐτὸν μάτην πρὸς τοὺς Ἕλληνας ὡς ἐπαγγειλάμενον αὐτοῖς πολλὰ καὶ μεγάλα, ψευσάμενον δέ· οὐδὲν γὰρ ὑπεσχῆσθαί φησιν οὐδὲ ἐψεῦσθαι, καὶ περὶ τούτων ἐλέγχους ἀπαιτεῖ. ἔπεμψαν δὲ μετὰ Φιλίππου καὶ Ἀργεῖοι καὶ Μεσσήνιοι πρέσβεις εἰς Ἀθήνας, αἰτιώμενοι καὶ οὗτοι τὸν δῆμον ὅτι Λακεδαιμονίοις καταδουλουμένοις τὴν Πελοπόννησον εὔνους τέ ἐστι καὶ συγκροτεῖ, αὐτοῖς δὲ περὶ ἐλευθερίας πολεμοῦσιν ἐναντιοῦται. ἀποροῦσιν οὖν οἱ Ἀθηναῖοι καὶ πρὸς τὸν Φίλιππον ἀποκρίσεων καὶ πρὸς τὰς πόλεις, ὅτι εὔνοι μέν εἰσι Λακεδαιμονίοις καὶ τὴν τῶν Ἀργείων καὶ Μεσσηνίων μετὰ

ARGUMENT.—τούτου τοῦ λ.] Delivered in B.C. 344.

ἐπαγγέλλεται] In § 28.

τῶν Φιλιππικῶν ἱστοριῶν] A History of Philip was written by Theopompus of Chios, in fifty-eight books: fifty-three of them were extant in the ninth century, and read by Photius. The popularity of this history is attested by the numerous quotations from it, and it is probable that Libanius refers to it in particular. There were other works — histories or biographies—treating of this period, by Satyrus the peripatetic philosopher, Duris of Samos, Anaximenes of Lampsacus (whose history of Philip is referred to by Harpocration s. v. Ἀλόννησος), and others.

ἔπεμψε πρέσβεις] Thirl. (vi. p. 10) follows the account here given, and agrees with Winiewski in thinking that Philip's embassy was headed by the celebrated Python of Byzantium, who, at some time during his mission, delivered a speech in defence of his master, which is mentioned by Dem. in 18. 173. Grote (11. 615, n. 4) cannot believe that any ambassadors from Philip were in Athens at the time, and makes the mission of Python the result of this speech. The speech does not decide the point. But there is no reason to reject this statement of Libanius, drawn as it is from the histories of the period.

ὡς ἐπαγγειλάμενον] through the ambassadors of the Athenians, Aeschines and Philocrates (cf. §§ 29, 30; 19. 20 sq.), and a letter in which he threw out hints of what he would do for them if alliance were granted him as well as peace: Ps. Dem. 7. 33; 19. 40.

καταδουλουμένοις] Grote, 11. 612; Thirl. 6. 8.

ΔΗΜΟΣΘΕΝΟΤΣ [6. 1

Φιλίππου σύστασιν καὶ μισοῦσι καὶ ὑποπτεύουσιν, οὐ μὴν ἀποφήνασθαι
δύνανται δίκαια πράττειν τοὺς Λακεδαιμονίους. πρὸς δὲ τὸν Φίλιππον
διημαρτήκασι μὲν ὧν ἤλπισαν, οὐ μὴν ὑπ' ἐκείνου γε αὐτοῦ δοκοῦσιν
ἐξηπατῆσθαι· οὔτε γὰρ ταῖς ἐπιστολαῖς ἐνέγραψεν ὁ Φίλιππος ἐπαγγελίαν
οὐδεμίαν, οὔτε διὰ τῶν ἰδίων πρέσβεων ἐποιήσατό τινα ὑπόσχεσιν, ἀλλ'
Ἀθηναίων τινὲς ἦσαν οἱ τὸν δῆμον εἰς ἐλπίδα καταστήσαντες ὡς Φίλιππος
Φωκέας σώσει καὶ τὴν Θηβαίων ὕβριν καταλύσει. διὰ τοῦτο ὁ Δημοσθένης τῶν
ἀποκρίσεων μνησθεὶς ἐπαγγέλλεται μὲν αὐτὸς δώσειν, φησὶ δὲ ὅτι δίκαιον ἦν
τοὺς τὴν δυσχέρειαν πεποιηκότας ἐκείνους καὶ τὰς ἀποκρίσεις ἀπαιτεῖσθαι, τοὺς
ἀπαιτήσαντας, φησί, τὸν δῆμον καὶ ἀνοίξαντας Φιλίππῳ Πύλας. ταῦτα δὲ εἰς
τὸν Αἰσχίνην αἰνίττεται, προκατασκευαζόμενος, ὥς φασι, τὴν κατ' αὐτοῦ
κατηγορίαν τῆς παραπρεσβείας, ἣν ὕστερον ἐνεστήσατο, καὶ προδιαβάλλων
αὐτὸν πρὸς τοὺς Ἀθηναίους.

1. "Οταν, ὦ ἄνδρες Ἀθηναῖοι, λόγοι γίγνωνται περὶ ὧν
Φίλιππος πράττει καὶ βιάζεται παρὰ τὴν εἰρήνην, ἀεὶ τοὺς
ὑπὲρ ἡμῶν λόγους καὶ δικαίους καὶ φιλανθρώπους ὁρῶ
φαινομένους, καὶ λέγειν μὲν ἅπαντας ἀεὶ τὰ δέοντα δοκοῦντας
τοὺς κατηγοροῦντας Φιλίππου, γιγνόμενον δ' οὐδὲν ὡς ἔπος
εἰπεῖν τῶν δεόντων οὐδ' ὧν ἕνεκα ταῦτ' ἀκούειν ἄξιον·

δίκαιον ἦν] Cf. § 28.
ὕστερον] In the following year,
B.C. 343.

§ 1] Compare the beginning of
the third Philippic.
In πρ. καὶ βιάζεται the latter
verb gives the kind of acts by which
Philip was infringing the peace. 9.
39, ἀπόλωλε καὶ νενόσηκεν ἡ Ἑλλάς:
9. 62, ἄρχουσι καὶ τυραννοῦσι: 19.
90, ἀπόλωλε καὶ γέγονεν ἀσθενὴς
(where see Mr. Shill.'s note): Aesch.
1. 95, ταῦτα μὲν ἀπολώλει καὶ
κατανενόθευτο καὶ κατωψοφάγητο.
"Whenever there is a discussion
about the acts, I should say the
acts of aggression, by which Philip
is infringing the peace, I always
observe that the speeches made on
our behalf..". With βιάζεται we
must in strictness understand πράττειν, as in 21. 11, λαμβανόντων
ἢ βιαζομένων, where Schäf. compares also 21. 40, μὴ.. ἐᾶτε ταῦτ'
αὐτὸν λέγειν, μηδ', ἂν βιάζηται..
φιλανθρώπους] "sympathetic,"

"generous" (cf. 7. 30), as exhibit-
ing an interest in the fortunes of the
Greeks affected by the aggressions
of Philip.
φαινομένους.. δοκοῦντας] "approve themselves as.. are thought
.."
δ'] "yet."
ὡς ἔπος εἰπεῖν] (S omits εἰπεῖν.)
Don. § 607 obs.; Madv. 151. "nothing, so to say," "nothing, or next
to nothing, that is proper, is done,
or for the sake of which it is worth
while to listen to these speeches."
The use of the phrase with πάντες,
οὐδέν, &c., in order to lower an absolute to a general statement, is
common and well known. Pl. Rep.
5. 456 B, πολὺ κρατεῖται ἐν ἅπασιν
ὡς ἔπος εἰπεῖν τὸ γένος τοῦ γένους,
γυναῖκες μέντοι πολλαὶ πολλῶν ἀνδρῶν βελτίους εἰς πολλά· τὸ δ' ὅλον
ἔχει ὡς σὺ λέγεις. Hence the use
in Rep. 1. 341 B, ποτέρως λέγεις τὸν
ἄρχοντα.. τὸν ὡς ἔπος εἰπεῖν (in the
popular sense) ἢ τὸν ἀκριβεῖ λόγῳ;
It is very seldom that we find in

ΚΑΤΑ ΦΙΛΙΠΠΟΥ Β.

2. ἀλλ' εἰς τοῦτο ἤδη προηγμένα τυγχάνει πάντα τὰ πράγματα τῇ πόλει ὥσθ', ὅσῳ τις ἂν μᾶλλον καὶ φανερώτερον ἐξελέγχῃ Φίλιππον καὶ τὴν πρὸς ὑμᾶς εἰρήνην παραβαίνοντα καὶ πᾶσι τοῖς Ἕλλησιν ἐπιβουλεύοντα, τοσούτῳ τὸ τί χρὴ ποιεῖν συμβουλεῦσαι χαλεπώτερον. 3. αἴτιον δὲ τούτων ὅτι πάντας, ὦ ἄνδρες Ἀθηναῖοι, τοὺς πλεονεκτεῖν ζητοῦντας ἔργῳ κωλύειν καὶ πράξεσιν οὐχὶ λόγοις δέον, πρῶτον μὲν ἡμεῖς οἱ παριόντες τούτων μὲν ἀφέσταμεν, καὶ γράφειν καὶ συμβουλεύειν, τὴν πρὸς ὑμᾶς ἀπέχθειαν ὀκνοῦντες, οἷα ποιεῖ δέ, ὡς δεινὰ καὶ χαλεπά, ταῦτα διεξερχόμεθα· ἔπειθ' ὑμεῖς οἱ καθήμενοι, ὡς μὲν ἂν εἴποιτε δικαίους λόγους καὶ λέγοντος

prose any such variation in the order of the words as in Pl. *Legg.* 12. 967 C, ἐπειδ' ὡς εἰπεῖν ἔπος. We have also ὡς λόγῳ εἰπεῖν, Herod. 2. 15; ὡς εἰπεῖν, Thuc. 1. 1.

§ 2. τῇ πόλει] a dat. of reference: Don. § 459. "But to this point now are all the affairs of the country brought, that the more convincingly and clearly .. the more it is .." On the part. παραβαίνοντα, 4. 37. After χαλεπώτερον Bekk. st. omits εἶναι with S, pr. m. On the omission, 1. 5.

§ 3. αἴτιον δέ] Madv. 197. For πάντας West. reads πάντες from "pr. S," i. e. ἡμεῖς οἱ π. and ὑμεῖς οἱ κ. But the accusative is required by the argument: "the reason is that whereas in all cases those who are seeking to aggrandize themselves ought to be stopped by deeds and actions," neither we the speakers nor you our hearers are prepared for such an energetic course in the case of Philip. Cf. 8. 73, δεῖ δ' ἔργον τῇ πόλει καὶ πράξεώς τινος.

οἱ παριόντες] The full phrase is παριέναι ἐπὶ τὸ βῆμα, Aesch. 1. 64, quoted on 1. 8. But of π. often occurs as a standing expression for "speakers," "the men of the platform," referred to in 4. 1, τῶν εἰωθότων . . Cf. 9. 182; Isocr. 8. 1, οἱ παριόντες εἰώθασι. Schöm. *Ass. of the Ath.* p. 111, Engl. Tr.

τούτων] explained by καὶ λέγειν καὶ συμβουλεύειν. On the omission of the article see 3. 12. "shrink from these (our proper) duties of making motions and giving advice."

τὴν πρὸς ὑ. ἀ.] "ἡ πρός τινα ἀ. duplicem habet significationem: subjectivam, *odium quo aliquem persequor;* objectivam, *quod est contra me apud aliquem*,"—Brémi, who illustrates the first sense by 18. 36, διὰ τὴν τοῦ ὑπούσαν ἀπέχθειαν πρὸς τοὺς Θηβαίους, the second by τὴν ἀπέχθειαν πρὸς Θηβαίους in the same section. Cf. Mr. Shill. *de F. Leg.* § 96; Isocr. 8. 167, δείσας τὴν πρὸς ὑμᾶς ἀπέχθειαν, "through fear of incurring your displeasure."

οἷα π. δέ] "but detail his doings, descanting on their heinous and atrocious character." 18. 41, ὁ τὰ Θηβαίων ὀδυρόμενος .. πάθη καὶ διεξιὼν ὡς οἰκτρά.

οἱ κ.] "our hearers," opp. to ἀναστάς as said of the speaker, 4. 1.

ὡς .. ἂν εἴποιτε] Madv. 137: infr. 37. "are better provided for making just speeches . . ." (Pl. *Gorg.* 448 D, καλῶς γε .. φαίνεται Πῶλος παρεσκευάσθαι εἰς λόγους), "but to hinder him from executing what he has now in hand you are wholly unprepared to exert yourselves."

D

ἄλλου συνείπτε, ἄμεινον Φιλίππου παρεσκεύασθε, ὡς δὲ κωλύσαιτ' ἂν ἐκεῖνον πράττειν ταῦτα ἐφ' ὧν ἐστὶ νῦν, παντελῶς ἀργῶς ἔχετε. 4. συμβαίνει δὴ πρᾶγμα ἀναγκαῖον, οἶμαι, καὶ ἴσως εἰκός· ἐν οἷς ἑκάτεροι διατρίβετε καὶ περὶ ἃ σπουδάζετε, ταῦτ' ἄμεινον ἑκατέροις ἔχει, ἐκείνῳ μὲν αἱ πράξεις ὑμῖν δ' οἱ λόγοι. εἰ μὲν οὖν καὶ νῦν λέγειν δικαιότερα ὑμῖν ἐξαρκεῖ, ῥᾴδιον, καὶ πόνος οὐδεὶς πρόσεστι τῷ πράγματι· 5. εἰ δ' ὅπως τὰ παρόντ' ἐπανορθωθήσεται δεῖ σκοπεῖν, καὶ μὴ προελθόντα ἔτι πορρωτέρω λήσει πάντας ἡμᾶς, μηδ' ἐπιστήσεται μέγεθος δυνάμεως πρὸς ἣν οὐδ' ἀντᾶραι δυνησόμεθα, οὐχ ὁ αὐτὸς τρόπος ὅσπερ πρότερον τοῦ βουλεύεσθαι, ἀλλὰ καὶ τοῖς λέγουσιν ἅπασι καὶ τοῖς ἀκούουσιν ὑμῖν τὰ βέλτιστα καὶ τὰ σώσοντα τῶν ῥᾴστων καὶ τῶν ἡδίστων προαιρετέον.

6. Πρῶτον μέν, εἴ τις, ὦ ἄνδρες Ἀθηναῖοι, θαρρεῖ ὁρῶν ἡλίκος ἤδη καὶ ὅσων κύριός ἐστι Φίλιππος, καὶ μηδένα οἴεται κίνδυνον φέρειν τοῦτο τῇ πόλει μηδ' ἐφ' ὑμᾶς πάντα παρα-

ἐφ' ὧν ἐστί] Cf. 4. 7. Arist. *Nic. Eth.* 9. 6. 3, οὗτοι γὰρ καὶ ἑαυτοῖς ὁμονοοῦσι καὶ ἀλλήλοις, ἐπὶ τῶν αὐτῶν ὄντες, ὡς εἰπεῖν.

§ 4. πρᾶγμα] "there follows a result."

ἐν οἷς] for this asyndeton cf. infr. 17, ἄρχειν βούλεται: 4. 14, ἐπειδὰν..: 9. 1.

διατρίβετε, κ.τ.λ.] "on which you employ yourselves, and in which you take a lively interest." Arist *Rhet.* 2. 2. 2, διατρίβουσιν ἐν τῷ τιμωρεῖσθαι τῇ διανοίᾳ. For ἔχει the Zurich editors and West. read ἔχειν, with S, depending on συμβαίνει.

ῥ., καὶ π. οὐδείς] Cf. on § 31,— "If then you are still satisfied with using juster arguments, it is easy and involves no trouble; but if it is our duty to consider how the present state of things is to be amended (cf. 3. 1), and we are to prevent its going still further unperceived by us all, and the sudden coming upon us of a mighty power which we shall not be able to withstand, then the manner of our deliberation is not the same.." After ὅσπερ one or two MSS. have καί, which would have been quite legitimate, notwithstanding Vömel says "nostro loco neganti conjunctio καί aliena esset." Cf. 3. 13.

§ 5. προελθόντα ἔτι] 3. 3; infr. § 33; 13. 203, τὸ πρᾶγμα ἤδη καὶ πορρωτέρω βαδίζει.

μέγεθος δ.] see note to 3. 25, καδάλλη .. ἱερῶν. Caes. *B. Civ.* 1. 64, "tantae magnitudini fluminis exercitum obicere."

ἀντᾶραι] 2. 24. Pl. *Euthyd.* p. 272 A, ταύτην (μάχην) νῦν ἐξειργάσθον, ὥστε μηδ' ἂν ἕνα αὐτοῖς οἷόν τ' εἶναι μηδ' ἀντᾶραι.

τοῖς λ.] Madv. 85.

§ 6. ὁρῶν] "though he sees," "sees without alarm."

φέρειν] "brings with it," "threatens." Soph. *El.* 1042, βλάβην. Pl. *Phaed.* 88 B, ὄλεθρον τῇ ψυχῇ.

ἐφ' ὑμᾶς π.] as infr. § 33, ὅτι

—8.]   ΚΑΤΑ ΦΙΛΙΠΠΟΥ Β.   35

σκευάζεσθαι, θαυμάζω, καὶ δεηθῆναι πάντων ὁμοίως ὑμῶν βούλομαι τοὺς λογισμοὺς ἀκοῦσαί μου διὰ βραχέων, δι' οὓς τἀναντία ἐμοὶ παρέστηκε προσδοκᾶν καὶ δι' ὧν ἐχθρὸν ἡγοῦμαι Φίλιππον, ἵν' ἐὰν μὲν ἐγὼ δοκῶ βέλτιον προορᾶν, ἐμοὶ πεισθῆτε, ἐὰν δ' οἱ θαρροῦντες καὶ πεπιστευκότες αὐτῷ, τούτοις προσθήσεσθε. 7. ἐγὼ τοίνυν, ὦ ἄνδρες Ἀθηναῖοι, λογίζομαι, τίνων ὁ Φίλιππος κύριος πρῶτον μετὰ τὴν εἰρήνην κατέστη; Πυλῶν καὶ τῶν ἐν Φωκεῦσι πραγμάτων. τί οὖν; πῶς τούτοις ἐχρήσατο; ἃ Θηβαίοις συμφέρει καὶ οὐχ ἃ τῇ πόλει, πράττειν προείλετο. τί δή ποτε; ὅτι πρὸς πλεονεξίαν, οἶμαι, καὶ τὸ πάνθ' ὑφ' ἑαυτῷ ποιήσασθαι τοὺς λογισμοὺς ἐξετάζων, καὶ οὐ πρὸς εἰρήνην οὐδ' ἡσυχίαν οὐδὲ δίκαιον οὐδέν, εἶδε τοῦτ' ὀρθῶς. 8. ὅτι τῇ μὲν ἡμετέρᾳ πόλει καὶ τοῖς ἤθεσι τοῖς ἡμετέροις οὐδὲν ἂν ἐνδείξαιτο τοσοῦτον οὐδὲ ποιήσειεν ὑφ' οὗ πεισθέντες ὑμεῖς τῆς ἰδίας ἕνεκ' ὠφελείας τῶν ἄλλων τινὰς Ἑλλήνων ἐκείνῳ προεῖσθε, ἀλλὰ καὶ τοῦ δικαίου

ταῦτ' ἐφ' ὑμᾶς ἐστιν, "that you are the objects of all." Very often with a dat., "with a view to the harm of." 19. 205, χρήματα "χουσιν ἐφ' ὑμῖν: 23. 137, καὶ ταῦτ' ἐφ' ἡμῖν ὄντα, "tend to our detriment." Isocr. (5. 73) complains of this line of argument,—περὶ σῆς δυνάμεως λέγουσιν, ὡς οὐχ ὑπὲρ τῆς Ἑλλάδος ἀλλ' ἐπὶ ταύτην αὐξάνεται, καὶ σὺ πολὺν χρόνον ἤδη ἡμῖν ἐπιβουλεύεις.

διὰ βραχέων] "to hear briefly from me." West thinks it somewhat surprising that διὰ βρ. should be joined with ἀκοῦσαι. He seems to have forgotten Virg. Aen. 2. 11, "Et breviter Trojae supremum audire laborem."

δι' οὓς] "propter quas (causa remotior quae dicitur); δι' ὧν per quas (causa est instrumenti instar), i.e. quibus permotus." Fr. Lys. 12. 87, εἰ διὰ μὲν τοῦ ὑμετέρου πλήθους . . ἡγοῦνται τοὺς τριάκοντα σῶσαι, διὰ δ' Ἐρατοσθένην. Dem. 5. 22, "which lead me (3. 1) to expect the contrary, and wherefore I look upon . ."

βέλτιον προορᾶν] "to see better into the future," "have the better foresight." F Ω T have βέλτιον τῶν ἄλλων, as in 5. 11.

προσθήσεσθε] Bekk. st. from S; Bekk. προσθῆσθε. If this reading is correct, the construction commenced with ἵν' εἰ is abandoned for a direct statement.

§ 7. ἐγὼ τοίνυν] "well, then, I reason—What did P. first make himself master of after the peace? P. and the settlement of the P. business."

Πυλῶν] 5. 20. Grote, 11. 482.
πρὸς . . ἐξ.] 1. 11. "forming his calculations by reference to ambition and the reduction . ."

εἶδε] 4. 5.
§ 8. τοῖς ἤθεσι] "a people of our character," "our principles."
ἐνδείξαιτο] Lat. "ostento:" "offer as a bait"—"could offer no bait tempting enough, could do nothing that would induce you to sacrifice . ."

τῶν ἄλλων τινάς] "de hāc collocatione pronominis indefiniti,

D 2

ΔΗΜΟΣΘΕΝΟΥΣ [Ο. 9

λόγον ποιούμενοι, καὶ τὴν προσοῦσαν ἀδοξίαν τῷ πράγματι φεύγοντες, καὶ πάνθ' ἃ προσήκει προορώμενοι, ὁμοίως ἐναντιώσεσθε, ἄν τι τοιοῦτον ἐπιχειρῇ πράττειν, ὥσπερ ἂν εἰ πολεμοῦντες τύχοιτε. 9. τοὺς δὲ Θηβαίους ἡγεῖτο, ὅπερ συνέβη, ἀντὶ τῶν ἑαυτοῖς γιγνομένων τὰ λοιπὰ ἐάσειν ὅπως βούλεται πράττειν ἑαυτόν, καὶ οὐχ ὅπως ἀντιπράξειν καὶ διακωλύσειν ἀλλὰ καὶ συστρατεύσειν ἂν αὐτοὺς κελεύῃ. καὶ νῦν τοὺς Μεσσηνίους καὶ τοὺς Ἀργείους ταὐτὰ ὑπειληφὼς εὖ ποιεῖ. ὃ καὶ μέγιστόν ἐστι καθ' ὑμῶν ἐγκώμιον, ὦ ἄνδρες Ἀθηναῖοι· 10. κέκρισθε γὰρ ἐκ τούτων τῶν ἔργων μόνοι τῶν πάντων μηδενὸς ἂν κέρδους τὰ κοινὰ δίκαια τῶν Ἑλλήνων προέσθαι, μηδ' ἀνταλλάξασθαι μηδεμιᾶς χάριτος μηδ' ὠφελείας τὴν εἰς τοὺς Ἕλληνας εὔνοιαν. καὶ ταῦτ' εἰκότως καὶ περὶ ὑμῶν οὕτως ὑπείληφε καὶ κατ' Ἀργείων καὶ Θηβαίων ὡς ἑτέρως, οὐ μόνον εἰς τὰ παρόντα ὁρῶν ἀλλὰ καὶ

quae Ionensibus propria dicitur esse, cf. 14. 6, τῶν ἰδίᾳ τι συμφερόντων: 20. 81, 133: 24. 2; Aesch. 3. 196" (Fr.). It is not uncommon in Thuc.: 1. 45, ἐς τῶν ἐκείνων τι χωρίων: 5. 82, τῶν ἐν Πελοποννήσῳ τινὲς πολέων. Antiph. de Caed. Her. § 21, εἰς τῇ Μηθυμναίας τι χωρίον.

ἀλλὰ καί] "but both out of a regard for justice and fear of the disgrace attaching to the thing, and in the exercise of a proper foresight, you would oppose him.." For the position of τῷ πράγματι cf. 18. 176, τὸν ἐφεστηκότα κίνδυνον τῇ πόλει: ib. 220, τὸν κατειληφότα κίνδυνον τὴν πόλιν: 25. 40, τοὺς γιγνομένους κύρας τῶν προβάτων. Madv. 9 a, r. On the fut. ind. ἐναντιώσεσθαι, Madv. 130 b.

ὁμοίως .. ὥσπερ ἄν] "just the same as if you were.." Madv. 139 c; Heind. Gorg. c. 76; Butt. Ind. Mid. κ. v. ὡς ἄν. Cf. 21. 60, 117, 225, βοηθεῖν ὁμοίως ὥσπερ ἂν αὐτῷ τις ἀδικούμενος.

§ 9. ὅπερ συνέβη] "which proved to be the case." Cf. 2. 5.

ἀντί κ.τ.λ.] "in return for what he was doing for them.." See 5. 21.

οὐχ ὅπως ... ἀλλὰ καί] "and so far from.. would even.." Madv. 212. 4; Don. § 571.

ταὐτά ὐ.] "under the same persuasion. For ποιεῖ the Zurich editors Vöm. and Fr. read ἐποίει from S. A reference to § 15 will serve to show that this is a mere blunder of the copyist.

καθ' ὑμῶν] " panegyric upon you." κατά is not often used as here to express a favourable judgment. Cf. however 18. 125; Aesch. 1. 157, 163; 3. 50, 125, 141—passages which I now find have been collected by Vöm. also.

§ 10. ἄν .. προέσθαι] Cf. 4. 13. "by these acts to be the only people in the world who would not for any (μηδενός being emphasized by ἄν).." μηδενὸς κ. is of course the gen. of price: 3. 22.

τὰ κ. δ. τῶν Ἑ.] 2. 24.

εἰς .. εὔνοιαν] Antiph. de Caed. Her. § 76, ἔργῳ τὴν εὔνοιαν ἐδείκνυε τὴν εἰς ὑμᾶς. Dem. 18. 54.

ὡς ἑτέρως] Lit., "how differently." Infr. 32; 18. 202, 306.

ΚΑΤΑ ΦΙΛΙΠΠΟΥ Β.

τὰ πρὸ τούτων λογιζόμενος. 11. εὑρίσκει γάρ, οἶμαι, καὶ ἀκούει τοὺς μὲν ὑμετέρους προγόνους, ἐξὸν αὐτοῖς τῶν λοιπῶν ἄρχειν Ἑλλήνων ὥστ' αὐτοὺς ὑπακούειν βασιλεῖ, οὐ μόνον οὐκ ἀνασχομένους τὸν λόγον τοῦτον, ἡνίκ' ἦλθεν Ἀλέξανδρος ὁ τούτων πρόγονος περὶ τούτων κῆρυξ, ἀλλὰ καὶ τὴν χώραν ἐκλιπεῖν προελομένους καὶ παθεῖν ὁτιοῦν ὑπομείναντας, καὶ μετὰ ταῦτα πράξαντας ταῦθ' ἃ πάντες μὲν ἀεὶ γλίχονται λέγειν, ἀξίως δ' οὐδεὶς εἰπεῖν δεδύνηται, διόπερ κἀγὼ παραλείψω δικαίως (ἔστι γὰρ μείζω τἀκείνων ἔργα ἢ ὡς τῷ λόγῳ τις ἂν εἴποι), τοὺς δὲ Θηβαίων καὶ Ἀργείων προγόνους τοὺς μὲν συστρατεύσαντας τῷ βαρβάρῳ, τοὺς δ' οὐκ ἐναντιωθέντας. 12. οἶδεν οὖν ἀμφοτέρους ἰδίᾳ τὸ λυσιτελοῦν ἀγαπήσοντας, οὐχ ὅ τι συνοίσει κοινῇ τοῖς Ἕλλησι σκεψομένους. ἡγεῖτ' οὖν, εἰ μὲν ὑμᾶς ἕλοιτο φίλους, ἐπὶ τοῖς

"He has naturally formed both this opinion of you, and that—how different—of..."

§ 11. ὥστ'...ὑπακούειν] "when they might.. so they would," "on condition they would." Madv. 166 b. "Sic Latine 'quum possent Graecis ita imperitare, ut ipsi dicto audientes essent regi.' Conf. Eur. *Phoen.* 514, ἂν ἔλθοιμ'... ὥστ' ἔχειν τυραννίδα. Plenissime h. e. junctis conditione et effectu: *ib.* 599, οὐκ ἂν ξυμβαίμεν ἄλλως ἢ 'πὶ τοῖς εἰρημένοις, ὥστ' ἐμὶ.. τῆσδ' ἄνακτ' εἶναι χθονός" (Schäf.). Cf. 18. 67, 81, 103; 21. 3 al.

οὐκ ἀνασχομένους] "did not put up with," "rejected with disdain."

Ἀλέξανδρος] Herod. 8. 140 sq. In 23. 200 Dem. makes Perdiccas king at the time of the Battle of Plataea.

λέγειν.. εἰπεῖν] In some passages these verbs are found together where there can be no intention to insist on any difference of meaning. Isocr. 15. 273, τὴν δύναμιν ἔχω μὲν εἰπεῖν, ὀκνῶ δὲ λέγειν: Id. 4. 11, τὸν δ' ἀκριβῶς ἐπιστάμενον λέγειν ἁπλῶς, οὐκ ἂν δυνάμενον εἰπεῖν. Here λέγειν might be understood of the contents of the speeches, and εἰπεῖν of the language used. "All earnestly desire to describe.. to do so in language worthy of the subject," "speak them as they deserve." Thuc. 3. 67, λόγοι ἔνεσι κοσμηθέντες. Cf. what Dem. had already said on this subject in 14. 1. On μέν.. δέ cf. 2. 24. S omits μέν, which is properly retained by Bekker, as also in § 13, ἐν μὲν τῇ μ. The same MS. omits μέν in 9. 2, ἢ μὲν πόλις, and ib. 5, τῆς μὲν ῥᾳθυμίας..

ἢ ὡς] Madv. 90, r. 4. "are great beyond any man's power to express them in words."

τοὺς μὲν.. τοὺς δ'] Madv. 50 a, r. 4. I's. Dem. 7. 41, ταύτην τὴν χώραν..τὴν μὲν..τὴν δὲ..9. 61; 19. 90; Thuc. 1. 89. Mr. K. well translates, "either joined the barbarian army, or.."

§ 12. ἰδίᾳ] "selfishly."

ἀγαπᾶν] rarely as here with the acc. In Thuc. 6. 18 the words οὐκ ἀγαπήσαντες, which followed ὑπεριδόντες, are now omitted on the authority of the best MSS. Cf. Heind., Pl. *Euthyd.* § 82.

ἐπὶ τοῖς δ.] "on condition his objects are just."

δικαίοις αἱρήσεσθαι, εἰ δ' ἐκείνοις προσθεῖτο, συνεργοὺς ἕξειν τῆς αὑτοῦ πλεονεξίας. διὰ ταῦτ' ἐκείνους ἀνθ' ὑμῶν καὶ τότε καὶ νῦν αἱρεῖται. οὐ γὰρ δὴ τριήρεις γε ὁρᾷ πλείους αὐτοῖς ἢ ὑμῖν οὔσας· οὐδ' ἐν μὲν τῇ μεσογείᾳ τιν' ἀρχὴν εὕρηκε, τῆς δ' ἐπὶ τῇ θαλάττῃ καὶ τῶν ἐμπορίων ἀφέστηκεν οὐδ' ἀμνημονεῖ τοὺς λόγους οὐδὲ τὰς ὑποσχέσεις ἐφ' αἷς τῆς εἰρήνης ἔτυχεν.

13. 'Αλλὰ νὴ Δί' εἴποι τις ἂν ὡς πάντα ταῦτ' εἰδὼς οὐ πλεονεξίας ἕνεκεν οὐδ' ὧν ἐγὼ κατηγορῶ τότε ταῦτ' ἔπραξεν, ἀλλὰ τῷ δικαιότερα τοὺς Θηβαίους ἢ ὑμᾶς ἀξιοῦν. ἀλλὰ τοῦτον καὶ μόνον πάντων τῶν λόγων οὐκ ἔνεστ'

καὶ τότε καὶ νῦν] "these considerations made him prefer them to you both then and now." In this case the verb is almost always in the present, even when τότε stands next to it. Soph. *Electr.* 917, καὶ νῦν θ' ὁμοίως καὶ τότ' ἐξεπίσταμαι. Dem. 18. 31. We find, however, Dem. 29. 38, παραδοῦναι καὶ τότε καὶ νῦν ἤθελον.

εὕρηκε] "invenit," "found"— as an ἕρμαιον or godsend. "nor having found an empire inland has he renounced . . ;" so that he can well dispense with the alliance of a maritime power like ourselves, as being out of our reach. "Sane de vero hic dominatu sermo est, sed illud εὕρηκε proverbiale quid sonat; nam ita fere locum circumscripserim, 'neque in mediterraneis subito praeclarum *sibi vinus est invenire principatum*, cujus gratiâ maritimum illum jam missum faceret.'" Butt. *Ind. Mid.* s. v. ἀρχή.

ἐπὶ τ. θ.] "over," "of the sea." Xen. *Cyrop.* 5. 3. 36, ἄρχων ἐπὶ τούτοις ἦν. Thuc. 6. 29, πέμπειν αὐτὸν ἐπὶ τοσούτῳ στρατεύματι, "in command of." Cf. 9. 2, τοὺς ἐπὶ τοῖς πράγμασιν ὄντας.

ἐφ' αἷς] "on the faith of which . ." Cp. §§ 28, 30. 18. 28, ἐπὶ ταύταις ταῖς ἐλπίσι τὴν εἰρήνην ἐποιεῖσθε: ib. 44; 19. 87.

§ 13. 'Αλλὰ νὴ Δί'] "yes, but,

some one may say . . .," "but it may be said . . .," anticipating an objection, as in Lat. "at," "at enim." Cf. 8. 9; 20. 58; al. Sometimes νὴ Δία precedes: 18. 117, νὴ Δί' ἀλλ' ἄδλιοι ἄρξα. In other passages γάρ follows νὴ Δία: 9. 68; 20. 56, νὴ Δί' ἀνάξιοι γάρ τινες τῶν εἰρημένων ταῦτ' ἦσαν: 23. 166. See other forms of "occupatio" in 1. 16; 4. 10.—Franke and Dind. refer εἰδὼς to Philip ("that though he knew all this [that the alliance with Thebes would be more to his advantage], it was not from selfishness nor the motives I attribute to him . ."). Schäf. and Redh. tr. τις "dicat aliquis quasi totum rerum hodiernarum statum perspectum habens." I prefer the former explanation.

ἐν . . . κατηγορῶ] observe the absence of a gen. of the person: cf. 19. 2, with Mr. Shilleto's note.

τῷ . . ἀξιοῦν] Madv. 115; Heind., *Phaed.* 60 B; Dem. 5. 21. "because the demands of the Thebans . . .," in claiming Orchomenus and Coronea.

τοῦτον καὶ μ.] "this is *just* the plea which of all others . . .," "of all pleas this is just . . . ." This *epitatic* use of καὶ has been noticed on 3. 1.

— 15.] ΚΑΤΑ ΦΙΛΙΠΠΟΥ Β. 39

αὐτῷ νῦν εἰπεῖν· ὁ γὰρ Μεσσήνην Λακεδαιμονίοις ἀφιέναι κελεύων πῶς ἂν Ὀρχομενὸν καὶ Κορώνειαν τότε Θηβαίοις παραδοὺς τῷ δίκαια νομίζειν ταῦτ᾽ εἶναι πεποιηκέναι σκήψαιτο;

14. Ἀλλ᾽ ἐβιάσθη νὴ Δία (τοῦτο γάρ ἐσθ᾽ ὑπόλοιπον) καὶ παρὰ γνώμην, τῶν Θετταλῶν ἱππέων καὶ τῶν Θηβαίων ὁπλιτῶν ἐν μέσῳ ληφθείς, συνεχώρησε ταῦτα. καλῶς. οὐκοῦν φασὶ μὲν μέλλειν πρὸς τοὺς Θηβαίους αὐτὸν ὑπόπτως ἔχειν, καὶ λογοποιοῦσι περιιόντες τινὲς ὡς Ἐλάτειαν τειχιεῖ· 15. ὁ δὲ ταῦτα μὲν μέλλει καὶ μελλήσει, ὡς ἐγὼ κρίνω, τοῖς Μεσσηνίοις δὲ καὶ τοῖς Ἀργείοις ἐπὶ τοὺς Λακεδαιμονίους συμβάλλειν οὐ μέλλει, ἀλλὰ καὶ ξένους εἰσπέμπει καὶ χρήματ᾽ ἀποστέλλει καὶ δύναμιν μεγάλην ἔχων αὐτός

Μεσσήνην] Grote, 11. 612.
ἀφιέναι] more fully in Thuc. i. 139, Αἰγιναν αὐτόνομον ἀφιέναι.
τότε] at the end of the Sacred War, when Philip restored to them Orchomenus and Coronea, which had been in the hands of the Phocians since B.C. 354, 353. 19. 112, 141. Cf. 5. 21, Θηβαίοις πρὸς μὲν τὸ τὴν χώραν κεκομίσθαι πέπρακταί τι, πρὸς δὲ τιμὴν καὶ δόξαν αἴσχιστα. The feeling of repugnance was caused by the manner in which they had become possessed of the towns. Cf. Grote, 10. 426.
σκήψαιτο] "how can he pretend to have done so because . . ."
§ 14. ἀλλ᾽ . . νὴ Δία] "but perhaps . . .," "but it may be said he was forced—for this plea is left . ." supr. § 13.
ἐν μ. ληφθείς] "surrounded by." Cf. 5. 22; Grote, 11. 587.
καλῶς] Ironical—"admirable!" "excellent!"
φασὶ μέν] "so they say he intends to regard the T. with suspicion." So 9. 63; 19. 132.
λογ. περιιόντες] 4. 10.
Ἐλάτειαν] the principal town in Phocis, and especially important in a military point of view—"ad defendendas, in quibus surgebat, angustias, quae Boeotiam versus propinquam et Thessaliam aperiebantur, opportunissima erat, ut qui eam teneret, brevi viâ praeter Thronium et Scarpheam ad Thermopylas perveniret (Livy 33, c. 3), et aditus in Boeotiam haberet" (Vom.). Hence the alarm at Athens when the news came in the year before the battle of Chaeronea, that Philip was fortifying the town. 18. 169.
§ 15. μ. καὶ μελλήσει] "this he intends, and will intend in my judgment," he will go no farther—there the matter will end. We might have expected τε καὶ here, but cf. 19. 89, χρήμαθ᾽ ἡμῖν πέρεστι καὶ περίεσται, with Mr. Shilleto's note.
τοῖς Μ.] a dat. commodi, as it is called—"in the interest of," "on behalf of." Madv. 34 and r. 1. 24. 88, δι᾽ ὅλου . . . τοῦ νόμου τῷ καταστήσαντι τοὺς ἐγγυητὰς ἅπαντα λέγει.
ἐπὶ . . συμβάλλειν] whether this constr. occurs elsewhere I don't know. σ. with πρός is not uncommon.
οὐ μ.] "he does not intend"—there is no intending about this, it is already being done.

ἐστι προσδόκιμος. τοὺς μὲν ὄντας ἐχθροὺς Θηβαίων Λακεδαιμονίους ἀναιρεῖ, οὓς δ' ἀπώλεσεν αὐτὸς πρότερον Φωκέας νῦν σώζει; 16. καὶ τίς ἂν ταῦτα πιστεύσειεν; ἐγὼ μὲν γὰρ οὐκ ἂν ἡγοῦμαι Φίλιππον, οὔτ' εἰ τὰ πρῶτα βιασθεὶς ἄκων ἔπραξεν οὔτ' ἂν εἰ νῦν ἀπεγίγνωσκε Θηβαίους, τοῖς ἐκείνων ἐχθροῖς συνεχῶς ἐναντιοῦσθαι, ἀλλ' ἀφ' ὧν νῦν ποιεῖ, κἀκεῖνα ἐκ προαιρέσεως δῆλός ἐστι ποιήσας. ἐκ πάντων δ', ἄν τις ὀρθῶς θεωρῇ, πάντα πραγματεύεται κατὰ τῆς πόλεως συντάττων. 17. καὶ τοῦτ' ἐξ ἀνάγκης τρόπον τιν' αὐτῷ νῦν γε δὴ συμβαίνει. λογίζεσθε γάρ. ἄρχειν βούλεται, τούτου δ' ἀνταγωνιστὰς μόνους ὑπείληφεν ὑμᾶς. ἀδικεῖ πολὺν ἤδη χρόνον, καὶ τοῦτο αὐτὸς ἄριστα σύνοιδεν ἑαυτῷ· οἷς γὰρ οὖσιν ὑμε-

ἐστι πρ.] "is expected." Thuc. 1. 14.

τοὺς μὲν ... σώζει] "when he is seeking to destroy the existing enemies of the T., the L., does he now mean to restore the P., whom he himself before annihilated," as some would have us believe? τοὺς ὄντας, opp. to οὓς ἀπώλεσεν. 8. 17, ἂν μὲν τοίνυν ἢ ..., opp. to τὸ διαλύεσθαι. 9. 56, ὅτ' ἂν ᾖ πόλις. The sentence is an example of the "argumentum ex contrario," or "contrarium" as it is called by the Auct. ad Her., who explains it at length 4. 15, 26. It is very often introduced by εἶτα (cf. 1. 24; supr. 13; 8. 20; 9. 13 al.), and generally appears in the form of two sentences connected by μέν and δέ, of which that with μέν, subordinate to the other (2. 24), contains some admitted fact, from which the inference is drawn.

§ 16. καὶ τίς] "but who can believe it?" "who pray can believe it?" καί being adversative, and expressing objection to the previous statement, as very often when used before πῶς, τίς, &c. 16. 8, καὶ τί ἂν ἄλλο βουλοίμεθα; 18. 235, καὶ πῶς ἔνι τοῦτο γενέσθαι; cf. Porson on Eur. Phoen. 1373.

ἐγὼ μὲν γάρ] Cf. 9. 15. "for my own part (so far from believing this) I do not even think that P., either if he were now giving up the T. (cf. 3. 33) would, .." ἄν .. ἄν with ἐναντιοῦσθαι. Cf. 1. 10.

βιασθείς] "because he was forced."

ποιήσας] Madv. 177 b.

συντάττων] here, as often, in the sense of "concocting a scheme." 32. 22, τοῦ σοφοῦ τοῦ ταῦτα πάντα συντεταχότος. "but his whole conduct rightly viewed shows that all his intrigues are directed against .." With this passage comp. 8. 43.

§ 17. καὶ τοῦτ'] 8. 41, καὶ τοῦτ' εἰκότως τρόπον τινὰ πράττει. On τρόπον τινά Madv. 31 d. For the asyndeton ἄρχειν β. cf. supr. § 4. "only consider: he desires to rule, and conceives you to be his only rivals in this!"

σύνοιδεν] "and of this he is himself perfectly conscious. For by those places of yours which he now holds it is that he secures himself in possession of..." Ps. Dem. 10. 12 has οἷς ... ἔχει χρῆσθαι, which is also the reading of some MSS. here. It seems to have arisen, as Fr. suggests, from ignorance of the attraction. Cf. Madv. 103.

—19.] ΚΑΤΑ ΦΙΛΙΠΠΟΥ Β. 41

τέροις ἔχει, τούτοις πάντα τἆλλα ἀσφαλῶς κέκτηται· εἰ γὰρ Ἀμφίπολιν καὶ Ποτίδαιαν προεῖτο, οὐδ' ἂν οἴκοι μένειν βεβαίως ἡγεῖτο. 18. ἀμφότερα οὖν οἶδε, καὶ ἑαυτὸν ὑμῖν ἐπιβουλεύοντα καὶ ὑμᾶς αἰσθανομένους· εὖ φρονεῖν δ' ὑμᾶς ὑπολαμβάνων δικαίως [ἂν] αὐτὸν μισεῖν νομίζει καὶ παρώξυνται, πείσεσθαί τι προσδοκῶν, ἂν καιρὸν λάβητε, ἂν μὴ φθάσῃ ποιήσας πρότερος. διὰ ταῦτ' ἐγρήγορεν, ἐφέστηκεν, ἐπὶ τῇ πόλει θεραπεύει τινὰς Θηβαίους καὶ Πελοποννησίων τοὺς ταὐτὰ βουλομένους τούτοις, 19. οὓς διὰ μὲν πλεονεξίαν τὰ παρόντα ἀγαπήσειν οἴεται, διὰ δὲ σκαιότητα τρόπων τῶν μετὰ ταῦτ' οὐδὲν προόψεσθαι. καίτοι σωφρονοῦσί γε καὶ μετρίως ἐναργῆ παραδείγματ' ἔστιν ἰδεῖν, ἃ καὶ πρὸς Μεσσηνίους καὶ πρὸς Ἀργείους ἔμοιγ' εἰπεῖν συνέβη, βέλτιον δ' ἴσως καὶ πρὸς ὑμᾶς ἐστιν εἰρῆσθαι.

Ἀμφ. καὶ Π.] Grote, II. 339, 331, 336.
§ 18. ἀμφ. . . . καὶ . . . καὶ] l. 14.
δικαίως [ἂν] . . νομίζει] Bekk. Others from S read ἂν νομίζοι. Schāf. rightly says, "particula delenda est, nata illa ex literis proximis. Certe scit Philippus se odio esse Atheniensibus." If ἂν . . . νομίζοι were read, ὑπολαμβάνων would = εἰ ὑπολαμβάνοι. Even if this were not in itself unmeaning here, the words καὶ παρώξυνται prove that the previous sentence is assertive, not hypothetical. δικαίως with νομίζει, "with reason."
παρώξυνται] "he is disturbed," "alarmed."
φθ. π. πρότερος] "unless he is beforehand with you by striking the first blow." On the aor. part., Madv. 183, r. 2.
ἐγρήγορεν] "he is awake." 19. 305, οἳ προσέχει τοῖς πράγμασιν ἤδη καὶ ἐγείρεται ἡ πόλις. Thuc. 7. 51. Fr. puts the comma after τῇ πόλει, but this seems weaker in itself, and leaves θεραπεύει without sufficient reference. "he is on the watch, he courts certain people against us

(supr. § 6)—the Thebans..."
ἐπὶ] Cf. supr. 6 on ἐφ' ἡμᾶς.
ταὐτὰ β.] a common expression to denote identity of political views. Thuc. 2. 79; 4. 79.
τούτοις] i. e. the Thebans.
§ 19. πλεονεξίαν] "cupidity."
διὰ . . σκ. τρ.] "through dulness of understanding." The ἀναισθησία of the Thebans was proverbial. 5. 15, εἰ καὶ πάνυ φησί τις αὐτοὺς ἀναισθήτους εἶναι. 18. 19, 43; 20. 109. Hor. 2 Epp. 1. 244.
τῶν μ. ταῦτ'] 1. 8.
καίτοι . . . γε] "yet surely persons of even moderate intelligence may see striking instances of them (i. e. the consequences of trusting P.)."
ἔμοιγ' . . . συνέβη] "it occurred to me," "I had occasion to..." This was in or before B.C. 344, when at his own suggestion Dem. was sent with other envoys on a mission to the cities of the Peloponnese. He refers to it in 18. 79—τὴν εἰς Π. πρεσβείαν ἔγραψα ὅτε πρῶτον ἐκεῖνος εἰς Π. παρεδύετο. Grote, II. 614; Diss. de Cor. p. 212.

ΔΗΜΟΣΘΕΝΟΥΣ [θ. 20

20. Πῶς γὰρ οἴεσθ', ἔφην, ὦ ἄνδρες Μεσσήνιοι, δυσχερῶς ἀκούειν Ὀλυνθίους, εἴ τίς τι λέγοι κατὰ Φιλίππου κατ' ἐκείνους τοὺς χρόνους ὅτ' Ἀνθεμοῦντα μὲν αὐτοῖς ἀφίει, ἧς πάντες οἱ πρότερον Μακεδονίας βασιλεῖς ἀντεποιοῦντο, Ποτίδαιαν δ' ἐδίδου τοῖς Ἀθηναίων ἀποίκους ἐκβαλών, καὶ τὴν μὲν ἔχθραν τὴν πρὸς ἡμᾶς αὐτὸς ἀνῄρητο, τὴν χώραν δ' ἐκείνοις ἐδεδώκει καρποῦσθαι; ἆρα προσδοκᾶν αὐτοὺς τοιαῦτα πείσεσθαι, ἢ λέγοντος ἄν τινος πιστεῦσαι οἴεσθε; 21. ἀλλ' ὅμως, ἔφην ἐγώ, μικρὸν χρόνον τὴν ἀλλοτρίαν καρπωσάμενοι πολὺν τῆς ἑαυτῶν ὑπ' ἐκείνου στέρονται, αἰσχρῶς ἐκπεσόντες, οὐ κρατηθέντες μόνον ἀλλὰ καὶ προδοθέντες ὑπ' ἀλλήλων καὶ πραθέντες οὐ

§ 20. Πῶς γάρ] Aquila Rom. *de Fig.* c. 9 (quoted by Redh.) refers to this passage: "Apostrophe, aversio, ubi quae ad alios dicta volumus, ad alios dicere videmur. Acutissimum exemplum in Philippicis Demosthenis, ubi quibus verbis populum Atheniensium monitum vult ea se dicit apud Graecos et Arcadas et Messenios concionatum invidiose." "well, I said, ye men of M., with what vexation... used to listen whenever any one...," "used to hear any one speak against Γ...."

Πῶς .. θ.] 1. 34.
ἀκούειν] for the benefit of "tirones" as he says, Vöm. remarks that the sentence in the direct form would be δυσχερῶς ἀκούοιεν ἄν, εἴ τίς τι λέγοι. As el here = as often as, ἀκούειν must be the inf. of the imperfect. Madv. 133. Cf. 9. 4. 45; 18. 43, οὐδὲ φωνὴν ἤκουον εἴ τις ἄλλο τι βούλοιτο λέγειν.

Ἀνθεμοῦντα] well named by Libanius τὸ τῶν ταλαιπώρων Ὀλυνθίων δέλεαρ. Cf. Grote, 11. 333. Here the word is feminine, in Thuc. 2. 99 masculine.

ἐδίδου] here not "offered" but "gave," defined by κατ' ἐκείνους τοὺς χρ.

τοὺς Ἀθ. ἀποίκους] Grote, 11.

334 sq. Ps. Dem. 7. 10. Observe the rhetorical ἀποίκους instead of κληρούχους, their placing Cleruchs in Potidaea being in direct violation of the stipulation at the formation of the new Confederacy (B.C. 378), that no Athenian citizen should possess or cultivate land out of Attica. Grote, 10. 335.

τὴν πρὸς ἡ.] Cf. § 3. "took upon himself the enmity they would incur with you," "your enmity."

τὴν χ.] the city, it would appear, had been destroyed. A. Schäf. 2. 23, note 5.

καρποῦσθαι] "to enjoy." Madv. 148 b. Thuc. 2. 27, ἔμενον Θυρέας οἰκεῖν καὶ τὴν γῆν νέμεσθαι.

λ... τινος = εἴ τις ἔλεγεν, ἂν going with πιστεῦσαι.

§ 21. στέρονται] Madv. 180, r. 1. "and yet, I said, after enjoying for a short time the land of others, they have been deprived for a long time of their own, shamefully expelled, not vanquished only, but..." The traitors were especially Lasthenes and Euthycrates, who are often mentioned—8. 40; 9. 55, 56; 18. 48; 19. 265, where he speaks of their being bribed. Grote, 11. 489. On the position of αὑτῶν cf. Don. p. 352, obs. 1; Madv. 11.

γὰρ ἀσφαλεῖς ταῖς πολιτείαις αἱ πρὸς τοὺς τυράννους αὗται λίαν ὁμιλίαι. 22. τί δ' οἱ Θετταλοί; ἆρ' οἴεσθ', ἔφην, ὅτ' αὐτοῖς τοὺς τυράννους ἐξέβαλλε καὶ πάλιν Νίκαιαν καὶ Μαγνησίαν ἐδίδου, προσδοκᾶν τὴν καθεστῶσαν νῦν δεκαδαρχίαν ἔσεσθαι παρ' αὐτοῖς, ἢ τὸν τὴν πυλαίαν ἀποδόντα τοῦτον τὰς ἰδίας αὐτῶν προσόδους παραιρήσεσθαι; οὐκ ἔστι ταῦτα. ἀλλὰ μὴν γέγονε ταῦτα καὶ πᾶσιν ἔστιν εἰδέναι. 23. ὑμεῖς δ', ἔφην ἐγώ, διδόντα μὲν καὶ ὑπισχνούμενον θεωρεῖτε Φίλιππον, ἐξηπατηκότα δ' ἤδη καὶ παρακεκρουμένον ἀπεύχεσθε, εἰ σωφρονεῖτε δή, ἰδεῖν.

ταῖς πολιτείαις] t. 5.
αἱ . . λίαν] 4. 17.
§ 22. τί δ' οἱ Θ.] 18. 48, τί δ' Ἀρίστιππος . . καὶ τί Περίλαος . . ," "then again the Thessalians, I said . . ," On the feelings of the T. towards Philip at this time cf. 18. 43. He restored Magnesia to them not long after the end of the Sacred War; and gratified them by the cession of Nicaea, one of the frontier towns near Thermopylae, which had been given up to him by Phalaecus B.C. 346. Thirl. 6. 12.
τοὺς τυράννους] 2. 14.
τὴν . . . δεκαδαρχίαν) Harpocr. s. v. says, Φίλιππος μέντοι παρὰ Θετταλοῖς δεκαδαρχίαν οὐ κατέστησεν, ὡς γέγραπται ἐν (" Φιλιππικῷ Δημοσθένους, ἀλλὰ τετραρχίαν, and so Dem. himself in 9. 26, καὶ τετραρχίας κατέστησεν. Vömel is right in thinking that the discrepancy is only apparent. After the expulsion of the tyrant family from Pherae, Philip, availing himself of the old division of the country into the four districts of Thessaliotis, Phthiotis, Pelasgiotis, and Histiaeotis, revived the distinction of the Tetrarchies, and put some of the chief Aleuadae at the head of the government. Dem. might therefore have used the same language as in 9. 26, but he skilfully adopts a term which would be more significant to his hearers, who remembered the Decarchies set by the Spartans (Grote, 9. 255), and were just then in fear of falling again under the Spartan rule. But whether he means by this that the general government of Thessaly was in the hands of a Decemvirate, or that each tetrarchy was governed by a board of ten, or that there were ten governors in each city, or lastly, used the expression simply in accommodation to his hearers, cannot be determined. The last supposition seems the most probable. At any rate he cannot have mentioned this particular point in his speech to the Messenians, as the arrangement had not been made at the time of his mission. Thirl. 6. p. 9.
τὸν . . τοῦτον] 2. 6; 9. 17, ὁ γὰρ . . οὗτος : ib. 18.
τὴν π.] "who restored to them the meeting at Pylae." 5. 23.
τὰς . . προσόδους] 1. 22. Thirl. 6. 14.
παραιρήσεσθαι] "take and appropriate."
πᾶσιν] "and are patent to all," "as all may see."
§ 23. διδόντα μέν] "and you, I said, behold Philip dispensing gifts and promises (to yourselves as to the Olynthians and Thessalians); pray, if you are indeed wise, that you may not awake (ἤδη) to find that he has deceived and cheated you (as he did them)."

ἔστι τοίνυν νὴ Δί', ἔφην ἐγώ, παντοδαπὰ εὑρημένα ταῖς πόλεσι πρὸς φυλακὴν καὶ σωτηρίαν, οἷον χαρακώματα καὶ τείχη καὶ τάφροι καὶ τἄλλα ὅσα τοιαῦτα. 24. καὶ ταῦτα μὲν ἔστω ἅπαντα χειροποίητα, καὶ δαπάνης προσδεῖται· ἓν δέ τι κοινὸν ἡ φύσις τῶν εὖ φρονούντων ἐν ἑαυτῇ κέκτηται φυλακτήριον, ὃ πᾶσι μέν ἐστιν ἀγαθὸν καὶ σωτήριον, μάλιστα δὲ τοῖς πλήθεσι πρὸς τοὺς τυράννους. τί οὖν ἐστὶ τοῦτο; ἀπιστία. ταύτην φυλάττετε, ταύτης ἀντέχεσθε· ἐὰν ταύτην σώζητε, οὐδὲν μὴ δεινὸν πάθητε. 25. τί ζητεῖτε; ἔφην. ἐλευθερίαν. εἶτ' οὐχ ὁρᾶτε Φίλιππον ἀλλοτριωτάτας ταύτῃ καὶ τὰς προσηγορίας ἔχοντα; βασιλεὺς γὰρ καὶ τύραννος ἅπας ἐχθρὸς ἐλευθερίᾳ καὶ νόμοις ἐναντίος. οὐ φυλάξεσθ' ὅπως, ἔφην, μὴ πολέμου ζητοῦντες ἀπαλλαγῆναι δεσπότην εὕρητε;

26. Ταῦτ' ἀκούσαντες ἐκεῖνοι, καὶ θορυβοῦντες ὡς ὀρθῶς λέγεται, καὶ πολλοὺς ἑτέρους λόγους παρὰ τῶν πρέσβεων καὶ παρόντος ἐμοῦ καὶ πάλιν ὕστερον ἀκούσαντες, ὡς ἔοικεν, οὐδὲν μᾶλλον ἀποσχήσονται τῆς Φιλίππου φιλίας οὐδ' ὧν ἐπαγγέλλεται. καὶ οὐ τοῦτό ἐστιν ἄτοπον, εἰ Μεσσή-

τοίνυν] "now there is, I continued.."
ταῖς π.] "devised by free states for." Madv. 38 g.
§ 24. καί, κ.τ.λ.] "now all these .. and require expense besides, but there is one common safeguard inherent in the nature of sensible men which .. for all, is especially so for democracies against despots."
τοῖς πλ. = ταῖς πολιτείαις, § 21. Cf. the definition in Thuc. 2. 43. For the plural, 18. 46; 23. 124.
ἀπιστία] 1. 5.
οὐδὲν μὴ .. π.] 4. 44.
§ 25. εἶτ'] 1. 24. "then do you not see that even the titles P. bears are utterly at variance with this?"
νόμοις] a grand characteristic of a free state. Aesch. 1. 4, διοικοῦνται δ' αἱ μὲν τυραννίδες καὶ ὀλιγαρχίαι τοῖς τρόποις τῶν ἐφεστηκότων, αἱ δὲ πόλεις αἱ δημοκρατούμεναι τοῖς νόμοις τοῖς κειμένοις. Cf. Thuc. 3. 62.

Hence νόμος is opposed to ὀλιγαρχία. Dem. 24. 75, τί ποτ' ἐστὶν ᾧ νόμος ὀλιγαρχίας διαφέρει; ib. 152, ἡ γὰρ πόλις ἡμῶν .. νόμοις καὶ ψηφίσμασι διοικεῖται. Cf. also 23. 138, 141.
πολέμου i. e. war with Sparta, the fear of which had caused them to apply to Philip for help.
ὅπως .. μή] Madv. 123.
§ 26. θορυβοῦντες ὡς] "though they heard these words, and loudly expressed their approbation of them, they will none the more, as it appears.." 8. 30, θορυβεῖτε ὡς εὖ λέγει; ib. 77. Arist. Rhet. 1. 2, θορυβοῦνται δὲ μᾶλλον οἱ ἐνθυμηματικοί.
πάλιν ὕστερον] from some of the other envoys, when he had left them to visit the other cities of the Peloponnesus.
On εἰ, "that," after ἄτοπον, Madv. 194 c. In 18. 64 Dem. asks with what party his censors would

—29.] ΚΑΤΑ ΦΙΛΙΠΠΟΥ Β. 45

νιοι καὶ Πελοποννησίων τινὲς παρ' ἃ τῷ λογισμῷ βέλ
τισθ' ὁρῶσί τι πράξουσιν 27. ἀλλ' ὑμεῖς οἱ καὶ συνιέντες
αὐτοὶ καὶ τῶν λεγόντων ἀκούοντες ἡμῶν ὡς ἐπιβουλεύεσθε,
ὡς περιστοιχίζεσθε, ἐκ τοῦ μηδὲν ἤδη ποιῆσαι λήσεθ', ὡς
ἐμοὶ δοκεῖ, πάντα ὑπομείναντες οὕτως ἡ παραυτίχ' ἡδονὴ
καὶ ῥᾳστώνη μεῖζον ἰσχύει τοῦ ποθ' ὕστερον συνοίσειν
μέλλοντος.

28. Περὶ μὲν δὴ τῶν ὑμῖν πρακτέων καθ' ὑμᾶς αὐτοὺς
ὕστερον βουλεύσεσθε, ἂν σωφρονῆτε· ἃ δὲ νῦν ἀποκρι
νάμενοι τὰ δέοντ' ἂν εἴητ' ἐψηφισμένοι, ταῦτ' ἤδη λέξω.
ἦν μὲν οὖν δίκαιον, ὦ ἄνδρες Ἀθηναῖοι, τοὺς ἐνεγκόντας
τὰς ὑποσχέσεις, ἐφ' αἷς ἐπείσθητε ποιήσασθαι τὴν εἰρή
νην, καλεῖν 29. οὔτε γὰρ αὐτὸς ἄν ποτε ὑπέμεινα πρεσ
βεύειν, οὔτ' ἂν ὑμεῖς οἶδ' ὅτι ἐπαύσασθε πολεμοῦντες, εἰ τοι

have wished the city to side? With that of the Thessalians and those who contributed to the disgrace of Hellas, or that which περιεωρακυίας ταῦτα γιγνόμενα ἐπὶ τῆς ἰδίας πλεονεξίας ἐλπίδι, ἣν ἂν Ἀρκάδας καὶ Μεσσηνίους καὶ Ἀργείους θείημεν:

τῷ λ.] "upon reflection," "to what their better judgment tells them is . ."

§ 27. ἀλλ' ὑμεῖς] the orator here deserts the construction commenced with ὅτοπον εἰ, and expresses himself more forcibly in a direct statement.

ὡς] "how."

περιστοιχίζεσθε] 4. 9.

ἐκ τοῦ . . . ποιῆσαι] Bekk. st.; Bekk., Dind., and Wesl. ποιεῖν. "in consequence of your doing nothing at once," "in consequence of shunning present exertion, will, before you are aware of it, as it seems to me, endure all things," and therefore the worst. πάντα opp. to οὐδέν. For ἐκ τοῦ S has ὅστε, which is adopted by Redh. Cf. 8. 53, γίγνεται ὑμῖν . . ἡ σχολὴ καὶ τὸ μηδὲν ἤδη ποιεῖν. On the aor. part. ὑπομείναντες, Madv. 183, r. 2.

ἡ π. ἡδονὴ] "non est ut vulgo explicant 'quae statim et sine labore paratur,' sed 'cujus in praesens est fructus citoque perit.'" Heind. Prot. p. 620. "the pleasure of the moment." Cf. 8. 70, τῆς παρ' ἡμέραν χάριτος.

§ 28. πρακτέων] the genitive plural of such verbals is rarely found. Isocr. 15. 59 has πολλῶν ἔτι μοι λεκτέων ὄντων.

καθ' ὑμᾶς αὐτούς] "by yourselves," when the ambassadors to whom an answer had to be given were gone. Grote, 11. 615.

ἃ δὲ νῦν] "but I will now give you such an answer as it would be proper for you to decide upon to-day." λέξω as in 4. 29, τοῦτ' ἤδη λέξω, and so often of the reading of public documents. Lat. "recito." Dind. and others rightly, I think, insert here the title 'Ἀνδόκρισις as in 4. 39, though the lemma is wanting in the MSS.

ἦν . . 8.] "it were just." Madv. 118 a; Don. p. 541.

τὰς ὑποσχέσεις] Grote, 11. 552. Allusion was made above to these promises of Philip: cf. 18. 41.

καλεῖν] i. e. to tell you what answer you ought to give.

§ 29. οἶδ' ὅτι] Madv. 193, r.

αὐτὰ πράξειν τυχόντα εἰρήνης Φίλιππον ᾤεσθε· ἀλλ' ἦν πολὺ τούτων ἀφεστηκότα τὰ τότε λεγόμενα. καὶ πάλιν γ' ἑτέρους καλεῖν. τίνας; τοὺς ὅτ' ἐγὼ γεγονυίας ἤδη τῆς εἰρήνης ἀπὸ τῆς ὑστέρας ἥκων πρεσβείας τῆς ἐπὶ τοὺς ὅρκους, αἰσθόμενος φενακιζομένην τὴν πόλιν, προὔλεγον καὶ διεμαρτυρόμην καὶ οὐκ εἴων προέσθαι Πύλας οὐδὲ Φωκέας, 30. λέγοντας ὡς ἐγὼ μὲν ὕδωρ πίνων εἰκότως δύστροπος καὶ δύσκολός εἰμί τις ἄνθρωπος, Φίλιππος δ', ἅπερ εὔξαισθ' ἂν ὑμεῖς, ἐὰν παρέλθῃ, πράξει, καὶ Θεσπιὰς μὲν καὶ Πλαταιὰς τειχιεῖ, Θηβαίους δὲ παύσει τῆς ὕβρεως, Χερρόνησον δὲ τοῖς αὑτοῦ τέλεσι διορύξει, Εὔβοιαν δὲ καὶ

τούτων] "but the representations then made were very different from what we see," i. e. what Philip is doing.
καὶ . . . γ'] 2. 10. "aye and summon others," i. e. Aeschines, Philocrates, and their associates. Grote, L c.
τοὺς . . λέγοντας] on the hyperbaton see 2. 16. "Those who, when I, after the conclusion of the peace, on my return (1. 8) from the second embassy, that for the oaths, finding they were practising an imposition on you, warned and protested and urged you not to . . . said that . . ." The embassy here mentioned was the second, sent in B.C. 346, of which, as of the first, Dem. was a member. For the expression τὴν ἐπὶ τοὺς ὅρκους cf. 19. 57. ἀπεδημήσαμεν ἐπὶ τοὺς ὅρκους: ib. 17, 96, αἱρεθεὶς ἐπὶ τοὺς ὅρκους.
προὔλεγον] Cf. 19. 65. Compare the account given in 5. 10; 18, 31 sq.
§ 30. ὡς ἐγὼ . . . εἰμί] 19. 45, ἐπανέστη δ' ὁ Φιλοκράτης μάλα ὑβριστικῶς, οὐδέν, ἔφη, θαυμαστὸν . . . μὴ ταὐτὰ ἐμοὶ καὶ Δημοσθένει δοκεῖν. οὗτος μὲν γὰρ ὕδωρ, ἐγὼ δὲ οἶνον πίνω· ὑμεῖς δὲ ἐγελᾶτε. Cf. Mr. Shill. in l. Philocrates was evidently a believer in the dictum of Cratinus, ὕδωρ δὲ πίνων χρηστὸν ἂν τέκοις; The last words of the quotation remind one of what Dem. says in 23. 206, ὑμεῖς δὲ . . τοὺς τὰ μέγιστ' ἀδικοῦντας καὶ φανερῶς ἐξελεγχομένους ἂν ἐν ᾖ δύο ἀστεῖα εἴπωσι . . ἀφίετε.
δ. . . . τις] "a sour and peevish (sort of) fellow." Arist. Eq. 45; Pl. Rep. 2. 358 A, ἐγώ τις, ὡς ἔοικε, δυσμαθής.
εἰμί] Cobet (Nov. Lect. p. 335) strangely objects to the pres. ind. : "non est bene Graecum quod legitur [Xen. Hell.] 2. 3. 45, ἃ δ' ἂν εἴπωσιν ὡς ἐγώ εἰμι οἷος δεῖ ποτε μεταβάλλεσθαι, sed requiritur ὡς ἐγὼ εἴην. Semper" (which surely begs the question) "Xenophon in tali re optativum ponit, qui prorsus est necessarium si quis quid ab alio dictum esse referri quod ipso judice mendacium est; in quâ re multi ἅρα addunt, ὡς ἄρα ἐγὼ εἴην. Idem remedium exspectat Dem. 21. 104, ἐτόλμα περὶ ἐμοῦ λέγειν ὡς ἐγὼ τὸ πρᾶγμ' εἰμὶ τοῦτο δεδρακώς, immo vero εἴην." This dictum, like many others of this great scholar, is far too sweeping. Cf. e. g. 8. 4. 73; 22. 2. Plat. Apol. 18 B, passages which sufficiently defend the pres. ind. here. ·
ἐὰν παρέλθῃ] "should he pass the Straits" of Thermopylae.
Θεσπιὰς] Cf. 5. 10; 19. 20 sq.
παύσει τῆς ὕ.] "humble the pride of the T." Cf. 19. 112, 220.
Χ . . . διορύξει] to protect it from

—32.] ΚΑΤΑ ΦΙΛΙΠΠΟΥ Β. 47

τὸν Ὠρωπὸν ἀντ' Ἀμφιπόλεως ὑμῖν ἀποδώσει· ταῦτα γὰρ ἅπαντα ἐπὶ τοῦ βήματος ἐνταῦθα μνημονεύετ' οἶδ' ὅτι ῥηθέντα, καίπερ ὄντες οὐ δεινοὶ τοὺς ἀδικοῦντας μεμνῆσθαι. 31. καὶ τὸ πάντων αἴσχιστον, καὶ τοῖς ἐκγόνοις πρὸς τὰς ἐλπίδας τὴν αὐτὴν εἰρήνην εἶναι ταύτην ἐψηφίσασθε οὕτω τελέως ὑπήχθητε. τί δὴ ταῦτα νῦν λέγω καὶ καλεῖν φημὶ δεῖν τούτους; ἐγὼ νὴ τοὺς θεοὺς τἀληθῆ μετὰ παρρησίας ἐρῶ πρὸς ὑμᾶς καὶ οὐκ ἀποκρύψομαι. 32. οὐχ ἵν' εἰς λοιδορίαν ἐμπεσὼν ἐμαυτῷ μὲν ἐξ ἴσου λόγον παρ'

the inroads of the Thracians. Expedients of this kind had been resorted to before. Plut. *Vit. Per.* c. 19, καὶ τὸν αὐχένα διαζώσας ἐρύμασι καὶ προβλήμασι ἐκ θαλάττης εἰς θάλατταν ἀπετείχισε τὰς καταδρομὰς τῶν Θρᾳκῶν τῶν περιεχυμένων τῇ Χερρονήσῳ. For the same purpose a wall was built across the neck of the Isthmus by Dercyllidas towards the end of the Peloponnesian War. Xen. *Hell.* 3. 2. 10. Cf. Pl. Dem. 7. 39.

τέλεσι] "at his own expense."

Ὠρωπόν] Cf. Grote, 11. 573. 19. 22, 220, 325 sq.

ἐνταῦθα] Bekk. with S, remarking however "praestat ἐνταυθὶ ei hoc loco et 23. 77 et 41. 23." Dind. has here, as elsewhere, ἐνταυθί. Cf. Mr. Shill. *de Fals. Leg.* § 356.

δεινοί] "famous for" (2. 20). For this trait in the character of the Athenians see 18. 99.

§ 31. τὸ π. αἴσχιστον] 2. 1; 3. 31.

τοῖς ἐκγόνοις] "should descend also (τὴν αὐτήν) to his descendants." Cf. 19. 48, 52 sq., where the clause is criticized. From these passages it is clear that by ἐκγόνοις are meant Philip's descendants, not "your descendants," as Mr. Kennedy and Grote (11. 575, note) think.

ὑπήχθητε] "were you led away."

ἐρῶ . . καὶ οὐκ ἀποκρύψομαι] a common form of expression, in which "Graeco more id quod antea affir-

mando expressum est rursus per negationem exprimitur" (Weber Aristocr. § 90); 6. 5, ῥᾴδιον καὶ πόνος οὐδείς .. ι 13. 10, ἐρῶ καὶ οὐκ ἀποκρύψομαι: 8. 73, λέξω .. καὶ οὐκ ἀποκρύψομαι: 18. 56; 19. 3; Soph. *El.* 929, ἡδὺς οὐδὲ μητρὶ δυσχερής. "and without reserve."

§ 32. λόγον . . . ποιήσω] West., Redhantz, &c., follow Schäfer, who translates, "non ut conviciatoribus congressus mihi quidem eandem apud vos audientiam faciam, quam vos, quâ estis levitate, adversariis meis praebetis." But Whiston rightly, I think, agrees with Mr. Kennedy in denying that ἐμαυτῷ λόγον ποιήσω can = ἵνα λόγου τύχω. Nor is the difficulty removed by the passage from 23. 81, quoted by Redhantz in support of Schäfer's view, ἀλλ' οὐδὲ τούτῳ λόγον οὐδὲ κρίσιν πεποίηκεν, said of the framer of a law. κρίσιν ποιεῖν τινι is a regular phrase, to which λόγον might legitimately be added, though ποιεῖν λόγον might in itself be an inadmissible expression. The meaning probably is, "it is not that I may fall a wrangling and draw upon myself a return in kind—provoke recrimination from my adversaries before you, and thus give them a fresh pretext for getting more from Philip by a display of zeal in defending him from my attack." He had alluded to the wrangling of the speakers before in 4. 44 : cf. 18. 3.

48   ΔΗΜΟΣΘΕΝΟΥΣ   [6. 33

ὑμῖν ποιήσω, τοῖς δ' ἐμοὶ προσκρούσασιν ἐξ ἀρχῆς καινὴν παρέσχω πρόφασιν τοῦ πάλιν τι λαβεῖν παρὰ Φιλίππου, οὐδ' ἵνα ὡς ἄλλως ἀδολεσχῶ. ἀλλ' οἶμαί ποθ' ὑμᾶς λυπήσειν ἃ Φίλιππος πράττει, μᾶλλον ἢ τὰ νυνί· 33. τὸ γὰρ πρᾶγμα ὁρῶ προβαῖνον, καὶ οὐχὶ βουλοίμην μὲν ἂν εἰκάζειν ὀρθῶς, φοβοῦμαι δὲ μὴ λίαν ἐγγὺς ᾖ τοῦτ' ἤδη. ὅταν οὖν μηκέθ' ὑμῖν ἀμελεῖν ἐξουσία γίγνηται τῶν συμβαινόντων, μηδ' ἀκούηθ' ὅτι ταῦτ' ἐφ' ὑμᾶς ἐστὶν ἐμοῦ μηδὲ τοῦ δεῖνος, ἀλλ' αὐτοὶ πάντες ὁρᾶτε καὶ εὖ εἰδῆτε, ὀργίλους καὶ τραχεῖς ὑμᾶς ἔσεσθαι νομίζω. 34. φοβοῦμαι δὴ μὴ τῶν πρέσβεων σεσιωπηκότων ἐφ' οἷς αὐτοῖς συνίσασι δεδωροδοκηκόσι, τοῖς ἐπανορθοῦν τι πειρωμένοις τῶν διὰ τούτους ἀπολωλότων τῇ παρ' ὑμῶν ὀργῇ περιπεσεῖν συμβῇ· ὁρῶ γὰρ ὡς τὰ πολλὰ ἐνίους οὐκ εἰς τοὺς αἰτίους ἀλλ' εἰς τοὺς ὑπὸ χεῖρα μάλιστα τὴν ὀργὴν ἀφιέντας. 35. ἕως οὖν ἔτι μέλλει καὶ συνίσταται τὰ πράγματα καὶ κατακούομεν

τοῖς . . ἐξ ἀρχῆς] Aeschines and Philocrates.

ὅτι ἄλλως] Bekk. st. from F S; Bekk. τὴν ἄλλως. "prate idly." ὡς must be understood as in ὡς ἑτέρως, supr. § 10; Soph. *El.* 1439, ὡς ἠλίως: Pl. *Cratyl.* 395 n, ἃ πρὸς τὸν Θυέστην ὡς ἁμὰ διεπράττετο.

ἢ τὰ νυνί] "than it does now."

§ 33. οὐχὶ βουλοίμην] similarly οὐ attaches itself to φημί, οἶμαι, προσποιοῦμαι, &c.,—a transposition of the negative foreign to our idiom, which requires that the negative should follow the verb. The deviation from the regular usage in Xen. *Anab.* 3. 2. 16, ὀνθότε καὶ πείραν ἤδη ἔχετε αὐτῶν, ὅτι θέλουσι καὶ πολλαπλάσιοι ὄντες μὴ δίχεσθαι ἡμᾶς, is surprising. West. omits μέν after βουλοίμην, with S. It is hardly necessary to point out how easily the preceding syllable might cause its omission. The meaning is, "and though I hope I may not be a true prophet, I fear this is now only too near." For the position of ἤδη cf. 4. 8.

ἀμελεῖν ἐξουσία] cf. 1, 15, ἀνάγκη ποιεῖν. "When the time comes that you have no longer the power to disregard what is happening, when you do not hear from me or another that these measures are directed against you, but you all see it yourselves, and are certain that it is so, I expect you will be wrathful and savage."

τοῦ δεῖνος] 2. 31.

§ 34. δεδωροδοκηκόσι] Bekk.; δεδωροδοκηκότες Dind. and West. Both constructions are legitimate (Madv. 178 *a*, r. 7). "I fear that as the Amb. have kept secret the purposes for which they know they were bribed . . . to fall under your anger." Cf. 18. 42.

τῇ παρ' ὑμῶν] Cf. on 1, 12, τῆς παρ' ἐκείνων εὐνοίας.

ὡς τὰ πολλά] "generally." Pl. *Rep.* 1. 330 c, ὡς τὸ πολύ.

τοὺς ὑπὸ χεῖρα] compare what he says in 1. 16.

§ 35. ἕως] "while therefore the storm is yet to come and is gathering." Cf. 18. 62, τοῦ φυομένου καὶ συνισταμένου πακοῦ.

—37.   ΚΑΤΑ ΦΙΛΙΠΠΟΥ Β.   49

ἀλλήλων, ἕκαστον ὑμῶν, καίπερ ἀκριβῶς εἰδότα, ὅμως ἐπαναμνῆσαι βούλομαι τίς ὁ Φωκέας πείσας καὶ Πύλας ὑμᾶς προέσθαι, ὧν καταστὰς ἐκεῖνος κύριος τῆς ἐπὶ τὴν Ἀττικὴν ὁδοῦ καὶ τῆς εἰς Πελοπόννησον κύριος γέγονε, καὶ πεποίηχ' ὑμῖν μὴ περὶ τῶν δικαίων μηδ' ὑπὲρ τῶν ἔξω πραγμάτων εἶναι τὴν βουλήν, ἀλλ' ὑπὲρ τῶν ἐν τῇ χώρᾳ καὶ τοῦ πρὸς τὴν Ἀττικὴν πολέμου, ὃς λυπήσει μὲν ἕκαστον ἐπειδὰν παρῇ, γέγονε δ' ἐν ἐκείνῃ τῇ ἡμέρᾳ. 36. εἰ γὰρ μὴ παρεκρούσθητε τόθ' ὑμεῖς, οὐδὲν ἂν ἦν τῇ πόλει πρᾶγμα· οὔτε γὰρ ναυσὶ δήπου κρατήσας εἰς τὴν Ἀττικὴν ἦλθεν ἄν ποτε στόλῳ Φίλιππος, οὔτε πεζῇ βαδίζων ὑπὲρ τὰς Πύλας καὶ Φωκέας, ἀλλ' ἢ τὰ δίκαι' ἂν ἐποίει καὶ τὴν εἰρήνην ἄγων ἡσυχίαν εἶχεν, ἢ παραχρῆμ' ἂν ἦν ἐν ὁμοίῳ πολέμῳ δι' ὃν τότε τῆς εἰρήνης ἐπεθύμησεν. 37. ταῦτ' οὖν ὡς μὲν ὑπομνῆσαι,

τίς ὁ ... πείσας] Aeschines is meant: cf. 18. 35 sq.
ὧν ε.] "to give up the P. and Pylae, by gaining the command of which he has become master of the road to Attica and that leading to the P." For the change of preposition cf. 1. 5; 3. 1 al. The importance to Athens of Phocis and Pylae is often insisted on : 19. 83, τίς .. οὐκ οἶδεν ὑμῶν ὅτι τῷ Φωκέων πολέμῳ καὶ τῷ κυρίους εἶναι Πυλῶν Φωκέας ἤ τε ἀπὸ Θηβαίων ἄδεια ὑπῆρχεν ὑμῖν, καὶ τὸ μηδέποτ' ἂν ἐλθεῖν εἰς Πελοπόννησον μηδ' εἰς Εὔβοιαν μηδ' εἰς τὴν Ἀττικὴν Φίλιππον μηδὲ Θηβαίους; ib. 180.
τῶν δικαίων] "your rights (as they might be affected by the peace) or your interests abroad, but about those at home (1. 15) and the war against Attica." περί and ὑπέρ here again without any real difference of meaning: cf. 1. 5.
γέγονε δ'] "nay, which has begun from that day," on which the Assembly was held to receive the report of the ambassadors. Cf. 19. 58; Grote, 11. 535.
§ 36. ναυσί] "at sea." On the fleet of Philip cf. 4. 21, and Grote there quoted. At the time when the First Philippic was delivered Dem. thought ten triremes sufficient to convoy the armament. Philip's naval power was much increased after that. Ps. Dem. 7. 16.
πεζῇ .. ὑπέρ] "nor by land marching beyond P. and P." βαδίζω is the regular antithesis to πλεῖν or going by sea. Cf. Mr. Shill. de F. Leg. § 171.
ὑπέρ] Xen. An. 1. 1. 9, τοὺς ὑπὲρ Ἑλλήσποντον οἰκοῦσι, where L. Dind. quotes Pl. Cratyl. 108 E, τοὺς ὑπὲρ Ἡρακλείας στήλας ἔξω κατοικοῦντας.
Φωκέας] as 9. 11 and passim, where we speak of the country only.
ἀλλ' ἤ] "but he would either have continued to act with justice, and, observing the peace, have kept quiet, or would at once have been involved in a war similar to that which made him anxious for the peace."
δι' ὅν] i. e. οἷος ἦν δι' ὅν.
§ 37. ὡς ... ὑπομνῆσαι] "what has been said is sufficient to serve as a reminder," "to awaken recollection" (Mr. K.). Madv. 151.

E

ΚΑΤΑ ΦΙΛΙΠΠΟΥ Β.

νῦν ἱκανῶς εἴρηται, ὡς δ' ἂν ἐξετασθείη μάλιστ' ἀκριβῶς, μὴ γένοιτο, ὦ πάντες θεοί· οὐδένα γὰρ βουλοίμην ἂν ἔγωγε, οὐδ' εἰ δίκαιός ἐστ' ἀπολωλέναι, μετὰ τοῦ πάντων κινδύνου καὶ τῆς ζημίας δίκην ὑποσχεῖν.

ὡς .. ἐν ἐξ.] Supr. § 4, "but how it might be .." "but that it should be exactly verified, avert it all ye gods!" If the fears he had expressed in § 33 sq. were verified, the traitors would indeed be punished, but their treason must issue in the ruin of their country.

μετά] 3. 36. "for no one would I wish to see punished, however much he deserves to die, to the danger and damage of all"—when his punishment involves the ruin of all.

ΚΑΤΑ ΦΙΛΙΠΠΟΥ Γ.

ΥΠΟΘΕΣΙΣ.—Ἁπλῆ τοῦ λόγου τούτου ἡ ὑπόθεσις· Φιλίππου γὰρ λόγῳ μὲν εἰρήνην ἄγοντος ἔργῳ δὲ πολλὰ ἀδικοῦντος, συμβουλεύει τοῖς Ἀθηναίοις ὁ ῥήτωρ ἀναστῆναι καὶ ἀμύνασθαι τὸν βασιλέα, ὡς κινδύνου μεγάλου καὶ αὐτοῖς ἐπικρεμαμένου καὶ πᾶσι κοινῇ τοῖς Ἕλλησιν.

1. Πολλῶν, ὦ ἄνδρες Ἀθηναῖοι, λόγων γιγνομένων ὀλίγου δεῖν καθ' ἑκάστην ἐκκλησίαν περὶ ὧν Φίλιππος, ἀφ' οὗ τὴν εἰρήνην ἐποιήσατο, οὐ μόνον ὑμᾶς ἀλλὰ καὶ τοὺς ἄλλους ἀδικεῖ, καὶ πάντων οἶδ' ὅτι φησάντων γ' ἄν, εἰ καὶ μὴ ποιοῦσι τοῦτο, καὶ λέγειν δεῖν καὶ πράττειν ὅπως ἐκεῖνος παύσεται τῆς ὕβρεως καὶ δίκην δώσει, εἰς τοῦθ' ὑπηγμένα πάντα τὰ

ARGUMENT.—This speech, as also that on the Chersonesus, delivered about three months before it, belongs to the year 342 B.C. The date is fixed by νῦν ἐπὶ Θρᾴκην ταμίετα, which Diod. Sic. refers to Ol. 109. 2, i. e. to the latter half of B.C. 343 or the first half of B.C. 342. Again, it is said in § 32, τίθησι τὰ Πύθια . . κἂν αὐτὸς μὴ παρῇ, τοὺς δούλους ἀγωνοθετήσοντας πέμπει. Philip presided himself at the celebration of the games in the summer or autumn (Thirl. 6. 5) of B.C. 346. This speech must therefore have been delivered towards the end of the autumn of B.C. 342 at the earliest. For the circumstances which led to it see Thirl. 6, p. 27; Grote, 11. 623.

§ 1. With the commencement of this speech cf. 6. 1 sq.

ὀλίγου δεῖν] Madv. 168 b. "many speeches are made in almost every assembly about the wrongs which .. and all would, I feel sure, ... still our affairs .."

ἀδικεῖ] Madv. 110, r. 1. The peace was concluded in March, B.C. 346.

οἶδ' ὅτι] 6. 28.

ποιοῦσι τοῦτο] Some have wrongly referred these words to φησάντων, as if the meaning were, "would say so, though they don't do so actually," a way in which ποιῶ is often used. Cf. Mr. Shill. de F. Leg. § 225 n. cr. But the meaning obviously is, "and all, though they do not actually direct every speech and measure to the one object of humbling and chastising Philip, would at any rate allow that this ought to be done."

ὅπως] with the fut. ind. after ποιεῖτε, as l. 2, ὅπως βοηθήσετε, where see the note.

π. τῆς ὕβρεως] 6. 30, Θηβαίους δὲ παύσει τῆς ὕβρεως.

ὑπηγμένα] "per negligentiam et socordiam eo deducta, ad conditionem tam lamentabilem delapsa" (Reiske) ; "brought to such a state by inadvertence and neglect." 23.

πράγματα καὶ προειμένα ὁρῶ ὥστε δέδοικα μὴ βλάσφημον μὲν εἰπεῖν ἀληθὲς δ' ᾖ· εἰ καὶ λέγειν ἅπαντες ἐβούλοντο οἱ παριόντες καὶ χειροτονεῖν ὑμεῖς ἐξ ὧν ὡς φαυλότατ' ἔμελλε τὰ πράγμαθ' ἔξειν, οὐκ ἂν ἡγοῦμαι δύνασθαι χεῖρον ἢ νῦν διατεθῆναι. 2. πολλὰ μὲν οὖν ἴσως ἐστὶν αἴτια τούτων, καὶ οὐ παρ' ἓν οὐδὲ δύο εἰς τοῦτο τὰ πράγματα ἀφῖκται, μάλιστα δ', ἄνπερ ἐξετάζητε ὀρθῶς, εὑρήσετε διὰ τοὺς χαρίζεσθαι μᾶλλον ἢ τὰ βέλτιστα λέγειν προαιρουμένους, ὧν τινὲς μέν, ὦ ἄνδρες Ἀθηναῖοι, ἐν οἷς εὐδοκιμοῦσιν αὐτοὶ καὶ δύνανται, ταῦτα φυλάττοντες οὐδεμίαν περὶ τῶν μελλόντων πρόνοιαν ἔχουσιν, ἕτεροι δὲ τοὺς ἐπὶ τοῖς πράγμασιν ὄντας αἰτιώμενοι καὶ διαβάλλοντες οὐδὲν ἄλλο ποιοῦσιν ἢ

173. συμβαίνει τοῖς χρόνοις εἰς τοῦθ' ὑπηγμένα τὰ πράγματ' ἤδη.

βλ. μὲν ... ἀληθὲς δ'] "I am afraid, though a severe thing to say, it is nevertheless true.." Infr. 5.

εἰ καί] With the asyndeton cf. 6. 4; καί with λέγειν. "had all the speakers (6. 3) meant to propose and you to pass measures intended to bring our affairs to ruin, I do not think.."

§ 2. ἴσως] "no doubt."

παρ' ἕν, κ.τ.λ.] 4. 10. "and it is not owing to one or two (either) that.." but διὰ τούς of *persons*. Fr. says, "i. e. οὐ παρ' ἓν οὐδὲ παρὰ δύο." No doubt the orator could have said so, but it would not be correct on that account to say that a second παρά is to be supplied here. As a matter of fact the second preposition is very often wanting: after οὐ μόνον.. ἀλλὰ καί, 19. 341; ἤ.. ἤ, 21. 114; ἤ, 20. 143 ὑπὲρ ἄλλου τινὸς ἢ τοῦ τῆς πόλεως ἀξιώματος. καί.. καί, Lys. 1. 2; καὶ ἐν δημοκρατίᾳ καὶ ὀλιγαρχίᾳ οὕτως.. ὥς, 19. 263; and in cases like 21. 155, κατὰ ταύτην τὴν ἡλικίαν ἣν ἐγὼ νῦν: 18. 134, ἀπὸ τῆς ἀγνοίας ἧσπερ, .. &c. An examination of such instances will prove to the young student that the principle which governs the omission is the same as in the case of the article, noticed on 2. 9. and that our own idiom is here also his best guide. "but if you only examine rightly, you will find that this is mainly owing to those who make it their study to please you (cf. 3. 24)."

τινὲς μέν] Eubulus and his friends.

ἐν οἷς] "in and by which." 18. 19, ἐν οἷς ἠμάρτανον οἱ ἄλλοι ... αὐτὸς παρεσκευάζετο: 23. 23, δωρεὰν ἐν ᾗ πολίτης γέγονεν: Lys. 26. 9, ἐν τῷ ἄρχειν.. ἢ πολιτεία σώζεται: infr. 64. "seeking to maintain a state of things through which they themselves enjoy power and repute.."

δύνανται = δυνατοί εἰσι (20. 191; 21. 207; 23. 174).

ἕτεροι] Aeschines and others who played into the hands of Philip.

τοὺς ἐπὶ.. ὄντας] "those who conduct public affairs." 6. 12; Thuc. 3. 11: cf. 2. 12. Infr. 56 we have τῶν ἐν τοῖς πράγμασι τινές.

οὐδὲν.. ἤ] "only aim at making ... and occupy herself with this, leaving P. free to.." "thus leaving P. at liberty.." West. Redh. and Fr. omit μέν after πόλει on the authority of S. Cf. 6. 33.

ΚΑΤΑ ΦΙΛΙΠΠΟΤ Γ.

ὅπως ἡ μὲν πόλις αὐτὴ παρ' αὑτῆς δίκην λήψεται καὶ περὶ τοῦτ' ἔσται, Φιλίππῳ δ' ἐξέσται καὶ λέγειν καὶ πράττειν ὅ τι βούλεται. 3. αἱ δὲ τοιαῦται πολιτεῖαι συνήθεις μέν εἰσιν ὑμῖν, αἴτιαι δὲ τῶν κακῶν. ἀξιῶ δ', ὦ ἄνδρες Ἀθηναῖοι, ἐάν τι τῶν ἀληθῶν μετὰ παρρησίας λέγω, μηδεμίαν μοι διὰ τοῦτο παρ' ὑμῶν ὀργὴν γενέσθαι. σκοπεῖτε γὰρ ὡδί. ὑμεῖς τὴν παρρησίαν ἐπὶ μὲν τῶν ἄλλων οὕτω κοινὴν οἴεσθε δεῖν εἶναι πᾶσι τοῖς ἐν τῇ πόλει ὥστε καὶ τοῖς ξένοις καὶ τοῖς δούλοις αὐτῆς μεταδεδώκατε, καὶ πολλοὺς ἄν τις οἰκέτας ἴδοι παρ' ὑμῖν μετὰ πλείονος ἐξουσίας ὅ τι βούλονται λέγοντας ἢ πολίτας ἐν ἐνίαις τῶν ἄλλων πόλεων, ἐκ δὲ τοῦ συμβουλεύειν παντάπασιν ἐξεληλάκατε. 4. εἶθ' ὑμῖν συμβέβηκεν ἐκ τούτου ἐν μὲν ταῖς ἐκκλησίαις τρυφᾶν καὶ κολακεύεσθαι πάντα πρὸς ἡδονὴν ἀκούουσιν, ἐν δὲ τοῖς πράγμασι καὶ τοῖς γιγνομένοις περὶ τῶν ἐσχάτων ἤδη κινδυνεύειν. εἰ μὲν οὖν καὶ νῦν οὕτω διάκεισθε, οὐκ ἔχω τί λέγω· εἰ δ' ἃ συμφέρει χωρὶς κολακείας ἐθελήσετε ἀκούειν, ἕτοιμος λέγειν. καὶ γὰρ εἰ πάνυ φαύλως τὰ πράγματα ἔχει καὶ πολλὰ προεῖται, ὅμως

περὶ τ. ἔσται] Xen. *An.* 3. 5. 7, οἱ μὲν ἄλλοι περὶ τὰ ἐπιτήδεια ἦσαν: Ps. Dem. 25. 61, περὶ τὴν .. συμφοράν .. γιγνόμενος; Ps. Dem. 13. 20, οἱ πολιτευόμενοι καὶ περὶ ταῦτα ὄντες.

§ 3. συνήθεις μέν .. &c.] supr. 3. "such courses of policy, though familiar, are .."

ὀργὴν γ.] Cf. 3. 3, and note 3. 10.

ἐπὶ .. τῶν ἄ.] "for only consider. So strongly do you hold that in all other cases freedom of speech ought to be enjoyed by all residents in the city without distinction (κοινήν), that you have granted a measure of it .." West. quotes Xen. *Rep. Ath.* 1. 12, διὰ τοῦτο οὖν ἰσηγορίαν καὶ τοῖς δούλοις πρὸς τοὺς ἐλευθέρους ἐποιήσαμεν καὶ τοῖς μετοίκοις πρὸς τοὺς ἀστούς, and Eur. *Phoen.* 390.

πολίτας] "than citizens," i. e. than the general body of citizens in oligarchies. Freedom of speech there might bring on those bold enough to indulge in it the fate pithily expressed by Critias in Xen. *Hell.* 2. 3. 16: ἐάν τινα αἰσθανώμεθα ἐναντίον τῇ ὀλιγαρχίᾳ, ὅσον δυνάμεθα ἐκποδὼν ποιούμεθα.

ἐκ δὲ τοῦ σ.] Comp. what he says in 3. 32.

§ 4. ἐν μὲν ταῖς .. κινδυνεύειν] The same words are found in 8. 34.

τρυφᾶν] Aesch. 3. 20, οἱ δ' ὑμέτεροι ῥήτορες τρυφῶσι; Dem. 19. 197; Arist. *Eq.* 1159. "you give yourselves airs and are flattered at hearing nothing but what is pleasant (1. 15), while in your affairs and circumstances you are in imminent peril."

οὐκ ἔχω τί λ.] "non habeo quod dicam," "I have nothing to say." Madv. 121.

ἕτοιμος] 4. 39. καὶ in καὶ γὰρ must be taken with εἰ. "for even if our affairs are in a wretched state, and many interests .."

ἐστιν, ἐὰν ὑμεῖς τὰ δέοντα ποιεῖν βούλησθ', ἔτι πάντα ταῦτα ἐπανορθώσασθαι. 5. καὶ παράδοξον μὲν ἴσως ἐστὶν ὃ μέλλω λέγειν, ἀληθὲς δέ· τὸ χείριστον ἐν τοῖς παρεληλυθόσι, τοῦτο πρὸς τὰ μέλλοντα βέλτιστον ὑπάρχει. τί οὖν ἐστὶ τοῦτο; ὅτι οὔτε μικρὸν οὔτε μέγα οὐδὲν τῶν δεόντων ποιούντων ὑμῶν κακῶς τὰ πράγματα ἔχει, ἐπεί τοι, εἰ πάνθ' ἃ προσῆκε πραττόντων οὕτω διέκειτο, οὐδ' ἂν ἐλπὶς ἦν αὐτὰ γενέσθαι βελτίω. νῦν δὲ τῆς μὲν ῥᾳθυμίας τῆς ὑμετέρας καὶ τῆς ἀμελείας κεκράτηκε Φίλιππος, τῆς πόλεως δ' οὐ κεκράτηκεν· οὐδ' ἥττησθε ὑμεῖς, ἀλλ' οὐδὲ κεκίνησθε.

6. Εἰ μὲν οὖν ἅπαντες ὡμολογοῦμεν Φίλιππον τῇ πόλει πολεμεῖν καὶ τὴν εἰρήνην παραβαίνειν, οὐδὲν ἄλλο ἔδει τὸν παριόντα λέγειν καὶ συμβουλεύειν ἢ ὅπως ἀσφαλέστατα καὶ ῥᾷστα αὐτὸν ἀμυνούμεθα· ἐπειδὴ δὲ οὕτως ἀτόπως ἔνιοι διάκεινται ὥστε πόλεις καταλαμβάνοντος ἐκείνου καὶ πολλὰ τῶν ὑμετέρων ἔχοντος καὶ πάντας ἀνθρώπους ἀδικοῦντος ἀνέχεσθαί τινων ἐν ταῖς ἐκκλησίαις λεγόντων πολλάκις ὡς ἡμῶν τινές εἰσιν οἱ ποιοῦντες τὸν πόλεμον, 7. ἀνάγκη

§ 5. παράδοξον] Cf. 3. 10. Comp. 18. 199; 19. 99; 24. 122. Lyc. § 49, εἰ δὲ δεῖ καὶ παραδοξότατον μὲν εἰπεῖν, ἀληθὲς δὲ .. Isocr. 12. 176 al. "now what I am going to say may sound paradoxical, but it is true." Cf. the very similar passage in 4. 2.

β ... καὶ .. ἀμελείας] a not unfrequent combination (Isocr. 2. 10, μὴ ῥᾳθυμεῖν μηδὲ ἀμελεῖν), hence the opposition in Arist. *Kh.* 1. 12. 10, καὶ τοὺς ῥᾳθύμους .. ἐπιμελοῦς γὰρ τὸ ἐπεξελθεῖν.

κεκίνησθε] "nay, you have not even moved," " stirred yourselves" —"far from being worsted, you have not appeared in the field at all." Some, in order to make a fuller opposition to ἥττησθ', understand κεκίνησθε in the sense of "loco moti estis." 8. 37 supports the view I have taken.

Sections 6 and 7, Εἰ μέν to πολεμεῖν δεῖ, are wanting in S. Bekk.

and Dind., rightly I think, retain them. As the words εἰ μὲν οὖν stand at the beginning of 6 and 8, it is probable that the omission arose from a mere oversight of the copyist, as Beuseler suggests.

§ 6. On ἔδει without ἄν, Madv. 118. "nothing else were it needful for the speaker to propose and advise but the safest and easiest way of .."

ἐπειδὴ .. δ.] "but since, at the very time when .. some are unreasonable enough .."

ἀνέχεσθαι] "to put up with," "tolerate."

τινές] the indefinite subject to οἱ π. Xen. *An.* 2. 4. 5, ὁ ἡγησόμενος οὐδεὶς ἔσται: Lys. 19. 57, εἰσὶ δέ τινες οἱ προαναλίσκοντες: Isocr. 8. 139; Dem. 24. 143. "that some of ourselves are the persons who are causing the war .." For the difference between ποιεῖν and ποιεῖσθαι πόλεμον cf. Don. p. 435.

—9.] ΚΑΤΑ ΦΙΛΙΠΠΟΥ Γ. 55

φυλάττεσθαι καὶ διορθοῦσθαι περὶ τούτου· ἔστι γὰρ δέος μὴ ποθ᾽ ὡς ἀμυνούμεθα γράψας τις καὶ συμβουλεύσας εἰς τὴν αἰτίαν ἐμπέσῃ τοῦ πεποιηκέναι τὸν πόλεμον. ἐγὼ δὴ τοῦτο πρῶτον ἁπάντων λέγω καὶ διορίζομαι, εἰ ἐφ᾽ ἡμῖν ἐστι τὸ βουλεύεσθαι περὶ τοῦ πότερον εἰρήνην ἄγειν ἢ πολεμεῖν δεῖ. 8. εἰ μὲν οὖν ἔξεστιν εἰρήνην ἄγειν τῇ πόλει καὶ ἐφ᾽ ἡμῖν ἐστι τοῦτο, ἵν᾽ ἐντεῦθεν ἄρξωμαι, φημὶ ἔγωγε ἄγειν ἡμᾶς δεῖν, καὶ τὸν ταῦτα λέγοντα γράφειν καὶ πράττειν καὶ μὴ φενακίζειν ἀξιῶ· εἰ δ᾽ ἕτερος τὰ ὅπλα ἐν ταῖς χερσὶν ἔχων καὶ δύναμιν πολλὴν περὶ αὑτὸν τοὔνομα μὲν τὸ τῆς εἰρήνης ὑμῖν προβάλλει, τοῖς δ᾽ ἔργοις αὐτὸς τοῖς τοῦ πολέμου χρῆται, τί λοιπὸν ἄλλο πλὴν ἀμύνεσθαι; φάσκειν δὲ εἰρήνην ἄγειν εἰ βούλεσθε, ὥσπερ ἐκεῖνος, οὐ διαφέρομαι. 9. εἰ δέ τις ταύτην εἰρήνην ὑπολαμβάνει ἐξ ἧς ἐκεῖνος πάντα τἆλλα λαβὼν ἐφ᾽ ἡμᾶς ἥξει, πρῶτον μὲν μαίνεται, ἔπειτα ἐκείνῳ παρ᾽ ὑμῶν, οὐχ ὑμῖν παρ᾽ ἐκείνου τὴν εἰρήνην λέγει·

§ 7. διορθοῦσθαι] Dind. in his notes adopts H. Wolf's tr., "cautione vehementer opus est, ut hoc recte constituatur," "should be set right." The next sentence shows that the meaning is probably the same—"to take security," "secure oneself"—as in 33. 11 (ἐπειδὴ ἔλαβον τοῦτον ἀδικοῦντα, διωρθωσάμην ὑπὲρ ἐμαυτοῦ καὶ τοῦ ξένου). The following words give the reason why such caution was necessary.

ὡς ἀ.] lit. "how we shall defend ourselves;" "a measure of defence," Mr. K.

ἐγὼ δή] "I first then discuss and settle this point, whether it is in our power to deliberate on the question of peace or war;" "is it in our power . . . on the question whether we ought . . . or go to war?"

§ 8. ταῦτα] i. e. that it is in our power to do so. On the plural, 1. 7; 2. 25.

πράττειν] "id agere, ut quod rogaverit decernatur ratumque fiat" (Fr.). "and I call upon . . to make a motion and take action, and not prevaricate."

τὰ . . ἐν ταῖς χ.] Madv. 8.

περὶ αὐτόν] "at the head of."

προβάλλει] "puts forward," as a cloak to hide his designs. In the middle voice (Thuc. 1. 37; 3. 63): "puts forward to you the name of peace, while he himself . ."

οὐ διαφέρομαι] "non repugno, non refragor. Usu congruit, etsi significatione differt, quod vulgo dicunt οὐδέν μοι διαφέρει" (Schäf.). φάσκειν emphatic—"if you choose to profess . . as he does, I have nothing to say against it," "I don't quarrel with it."

§ 9. ταύτην εἰρήνην] "calls that a peace which will enable him after he has . ." On ταύτην, Madv. 11, r. 1.

ἐξ ἧς] 1. 7; 6. 27, ἐκ τοῦ μηδέν . .

πρῶτον μὲν . . ἔπειτα] cf. 2. 1. "he is mad, and besides he talks about a peace which is observed on your part towards him . ."

ΔΗΜΟΣΘΕΝΟΥΣ [9. 10

τοῦτο δ' ἐστὶν ὃ τῶν ἀναλισκομένων χρημάτων πάντων Φίλιππος ὠνεῖται, αὐτὸς μὲν πολεμεῖν ὑμῖν, ὑφ' ὑμῶν δὲ μὴ πολεμεῖσθαι.

10. Καὶ μὴν εἰ μέχρι τούτου περιμενοῦμεν, ἕως ἂν ἡμῖν ὁμολογήσῃ πολεμεῖν, πάντων ἐσμὲν εὐηθέστατοι· οὐδὲ γὰρ ἂν ἐπὶ τὴν Ἀττικὴν αὐτὴν βαδίζῃ καὶ τὸν Πειραιᾶ, τοῦτ' ἐρεῖ, εἴπερ οἷς πρὸς τοὺς ἄλλους πεποίηκε δεῖ τεκμαίρεσθαι. 11. τοῦτο μὲν γὰρ Ὀλυνθίοις τετταράκοντ' ἀπέχων τῆς πόλεως στάδια εἶπεν ὅτι δεῖ δυοῖν θάτερον, ἢ 'κείνους ἐν Ὀλύνθῳ μὴ οἰκεῖν ἢ αὑτὸν ἐν Μακεδονίᾳ, πάντα τὸν ἄλλον χρόνον, εἴ τις αὐτὸν αἰτιάσαιτό τι τοιοῦτον, ἀγανακτῶν καὶ πρέσβεις πέμπων τοὺς ἀπολογησομένους· τοῦτο δ' εἰς Φωκέας ὡς πρὸς συμμάχους ἐπορεύετο, καὶ πρέσβεις Φωκέων ἦσαν οἳ παρηκολούθουν αὐτῷ πορευομένῳ, καὶ παρ' ἡμῖν ἤριζον πολλοὶ Θηβαίοις οὐ λυσιτελήσειν τὴν ἐκείνου πάροδον. 12. καὶ μὴν καὶ Φερὰς πρώην ὡς φίλος καὶ σύμμαχος εἰς Θετταλίαν ἐλθὼν ἔχει καταλαβών, καὶ τὰ τελευταῖα τοῖς

τῶν .. χρ.] 3. 22. "with all the treasure he is lavishing."

αὐτὸς μέν, κ.τ.λ.] explanatory of τοῦτο. infr. 23; 3. 7. On the nom. αὐτός with the inf., 4. 7.

§ 10. εἰ .. περιμενοῦμεν .. ἐσμέν] cf. 1. 19. "if we mean to wait .. we are the most simple of men."

βαδίζῃ] 6. 36. "is in full march .." 1. 12 and 25.

§ 11. τοῦτο μέν] "for example."
'Ολ.] cf. 8. 58, οὐδ' (did he admit that he was at war) Ὀλυνθίοις ἐξ ἀρχῆς, ἕως ἐν αὐτῇ τῇ χώρᾳ τὸ στράτευμα παρῆν ἔχων.

δεῖ δ. θ.] "there was no choice, but they must . . ." Cf. Mr. Shill. de F. Leg. § 166. 18. 139, καίτοι δυοῖν αὐτῷ ἀνάγκη θάτερον ἢ μηδὲν "he has only one alternative." The force of μή is extended to ἐν Μακεδονίᾳ. Cobet (N. Lect. p. 661) inserts μή after αὐτόν.

ἢ 'κείνους] Bekk. st. ἢ κείνους. Cf. 4. 4.

π. τὸν ἄλλον χ.] "though before that whenever any one accused him

of . . he was indignant . . ." ἀγανακτῶν and πέμπων represent the imperfects required after the opt. of indefinite frequency—εἴ τις .. αἰτιάσαιτο; cf. 6. 20. τὸν ἄλλον χρ. is sometimes, but rarely, used also of future time. Dem. 22. 3; Lyc. § 79.

ὡς πρός] "again he marched into Phocis (6. 36) as if to allies (he pretended to regard them in that light till he had them at his mercy), and there were . . . . who accompanied him on his march." Grote, 11. 587.

οὐ λ.] his passage of the Straits "would not benefit:" a meiosis. 3. 1; cf. 6. 30.

§ 12.] ἔχει has here its full force. He not only seized Pherae, but at 'that time held it with his troops. Madv. 180 d. On the subject here mentioned see Thirl. 6, p. 13. Ps. Dem. 7. 32, Φεραίων μὲν ἀφῄρηται τὴν πόλιν καὶ φρουρὰν ἐν τῇ ἀκροπόλει κατέστησεν, ἵνα δὴ αὐτόνομοι ὦσι. 8. 59.

τὰ τελ.] 2. 7.

ΚΑΤΑ ΦΙΛΙΠΠΟΥ Γ.

ταλαιπώροις Ὠρείταις τουτοισὶ ἐπισκεψομένους ἔφη τοὺς στρατιώτας πεπομφέναι κατ᾽ εὔνοιαν πυνθάνεσθαι γὰρ αὐτοὺς ὡς νοσοῦσι καὶ στασιάζουσι, συμμάχων δ᾽ εἶναι καὶ φίλων ἀληθινῶν ἐν τοῖς τοιούτοις καιροῖς παρεῖναι. 13. εἶτ᾽ οἴεσθ᾽ αὐτόν, οἳ ἐποίησαν μὲν οὐδὲν ἂν κακόν, μὴ παθεῖν δ᾽ ἐφυλάξαντ᾽ ἂν ἴσως, τούτους μὲν ἐξαπατᾶν αἱρεῖσθαι μᾶλλον ἢ προλέγοντα βιάζεσθαι, ὑμῖν δ᾽ ἐκ προρρήσεως πολεμήσειν, καὶ ταῦθ᾽ ἕως ἂν ἑκόντες ἐξαπατᾶσθε; οὐκ ἔστι ταῦτα· 14. καὶ γὰρ ἂν ἀβελτερώτατος εἴη πάντων ἀνθρώπων, εἰ τῶν ἀδικουμένων ὑμῶν μηδὲν ἐγκαλούντων αὐτῷ, ἀλλ᾽ ὑμῶν αὐτῶν τινὰς αἰτιωμένων, ἐκεῖνος ἐκλύσας τὴν πρὸς ἀλλήλους ἔριν ὑμῶν καὶ φιλονεικίαν ἐφ᾽ ἑαυτὸν προείποι τρέπεσθαι, καὶ τῶν παρ᾽ ἑαυτοῦ μισθοφορούντων τοὺς λόγους ἀφέλοιτο, οἷς ἀναβάλλουσιν ὑμᾶς, λέγοντες ὡς ἐκεῖνός γε οὐ πολεμεῖ τῇ πόλει.

15. Ἀλλ᾽ ἔστιν, ὦ πρὸς τοῦ Διός, ὅστις εὖ φρονῶν ἐκ τῶν

τοὺς .. Ὦ. depends, I think, on ἔφη: "and lastly he told the wretched people of Oreus .. out of good will to visit them .." infr. §§ 27, 33. On the *anaphorical* use of the demonstrative τουτοισὶ see Mr. Shill. *de F. Leg.* § 213; Cobet, *N. Lect.* p. 629. Dem. 23. 111, ἔστι δήπου Φίλιππος .. τουτονὶ τὸν Μακεδόνα, and passim.
ἐπισκεψομένους] to pay them a sick visit. 54. 12, λέγε τὴν τῶν ἰατρῶν μαρτυρίαν καὶ τὴν τῶν ἐπισκοπούντων: 59. 56, ἐβάδιζον ... γὰρ πρὸς αὐτὸν ὡς ἡσθείη ... τὰ πρόσφορα τῇ νόσῳ φέρουσαι καὶ ἐπισκοπούμεναι.
αὐτούς] Madv. 191. In νοσοῦσι καὶ σ. the particular kind of illness is added co-ordinately with καί, as in 6. 1, "suffering from internal disorders." Pl. *Rep.* 5. 470 C, νοσεῖν δ᾽ ἂν τῷ τοιούτῳ τὴν Ἑλλάδα καὶ στασιάζειν, καὶ στάσιν τὴν τοιαύτην ἐχθρὰν κλητέον: ib. B, ἐπὶ γὰρ τῇ τοῦ οἰκείου ἐχθρᾷ στάσις εἴληπται, ἐπὶ δὲ τῇ τῶν ἀλλοτρίων πόλεμος. Cf. 18. 45. αἱ δὲ πόλεις ἐνόσουν: Soph. *El.* 1070 al.

§ 13. εἶτ᾽] 1. 24.
οἳ .. μὲν .. δ᾽] The stress of the sentence is upon the clause introduced by δέ: cf. 2. 24. "do you then think that when he chose to deceive, rather than by giving them warning overpower by force, those who would have done him no harm (i. e. had he given them warning and formally declared war against them), though they might perhaps have taken measures to escape suffering it, he will make a formal declaration of war against *you*, and that so long as .. Impossible!" Cf. note to 6. 15, τοὺς μὲν ὄντας ...
ἐκ πρ.] "ex edicto." Livy 1. 27.
§ 14. τινάς] "some of yourselves," i. e. of course those who saw through his designs and warned them against him.
ἀναβάλλουσιν] "put you off," "amuse you." Cf. note to 4. 14.
ἐκεῖνός γε] however it may be with others, "he at any rate."
§ 15. ὦ πρὸς τοῦ Δ.] An exclamation of impatience. 24. 157.

ὀνομάτων μᾶλλον ἢ τῶν πραγμάτων τὸν ἄγοντ' εἰρήνην ἢ
πολεμοῦνθ' ἑαυτῷ σκέψαιτ' ἄν; οὐδεὶς δήπου. ὁ τοίνυν
Φίλιππος ἐξ ἀρχῆς, ἄρτι τῆς εἰρήνης γεγονυίας, οὔπω
Διοπείθους στρατηγοῦντος οὐδὲ τῶν ὄντων ἐν Χερρονήσῳ
νῦν ἀπεσταλμένων, Σέρριον καὶ Δορίσκον κατελάμβανε
καὶ τοὺς ἐκ Σερρίου τείχους καὶ Ἱεροῦ ὄρους στρατιώτας
ἐξέβαλλεν, οὓς ὁ ὑμέτερος στρατηγὸς κατέστησεν. καίτοι
ταῦτα πράττων τί ἐποίει; εἰρήνην μὲν γὰρ ὀμωμόκει.
καὶ μηδεὶς εἴπῃ, 16. τί δὲ ταῦτ' ἐστίν, ἢ τί τούτων μέλει
τῇ πόλει; εἰ μὲν γὰρ μικρὰ ταῦτα ἢ μηδὲν ὑμῖν αὐτῶν

φέρε γὰρ πρὸς Διὸς ἔστιν ὅστις ἂν
ἢ πρότερός ἐστ' ἐψήφισεν .. "but,
in heaven's name, would any sane
man judge from words rather than
deeds (§ 8), who is .." Cf. supr.
§ 2, note to οὐ παρ' ἕν.

ὁ τοίνυν] "well then, P. at the
beginning, immediately after the
conclusion of the peace (explanatory
of ἐξ ἀρχῆς), before D. was yet
general or those who are now ..
had been sent, was .." Cf. 8. 6.—
Scribium and Doriscus are often
mentioned by Dem.: 8. 64; 18.
27, 70; Ps. Dem. 7. 37. Hence
the sneer of Aesch. 3. 82, αὐτὸς
(Dem.) ἐστιν .. ὁ πρῶτος ἐξευρὼν
Σέρριον Τεῖχος καὶ Δόρισκον καὶ
Ἐργίσκην καὶ Μουργίσκην (Schulz
has Μύρτηνον, as in Dem. 18. 27)
καὶ Γάνος καὶ Γανίδα, χωρία ἂν οὐδὲ
τὰ ὀνόματα ᾔδειμεν πρότερον.

τοὺς ἐκ] 1. 15.
Ἱεροῦ Ὄρους] Cf. 19. 156. Why
Dem. attached such importance to
these places, he explains in 19. 180,
also 18. 27.

ὁ ὑμ. στρ.] Chares.
τ. πράττων τί ἐποίει] 'quan-
quam haec agens quid faciebat."
If these were not acts of hostility,
whatever his professions may be,
what were they? Pl. Crit. p. 52
A, καὶ φήσεις ταῦτα ποιῶν δίκαια
πράττειν;

μὲν γάρ] 3. 10, ἐγὼ μὲν γὰρ ..
R. 37. ἐγὼ μὲν γὰρ οὐχ ὁρῶ: infr.
16; 21. 158. In these cases γάρ

refers to the previous question, while
μέν emphasizes the word to which
it is attached.

ὀμωμόκει] Bekk.; Dind. &c. ὀμωμόκει. Cf. Mr. Shill. de F. Leg.
66, 295; 18. 32, ἐπειδὴ γὰρ ὤμοσε
τὴν εἰρήνην. Though the treaty of
peace had been concluded when
Philip took the towns mentioned,
he had not yet taken the oaths to
the Athenian ambassadors. In 18.
30 Dem. makes it a charge against
the ambassadors, that instead of
hurrying to Philip's camp, they gave
him the opportunity of making these
conquests by delaying three months
in Macedonia. Here, where his
object is to make out as strong a
case as possible against Philip, he
naturally suppresses this side of the
case.

§ 16. τί δέ] On this use of δέ
cf. Mr. Shill. de F. Leg. § 54 n.
crit. 8. 70, εἴ τις ἔροιτό με Εἰπέ μοι,
σὺ δὲ τί ..: 28. 28, and so passim.
"what do they signify? or how
does any of these things concern
us?"

τί .. ταῦτ' ἐστίν] Madv. 95 δ,
note. "whether these things were
really insignificant, or did not concern you, would be another question," with which we have nothing
to do; the matter before us is the
quality, and not the insignificance or
the reverse of the majority of them.
18. 44, ἕτερος λόγος οὗτος: 38. 8,
ἄλλος ἂν ἦν λόγος.

ΚΑΤΑ ΦΙΛΙΠΠΟΥ Γ. [—17.] 59

ἔμελεν, ἄλλος ἂν εἴη λόγος οὗτος· τὸ δ' εὐσεβὲς καὶ τὸ δίκαιον ἄν τ' ἐπὶ μικροῦ τις ἄν τ' ἐπὶ μείζονος παραβαίνῃ, τὴν αὐτὴν ἔχει δύναμιν. φέρε δὴ νῦν, ἡνίκ' εἰς Χερρόνησον, ἣν βασιλεὺς καὶ πάντες οἱ Ἕλληνες ὑμετέραν ἐγνώκασιν εἶναι, ξένους εἰσπέμπει καὶ βοηθεῖν ὁμολογεῖ καὶ ἐπιστέλλει ταῦτα, τί ποιεῖ; 17. φησὶ μὲν γὰρ οὐ πολεμεῖν, ἐγὼ δὲ τοσούτῳ δέω ταῦτα ποιοῦντα ἐκεῖνον ἄγειν ὁμολογεῖν τὴν πρὸς ὑμᾶς εἰρήνην, ὥστε καὶ Μεγάρων ἁπτόμενον καὶ ἐν Εὐβοίᾳ τυραννίδα κατασκευάζοντα καὶ νῦν ἐπὶ Θρᾴκην παριόντα καὶ τὰ ἐν Πελοποννήσῳ σκευωρούμενον καὶ πάνθ', ὅσα πράττει μετὰ τῆς δυνάμεως, ποιοῦντα λύειν φημὶ τὴν εἰρήνην καὶ πολεμεῖν ὑμῖν, εἰ μὴ καὶ τοὺς τὰ μηχανήματα ἐφιστάντας εἰρήνην ἄγειν φήσετε, ἕως ἂν αὐτὰ τοῖς τείχεσιν ἤδη προσάγωσιν. ἀλλ' οὐ φήσετε· ὁ γάρ, οἷς ἂν ἐγὼ ληφθείην, ταῦτα πράττων καὶ κατασκευαζόμενος, οὗτος ἐμοὶ πολεμεῖ,

ἐπὶ μ.] "in a small matter." 2. 1.

τὴν αὐτὴν.. 8.] "comes to the same thing." Mr. K. less correctly, "religion and justice have the same obligation." Cf. Antiph. *de Caed. Her.* § 92, καὶ μὴν τὴν ἴσην γε δύναμιν ἔχει, ὅστις τε ἂν τῇ χειρὶ ἀποκτείνῃ ἀδίκως καὶ ὅστις τῇ ψήφῳ.

φέρε] Cf. 4. 10, εἰσί μοι.

βασιλεύς, as applied to the king of Persia, having become as it were a proper name, is generally used without the article. Madv. 8, r. 2 b. The *Chersonese* had not of course been declared to be theirs by any formal act, but by allowance of their occupation of it, and the recognition of it, in negotiations, &c., as a part of their ἀρχή. Cf. Aesch. 2. 73, χερρόνησον.... τὴν οὖσαν ὁμολογημένως 'Αθηναίων. Comp. the similar language about Amphipolis in 19. 253 and Ps. Dem. 7. 29.

ἐπιστέλλει τ.] "writes us word to that effect," "writes to tell us so."

§ 17. φησὶ μὲν γάρ] Cf. § 15. "he *says* of course..." West.

reads φησί.. "you (his apologist) say.."

τοσούτῳ] Bekk. st. (Bekk. τοσούτου), as in 18. 111, τοσούτῳ γὰρ δέω λέγειν.

Μεγάρων] Grote, 11. 622.

ἐν Εὐβοίᾳ] 8. 36; infr. 57 sq. 19. 326.

ἐπὶ Θρᾴκην] Grote, l. c.

τὰ ἐν Π.] 6. 15. Grote, 11. 611 sq. "but so far from admitting that he is by this conduct.. I assert that his attempt to seize M.... all his movements with his army are so many infractions of the peace and acts of hostility against you." Comp. with this passage 18. 71.

εἰ μή] "unless indeed you will maintain that even those who are planting their engines.. till they actually (ἤδη) bring them up to.." 18. 87, χαράκωμα βαλλόμενος πρὸς τῇ πόλει καὶ μηχανήματ' ἐπιστήσας ἐπολιόρκει.

πράττων] "is contriving and preparing the means for my capture.. though he be not yet throwing dart or shooting arrow."

κἂν μήπω βάλλῃ μηδὲ τοξεύῃ. 18. τίσιν οὖν ὑμεῖς κινδυ-
νεύσαιτ' ἄν, εἴ τι γένοιτο; τῷ τὸν Ἑλλήσποντον ἀλλο-
τριωθῆναι, τῷ Μεγάρων καὶ τῆς Εὐβοίας τὸν πολεμοῦνθ'
ὑμῖν γενέσθαι κύριον, τῷ Πελοποννησίους τἀκείνου φρονῆσαι.
εἶτα τὸν τοῦτο τὸ μηχάνημα ἐπὶ τὴν πόλιν ἱστάντα, τοῦτον
εἰρήνην ἄγειν ἐγὼ φῶ πρὸς ὑμᾶς; 19. πολλοῦ γε καὶ δεῖ,
ἀλλ' ἀφ' ἧς ἡμέρας ἀνεῖλε Φωκέας, ἀπὸ ταύτης ἔγωγ' αὐτὸν
πολεμεῖν ὁρίζομαι. ὑμᾶς δέ, ἐὰν μὲν ἀμύνησθε ἤδη, σωφρο-
νήσειν φημί, ἐὰν δ' ἐάσητε, οὐδὲ τοῦθ' ὅταν βούλησθε δυνήσεσθε ποιῆσαι. καὶ τοσοῦτόν γε ἀφέστηκα τῶν ἄλλων, ὦ
ἄνδρες Ἀθηναῖοι, τῶν συμβουλευόντων ὥστε οὐδὲ δοκεῖ μοι
περὶ Χερρονήσου νῦν σκοπεῖν οὐδὲ Βυζαντίου, 20. ἀλλ'
ἐπαμῦναι μὲν τούτοις καὶ διατηρῆσαι μή τι πάθωσι, βουλεύεσθαι μέντοι περὶ πάντων τῶν Ἑλλήνων ὡς ἐν κινδύνῳ
μεγάλῳ καθεστώτων. βούλομαι δ' εἰπεῖν πρὸς ὑμᾶς ἐξ ὧν
ὑπὲρ τῶν πραγμάτων οὕτω φοβοῦμαι, ἵν' εἰ μὲν ὀρθῶς λογί-

§ 18. τίσιν .. κ. ἐν] Ps. Dem.
10. 3, πᾶσι τοῖς οὖσι .. κινδυνεύσων:
Thuc. 2. 65, μηδὲ τῇ πόλει κινδυν-
εύοντας: Id. 6. 9: the dat. expressing the stake risked. "what
then are the risks you would run
should any thing happen (i. e. in
event of a war breaking out)? The
risk of the alienation of the H. (cf.
19. 180. This would make him τῆς
σιτοπομπείας Ἑλλήνων κύριος, as he
says in 18. 241); of the power at
war with you becoming master of
.."
τἀκείνου φρ.] "taking his side,"
"siding with him." Thuc. 3. 68;
5. 84 al.
τοῦτο τὸ μ.] "such an engine as
this." Cf. Mr. Shill. *de F. Leg.*
§ 15.
φῶ) "am I to say?" "can I
allow?" Madv. 121.
§ 19. π. γε καὶ δεῖ] Bekk. st.
from F S T Ω. Bekk. and Dind.
π. γε καὶ δέω, as in Aesch. *Prom.*
1002; Dem. 5. 14. "far from
it; on the contrary, from the day
he destroyed..." The question

whether it was possible for them
ἄγειν εἰρήνην (§ 8) is thus settled.
For δυνήσεσθε Reiske and Cobet
propose δυνήσεσθαι, a needless cor-
rection for the sake of symmetry.
Observe the emphatic position of
ὑμᾶς. "if you defend yourselves
at once, I say you will act wisely,
but if you let it pass (put it off) you
will not be able to do as much as
that .." ἐάσητε, Bekk. st. from S;
ἀναβάλησθε, Bekk.
καὶ .. γε] 6. 29.
ἀφέστηκα] "dissent from."
οὐδὲ δ.] "that in my opinion you
ought not to think about either the
C. or B. You should send them
aid indeed, and watch that they
come to no harm, but *deliberate*
about all Hellas .." Cf. Grote, 11.
624. Comp. the similar language
in 15. 13, οὐ γὰρ ὑπὲρ Ῥοδίων βου-
λευτέον ... μόνον, ἀλλ' ὑπὲρ ὑμῶν
αὐτῶν καὶ τῶν ἄλλων Ἑλλήνων.
§ 20. ἐξ ὧν] "the reasons which
lead me," "why." 1. 7, ἐκ τῶν
ἐγκλημάτων: 2. 9 al.

—22.] ΚΑΤΑ ΦΙΛΙΠΠΟΥ Γ. 61

ζομαι, μετάσχητε τῶν λογισμῶν καὶ πρόνοιάν τιν᾽ ὑμῶν γ᾽
αὐτῶν, εἰ μὴ καὶ τῶν ἄλλων ἄρα βούλεσθε, ποιήσησθε, ἂν δὲ
ληρεῖν καὶ τετυφῶσθαι δοκῶ, μήτε νῦν μήτ᾽ αὖθις ὡς ὑγιαί-
νοντί μοι προσέχητε.

21. Ὅτι μὲν δὴ μέγας ἐκ μικροῦ καὶ ταπεινοῦ τὸ κατ᾽
ἀρχὰς Φίλιππος ηὔξηται, καὶ ἀπίστως καὶ στασιαστικῶς
ἔχουσι πρὸς αὑτοὺς οἱ Ἕλληνες, καὶ ὅτι πολλῷ παρα-
δοξότερον ἦν τοσοῦτον αὐτὸν ἐξ ἐκείνου γενέσθαι ἢ νῦν, ὅθ᾽
οὕτω πολλὰ προείληφε, καὶ τὰ λοιπὰ ὑφ᾽ αὑτῷ ποιήσασθαι,
καὶ πάνθ᾽ ὅσα τοιαῦτ᾽ ἂν ἔχοιμι διεξελθεῖν, παραλείψω.
22. ἀλλ᾽ ὁρῶ συγκεχωρηκότας ἅπαντας ἀνθρώπους, ἀφ᾽
ὑμῶν ἀρξαμένους, αὐτῷ ὑπὲρ οὗ τὸν ἄλλον ἅπαντα χρόνον
πάντες οἱ πόλεμοι γεγόνασιν οἱ Ἑλληνικοί. τί οὖν ἐστι
τοῦτο; τὸ ποιεῖν ὅ τι βούλεται, καὶ καθ᾽ ἕνα οὑτωσὶ περι-

εἰ μὴ .. ἐρα] "*nisi forte*," "unless perhaps..." Jelf, 788. 5. "however disinclined to do so for others" (Mr. K.).

τετυφῶσθαι] Harpocr. s. v., τετύφωμαι, ἀντὶ τοῦ ἐμβρόντημαι, ἔξω τῶν φρενῶν γέγονα, ἤτοι ὑπὸ τῆς Βροντῆς, ἢ ἀπὸ τῶν ἐπὶ τὸν Τυφῶνα ἀναφερομένων σηπτῶν, ἢ ἀπὸ τῶν Τυφωνικῶν καλουμένων πνευμάτων, ἃ δὴ καὶ αὐτὰ ἐξίστησιν ἀθρόως καταρραγέντα· Ἀλκαῖος "πάμπαν δὲ τυφὼς ἒκ σ᾽ ἔλιτο φρένας." Δημοσθένης ὑπὲρ Κτησιφῶντος (§ 4). 19. 219; 33. 137. "but if you think I talk nonsense and am dreaming (am besotted), you may regard me as out of my senses, and not listen to me either now or at any future time."

ὑγιαίνοντι] 8. 36. Pl. *Lys.* 205 A, οὐχ ὑγιαίνει ἀλλὰ ληρεῖ τε καὶ μαίνεται.

§ 21. Ὅτι μὲν ... ἀλλ᾽] Cf. 3. 27.

μέγας] 1. 28.

ἐκ μ. καὶ τ.] "from a humble and mean beginning." 3. 29, ἐκ πτωχῶν: 18. 131, ἐλεύθερος ἐκ δούλου.

ἀπίστως, κ.τ.λ.] Cf. 18. 21, where this is forcibly dwelt on; also § 61

and 14. 36.

αὐτοῖς] 4. 10.

ἐξ ἐ.] "from that origin." Isocr. 5. 115, ῥᾷον γάρ ἐστιν ἐκ τῶν παρόντων κτήσασθαι τὴν καλλίστην (δόξαν) ἥπερ ἐξ ὧν παρέλαβες ἐπὶ τὴν νῦν παροῦσαν προελθεῖν. "that it would be now for him, after making so many acquisitions, to reduce under his power what is left—these and all other topics of the kind I might enlarge on.."

§ 22. ἀφ᾽ ὑμῶν ἀρξ.] "participium ἀρξάμενος usurpatur in multitudine aliquâ ab unâ re, tanquam a principio, definiendâ; Lat. *si incipias ab* .. Ponitur autem plerumque in eo et numero et casu in quo illud ipsum quod ita definitive enuntiatum est. Vid. Heind. *ad Gorg.* 60 .. Gorg. l. c. ἔστις ὅστις Ἀθηναίων ἀπὸ σοῦ ἀρξάμενος δόξαιτ᾽ ἄν." Dutt. *Ind. Pl. Mino*; Madv. 176 c, r.

ὑπὲρ οὗ] "a privilege which has been the subject of .."

καθ᾽ ἕνα] Cf. 4. 20.

οὑτωσί] 4. 11. In 8. 6 he had already pointed out that all this was with the object of attacking them.

κόπτειν καὶ λωποδυτεῖν τῶν Ἑλλήνων, καὶ καταδουλοῦσθαι τὰς πόλεις ἐπιόντα. 23. καίτοι προστάται μὲν ὑμεῖς ἑβδομήκοντα ἔτη καὶ τρία τῶν Ἑλλήνων ἐγένεσθε, προστάται δὲ τριάκοντα ἑνὸς δέοντα Λακεδαιμόνιοι· ἴσχυσαν δέ τι καὶ Θηβαῖοι τουτουσὶ τοὺς τελευταίους χρόνους μετὰ τὴν ἐν Λεύκτροις μάχην. ἀλλ' ὅμως οὔθ' ὑμῖν οὔτε Θηβαίοις οὔτε Λακεδαιμονίοις οὐδεπώποτε, ὦ ἄνδρες Ἀθηναῖοι, συνεχωρήθη τοῦθ' ὑπὸ τῶν Ἑλλήνων, ποιεῖν ὅ τι βούλοισθε, οὐδὲ πολλοῦ δεῖ. 24. ἀλλὰ τοῦτο μὲν ὑμῖν, μᾶλλον δὲ τοῖς τότ' οὖσιν Ἀθηναίοις, ἐπειδή τισιν οὐ μετρίως ἐδόκουν προσφέρεσθαι, πάντες ᾤοντο δεῖν, καὶ οἱ μηδὲν ἐγκαλεῖν ἔχοντες αὐτοῖς, μετὰ τῶν ἠδικημένων πολεμεῖν, καὶ πάλιν Λακεδαιμονίοις ἄρξασι καὶ παρελθοῦσιν εἰς τὴν αὐτὴν δυναστείαν ὑμῖν, ἐπειδὴ πλεονάζειν ἐπεχείρουν καὶ πέρα τοῦ μετρίου τὰ

περικόπτειν] ß. 9, δεινὰ δὲ ποιοῦσιν οἱ ξένοι περικόπτοντες τὰ ἐν Ἑλλησπόντῳ.

λωποδυτεῖν] as if he were a common footpad, "plundering and robbing the Greeks one after another in the way he is doing, and of attacking.."

§ 23. προστάται) implying, as Redh. rightly points out, a legitimate authority as ἡγεμόνες, ἰσχύειν one founded on power and success in war. In 3. 24 (where see the note) the Athenian Hegemony is said to have lasted forty-five years, i. e. to the beginning of the Peloponnesian War. Here the orator adds the twenty-eight years of the Peloponnesian War in order to make the contrast dwelt on in § 25 more striking.

Λακεδαιμόνιοι] from the end of the Peloponnesian War, B.C. 405, to their defeat at Naxos by Chabrias, B.C. 376.

ἴσχυσαν] note to 2. 9. "attained some degree of power in these latter times."

ποιεῖν] Schäf. says, "omisit articulum Bekker. Malim servatum; confer § 12 (τὸ ποιεῖν). Omnino quoties eadem in periodo τοῦτο explicatur per infinitivum mox sequentem, in prosâ quidem oratione vix puto infinitivum posse carere articulo." But cf. 3. 12; Madv. 165 b.

On οὐδὲ ᾧ δεῖ Schäf. (on p. 110. 10) rightly remarks that the effect of οὐδὲ, due to the preceding negative, is "non ut tollatur vis formulae affirmans, sed ut augeatur negans enuntiationis. Simile Eur. Phoen. 1600, οὐκ ἂν προδοίην οὐδὲ περ πράσσων κακῶς." Cf. Mr. Shill. de F. Leg. § 33. "far otherwise, on the contrary, when." "so far from that, when you .. appeared .. even those who had no complaint against them (1. 7, ἐκ τῶν .. ἐγκλημάτων) thought it their duty .."

§ 24. οὐ μ.] a litotes, οὐ being privative: cf. 3. 1, "harshly." 18. 18, οἷς γὰρ ηὐτυχήκεσαν ἐν Λεύκτροις οὐ μετρίως ἐχρήσαντο.

On καὶ πάλιν after πρῶτον μὲν cf. Herm. Vig. p. 702. "again, as soon as the L. when they became masters.."

ἄρξασι] an ingressive aorist, as ἴσχυσαν above.

παρελθοῦσιν] "came into," "succeeded to." Thuc. 1. 89, ἦλθον ἐπὶ τὰ πράγματα.

—26.] ΚΑΤΑ ΦΙΛΙΠΠΟΥ Γ. 63

καθεστηκότα ἐκίνουν, πάντες εἰς πόλεμον κατέστησαν, καὶ οἱ μηδὲν ἐγκαλοῦντες αὐτοῖς. 25. καὶ τί δεῖ τοὺς ἄλλους λέγειν; ἀλλ' ἡμεῖς αὐτοὶ καὶ Λακεδαιμόνιοι, οὐδὲν ἂν εἰπεῖν ἔχοντες ἐξ ἀρχῆς ὅ τι ἠδικούμεθ' ὑπ' ἀλλήλων, ὅμως ὑπὲρ ὧν τοὺς ἄλλους ἀδικουμένους ἑωρῶμεν, πολεμεῖν ᾠόμεθα δεῖν. καίτοι πάνθ' ὅσα ἐξημάρτηται καὶ Λακεδαιμονίοις ἐν τοῖς τριάκοντ' ἐκείνοις ἔτεσι καὶ τοῖς ἡμετέροις προγόνοις ἐν τοῖς ἑβδομήκοντα, ἐλάττονά ἐστιν, ὦ ἄνδρες Ἀθηναῖοι, ὧν Φίλιππος ἐν τρισὶ καὶ δέκα οὐχ ὅλοις ἔτεσιν οἷς ἐπιπολάζει ἠδίκηκε τοὺς Ἕλληνας, μᾶλλον δὲ οὐδὲ πέμπτον μέρος τούτων ἐκεῖνα. 26. Ὄλυνθον μὲν δὴ καὶ Μεθώνην καὶ Ἀπολλωνίαν καὶ δύο καὶ τριάκοντα πόλεις ἐπὶ Θρᾴκης ἑῶ, ἃς ἁπάσας οὕτως ὠμῶς ἀνῄρηκεν ὥστε μηδ' εἰ πώποτ' ᾠκήθησαν προσελθόντ' εἶναι ῥᾴδιον εἰπεῖν· καὶ τὸ Φωκέων ἔθνος τοσοῦ-

ἐκίνουν] a technical word in this case: "began to change the established order of things in an arbitrary manner.." πέρα τοῦ μ. = οὐ μετρίως above. The policy of the L. is concisely given by Thuc. 1. 19. Cf. Thuc. 1. 76 in.

§ 25. καὶ τί δεῖ . . ἀλλ'] a common form of "transitio:" infr. § 59; 23. 114, καὶ τί δεῖ Φίλιππον λέγειν ἢ τιν' ἄλλον, ἀλλ' :." Isocr. 6. 104, καὶ τί δεῖ τὸ πόρρω λέγειν, ἀλλὰ ." "but what need to speak of the rest? We ourselves and the L.."

ἂν ... ἔχοντες] i. e. ἂν εἴχομεν. 3. 8; Madv. 184 a. "though we could not at the outset specify any thing in which.."

ὑπὲρ ὧν] i. e. ἐκείνων ἅ. "thought it our duty to go to war to redress the wrongs.." Cf. 18. 96.

ἐξημάρτηται) (ἠδίκηκε—the faults of themselves and the Spartans) (the wrongs done by Philip.

ἐν τρισὶ .. οἷς] Cf. note on § 2, παρ' ἥν.

οὐχ ὅλοις] As this speech was delivered in the summer of D.C. 341, the thirteen incomplete years, reckoning inclusively, will carry us back to the taking of Methone (B.C. 353), referred to in the next section.

ἐπιπολάζει] "invidiose et cum contemptu dictum" (Schäf.). Not necessarily so: Isocr. 8. 107, ὅσῳ ἡμᾶς (the Athenians) οὐ πολλοῖς ἔτεσιν ὕστερον ἐπιπολάσαι καὶ κυρίους γενέσθαι τῆς ἐκείνων (the Spartans) σωτηρίας; and 5. 61, τὰς μὲν ἀτιμασθήσεσθαι, τὰς δ' ἐπιπολάσειν τῶν Ἑλληνίδων πόλεων. "he has been in the ascendant," "has been uppermost."

§ 26. ἐπὶ Θ.] "on the T. coast," a term well known to the readers of Thucydides as applied to the coast from Thessaly to the Hellespont. See Arn. on Thuc. 1. 57; Mure, 5, p. 32.

προσελθόντ'] "Olynthus ... I pass over, all which he has so cruelly destroyed, that on visiting the spot it is not easy to say whether.." Appian, Bell. Civ. 4. 102, says, Φίλιππος ὁ Ἀμύντου τούς τ' ἄλλους καὶ Χαλκιδέας ἀνίστησεν, ὡς μηδὲν ἔτι πλὴν αἱμάτιδα μόνον ἱερῶν ὁρᾶσθαι.

καὶ τὸ Φ.] "also of the P., so great a nation exterminated, I say nothing. But .."

τον ἀνῃρημένον σιωπῶ. ἀλλὰ Θετταλία πῶς ἔχει; οὐχὶ τὰς πολιτείας καὶ τὰς πόλεις αὐτῶν παρῄρηται καὶ τετραρχίας κατέστησεν, ἵνα μὴ μόνον κατὰ πόλεις ἀλλὰ καὶ κατ' ἔθνη δουλεύωσιν; 27. αἱ δ' ἐν Εὐβοίᾳ πόλεις οὐκ ἤδη τυραννοῦνται, καὶ ταῦτα ἐν νήσῳ πλησίον Θηβῶν καὶ Ἀθηνῶν; οὐ διαρρήδην εἰς τὰς ἐπιστολὰς γράφει " ἐμοὶ δ' ἐστὶν εἰρήνη πρὸς τοὺς ἀκούειν ἐμοῦ βουλομένους;" καὶ οὐ γράφει μὲν ταῦτα, τοῖς δ' ἔργοις οὐ ποιεῖ, ἀλλ' ἐφ' Ἑλλήσποντον οἴχεται, πρότερον ἧκεν ἐπ' Ἀμβρακίαν, Ἦλιν ἔχει τηλικαύτην πόλιν ἐν Πελοποννήσῳ, Μεγάροις ἐπεβούλευσε πρῴην, οὔθ' ἡ Ἑλλὰς οὔθ' ἡ βάρβαρος τὴν πλεονεξίαν χωρεῖ τἀνθρώπου. 28. καὶ ταῦθ' ὁρῶντες οἱ Ἕλληνες

ἀλλά] supr. § 25.
πολιτείας, which in t. 5 we had used in the sense of "free states," here means "constitutions." cf. 20. 15. In his last edition, Dind., following Schäfer, brackets the words καὶ τὰς πόλεις, which are omitted by Dionysius in his citation of the passage. But there is surely no need to reject on such slender grounds the reading of the MSS. Philip took from them their cities by putting garrisons in them. Cf. supr. § 12. "their constitutions, nay, their cities."
τετραρχίας] see on 6. 22.
δουλεύωσιν] Cf. 2. 24, τύχωσι. The effect contemplated was still realized at the time of speaking. "that they might be (as they now are) his subjects not only by cities but by tribes."
§ 27. ἐν Εὐβοίᾳ] infr. § 57; supr. 17.
εἰς.. γράφει] "writes in.." So regularly: infr. 41, κατίθεντ' εἰς στήλην; 19. 40 and 49. On δ' after ἐμοί, supr. 16.
μέν.. δ'] "and he does not write this without carrying it into act." Madv. 189. Comp. the well-known passage 18. 179, οὐκ εἶπον μὲν ταῦτα, οὐκ ἔγραψα δέ, οὐδ' ἔγραψα μέν, οὐκ ἐπρέσβευσα δέ, οὐδ' ἐπρέσβευσα μέν,

οὐκ ἔπεισα δὲ Θηβαίους—which Quintil. (9. 3. 35) translates, "Non enim dixi quidem sed non scripsi; nec scripsi quidem, sed non obii legationem, nec obli quidem sed non persuasi Thebanis." Cf. Diss. de Cor. p. 348; Dem. 15. 16; Lys. 10. 8. The negative prefixed denies in this case, not the separate clauses, but the combination of them: cf. infr. 57.
ἀλλ'] "no! he is gone.." supr. 17.
Ἀμβρακίαν] infr. 34 and 72. Pa. Dem. 7. 32 connects with this expedition against Ambracia the capture of the three towns of the district of Cassopia, which claimed to be colonies of Elis. His pretext for attacking Ambracia may have been that it supported these towns in their refusal to acknowledge the authority of his brother-in-law Alexander. His real object no doubt was to open a way to the western side of the Peloponnese, with which view he had won over the Aetolians by promising to take Naupactus from the Achaeans and give it to them. Infr. 34; Thirl. 6. 17.
Ἦλιν] Thirl. ibid.; Dem. 19. 160.
Μεγάροις] supr. 17.
χωρεῖ] "cannot contain the am-

ΚΑΤΑ ΦΙΛΙΠΠΟΥ Γ.

ἅπαντες καὶ ἀκούοντες οὐ πέμπομεν πρέσβεις περὶ τούτων πρὸς ἀλλήλους καὶ ἀγανακτοῦμεν, οὕτω δὲ κακῶς διακείμεθα καὶ διορωρύγμεθα κατὰ πόλεις ὥστ᾽ ἄχρι τῆς τήμερον ἡμέρας οὐδὲν οὔτε τῶν συμφερόντων οὔτε τῶν δεόντων πρᾶξαι δυνάμεθα, οὐδὲ συστῆναι, οὐδὲ κοινωνίαν βοηθείας καὶ φιλίας οὐδεμίαν ποιήσασθαι, 29. ἀλλὰ μείζω γιγνόμενον τὸν ἄνθρωπον περιορῶμεν, τὸν χρόνον κερδᾶναι τοῦτον ὃν ἄλλος ἀπόλλυται ἕκαστος ἐγνωκώς, ὡς γ᾽ ἐμοὶ δοκεῖ, οὐχ ὅπως σωθήσεται τὰ τῶν Ἑλλήνων σκοπῶν οὐδὲ πράττων, ἐπεὶ ὅτι γε ὥσπερ περίοδος ἡ καταβολὴ πυρετοῦ ἤ τινος ἄλλου κακοῦ καὶ τῷ πάνυ πόρρω δοκοῦντι νῦν ἀφεστάναι προσέρχεται, οὐδεὶς ἀγνοεῖ. 30. καὶ μὴν κἀκεῖνό γε ἴστε, ὅτι ὅσα μὲν ὑπὸ Λακεδαιμονίων ἢ ὑφ᾽ ἡμῶν ἔπασχον οἱ Ἕλληνες, ἀλλ᾽ οὖν ὑπὸ γνησίων γε ὄντων τῆς Ἑλλάδος ἠδικοῦντο, καὶ τὸν αὐτὸν

bition of the man." 21. 200, ἡ πόλις αὐτὸν οὐ χωρεῖ: Aesch. 3. 164, τὴν δὲ σὴν ἀηδίαν ἡ πόλις οὐκ ἐχώρει.

§ 28. καί] "and yet."

ἀγανακτοῦμεν] "express indignation."

διορωρύγμεθα] "tanquam fossis interjectis et vallis separati" (II. Wolf). "entrenched in our separate cities" (Mr. K.). Cf. the fine passage in 18, 61, where Dem. describes how this was brought about by the arts of Philip.

τῆς τ. ἡ.] "that to this day we are unable to effect any thing required by our interest or duty, or unite or form any combination for succour and friendship."

§ 29. μεῖζω γ.] "growing greater and greater."

κερδᾶναι] "each resolved, so at least it appears to me, to count the time as gained (lucro apponere) in which another is destroyed, not taking thought or exerting himself for the saving of Greece." With this section comp. 18. 45.

ἐπεὶ . . . γε] added to give the reason of the foregoing. Ps. Dem. 7. 11; Pl. Prot. 333 C, αἰσχυνοίμην ἂν ἔγωγ᾽ . . . τοῦτο ὁμολογεῖν ἐπεὶ πολλοί γέ φασι τῶν ἀνθρώπων: Symp. 187 A, ὥσπερ ἴσως καὶ Ἡράκλειτος βούλεται λέγειν, ἐπεὶ τοῖς γε ῥήμασιν οὐ καλῶς λέγει. In all such examples ἐπεί preserves its causal sense, though it is convenient to translate "for," "though"—"for that, like the recurrence or periodic attack of a fever . . he is coming upon such even as seem at present to be very far removed, no one can be ignorant." περιοδικὰ νοσήματα καλοῦσιν οἱ ἰατροὶ τὰ τεταγμένως ἀνιέμενα καὶ αὖθις ἐπιτεινόμενα, οἶον τριταίους ἢ τεταρταίους καὶ γὰρ ἐπὶ τούτων οἱ κάμνοντες δοκοῦσιν ἐν ταῖς τῶν ἀνέσεων ἡμέραις μηδὲν νοσεῖν ἀλλ᾽ ὑγιεῖς εἶναι. Harpocr.

§ 30. ὑφ᾽ . . . ἔπασχον] cf. note to s. 9.

ἀλλ᾽ οὖν . . . γε] "yet at any rate," "at all events," often both after hypothetical and categorical statements. Isocr. 4. 171, εἰ δὲ καὶ προσείχον, ἀλλ᾽ οὖν τούς γε λόγους ὥσπερ χρησμοὺς . . . ἂν κατέλιπαν: Dem. 16. 31; Aesch. 3. 86, τοὺς μὲν πρώτους χρόνους, ἀλλ᾽ οὖν προσεποιοῦνθ᾽ ὑμῶν εἶναι φίλοι: ib. § 11 al. "were at all events inflicted by those who were genuine sons of Hellas."

66 ΔΗΜΟΣΘΕΝΟΥΣ [O. 31

τρόπον ἄν τις ὑπέλαβε τοῦθ' ὥσπερ ἂν εἰ υἱὸς ἐν οὐσίᾳ πολλῇ γεγονὼς γνήσιος διῴκει τι μὴ καλῶς μηδ' ὀρθῶς, κατ' αὐτὸ μὲν τοῦτο ἄξιον μέμψεως εἶναι καὶ κατηγορίας, ὡς δ' οὐ προσήκων ἢ ὡς οὐ κληρονόμος τούτων ὧν ταῦτα ἐποίει, οὐκ ἐνεῖναι λέγειν. 31. εἰ δέ γε δοῦλος ἢ ὑποβολιμαῖος τὰ μὴ προσήκοντα ἀπώλλυε καὶ ἐλυμαίνετο,'Ηράκλεις ὅσῳ μᾶλλον δεινὸν καὶ ὀργῆς ἄξιον πάντες ἂν ἔφησαν εἶναι. ἀλλ' οὐχ ὑπὲρ Φιλίππου καὶ ὧν ἐκεῖνος πράττει νῦν, οὐχ οὕτως ἔχουσιν, οὐ μόνον οὐχ ῞Ελληνος ὄντος οὐδὲ προσήκοντος οὐδὲν τοῖς ῞Ελλησιν, ἀλλ' οὐδὲ βαρβάρου ἐντεῦθεν ὅθεν καλὸν εἰπεῖν, ἀλλ' ὀλέθρου Μακεδόνος, ὅθεν οὐδ' ἀνδράποδον σπουδαῖον οὐδὲν ἦν πρότερον.

32. Καίτοι τί τῆς ἐσχάτης ὕβρεως ἀπολείπει; οὐ πρὸς τῷ πόλεις ἀνῃρηκέναι τίθησι μὲν τὰ Πύθια, τὸν κοινὸν τῶν

ὥσπερ ἂν] i. e. ὑπέλαβεν. "and it would have been regarded in the same light as if a legitimate son born to a large estate... that on that particular ground.. but that it could not be said he had no title or was not heir to the property he was thus dealing with." Cob. (*Nov. l.*, p. 228) without reason proposes to expunge ἐν οὐσίᾳ πολλῇ, and also γνήσιος, which is required by the preceding γνήσιος, and ὑποβολιμαῖος which follows.

τούτων] referring to the collective τι. 2. 18.

§ 31. 84 γε] "on the other hand," "on the contrary."

ὑποβ.] cf. 21. 149. where Demosthenes accuses Meidias of being such.

τὰ μὴ πρ.] "a property to which he had no right." Madv. 207. Cf. Thuc. 2. 61, where τῆς ὑπαρχούσης δόξης, "the reputation which is a man's own," is opposed to τῆς μὴ προσηκούσης, "the assumption of one to which he had no right or title."

Ἡράκλεις] "good heavens!"

οὐχ... οὐχ] Comp. 21. 165, οὐ μὴν Νικήρατός γε οὗτως... οὐδ' Εὐκτήμων.. οὐχ οὕτως: Aesch. 3.

194, ἀλλ' οὐχὶ ὁ Κέφαλος.. οὐχ οὕτως.

ἂν] i. e. ὑπὲρ τούτων ἃ. Isocr. 5. 83, περὶ μὲν οὖν τῶν ἐμῶν καὶ ὧν σοι πρακτέον ἐστί. Thuc. 5. 87.

οὕτως ἔχουσιν] "feel thus, though he is not only no Hellene (not a γνήσιος υἱός) or in any way connected with Hellas (not even an ὑποβολιμαῖος), but not even a barbarian (3. 16) from a place creditable to name, but a pestilent fellow of Macedonia, a country from which..."

ὀλέθρου] used adjectively as in 18. 127, ὄλεθρος γραμματεύς. 23. 202.

σπουδαῖον] "decent," "respectable."

§ 32. ὕβρεως] cf. 8. 62.

ἀπολείπει] i. e. Philip: "what is wanting to make his insolence complete." Mr. K.

πόλεις] "cities of Hellas." supr. 26.

τίθησι... τὰ Π.] 5. 22. Two months after the surrender of the Phocians, Philip was nominated by the Amphictyonic Council President of the Pythian Games in conjunction with the Thebans and Thessalians (B.C. 346). The Athenians refused

Ἑλλήνων ἀγῶνα, κἂν αὐτὸς μὴ παρῇ, τοὺς δούλους ἀγωνοθετήσοντας πέμπει; [κύριος δὲ Πυλῶν καὶ τῶν ἐπὶ τοὺς Ἕλληνας παρόδων ἐστί, καὶ φρουραῖς καὶ ξένοις τοὺς τόπους τούτους κατέχει; ἔχει δὲ καὶ τὴν προμαντείαν τοῦ θεοῦ, παρώσας ἡμᾶς καὶ Θετταλοὺς καὶ Δωριέας καὶ τοὺς ἄλλους Ἀμφικτύονας, ἧς οὐδὲ τοῖς Ἕλλησιν ἅπασι μέτεστιν;] 33. γράφει δὲ Θετταλοῖς ὃν χρὴ τρόπον πολιτεύεσθαι; πέμπει δὲ ξένους τοὺς μὲν εἰς Πορθμόν, τὸν δῆμον ἐκβαλοῦντας τὸν Ἐρετριέων, τοὺς δ' ἐπ' Ὠρεόν, τύραννον Φιλιστίδην καταστήσοντας; ἀλλ' ὅμως ταῦθ' ὁρῶντες οἱ Ἕλληνες ἀνέχονται, καὶ τὸν αὐτὸν τρόπον ὥσπερ τὴν χάλαζαν ἔμοιγε δοκοῦσι θεωρεῖν, εὐχόμενοι μὲν μὴ καθ' ἑαυτοὺς ἕκαστοι γενέσθαι, κωλύειν δὲ οὐδεὶς ἐπιχειρῶν. 34. οὐ μόνον δ' ἐφ' οἷς ἡ Ἑλλὰς ὑβρίζεται ὑπ' αὐτοῦ, οὐδεὶς

to send Theori on the occasion (19. 128). Though Dem. here resents this assumption on the part of Philip, he had advised the recognition of his Amphictyonic dignity. Grote, 11. 602.

τῶν Ἑ.] to whom he did not belong.

δούλους] "Intelligendi Macedonum proceres, quos orator δημοκρατικῶς lasciviens dicit δούλους" (Schäf.). They might, according to Greek views, be called so, because Philip was an absolute king. 19. 69, καὶ ὁ μὲν Ἀντίπατρος καὶ ὁ Παρμενίων δεσπότῃ διακονοῦντες. Cf. Eur. *Hel.* 276, τὰ βαρβάρων γὰρ δοῦλα πάντα πλὴν ἑνός. The passage κύριοι δὲ ... μέτεστιν, omitted by S, pr. m., is enclosed by Bekker in brackets. Before κύριοι we must supply οὐ from the preceding sentence.

τῶν ἐπὶ, κ.τ.λ.] "the passes into H." 6. 35, τῆς ἐπὶ τὴν Ἀττικὴν ὁδοῦ. He secured the pass by taking possession of Alponus, Thronium, and Nicaea, τὰ τῶν παρόδων τῶν εἰς Πύλας χωρία κύρια, Aesch. 2. 132; Grote, 11. 591, 602. The privilege of προμαντεία was transferred to Philip by the Amphic-

tyons. This is made the subject of complaint in 19. 327, ἡ δὲ πόλις τὴν προμαντείαν ἀφῄρηται. Cf. *Gr. and R. Ant.* s. v. Oraculum.

§ 33. γράφει δὲ] sc. οὐ from § 32.

Πορθμόν] Grote, 11. 622.

ἐπ' Ὠρεόν] Grote, 11. 621. "to set up P. as despot." Cf. § 57.

ὁρῶντες] Madv. 177 a.

τὸν αὐτὸν τ. ὥσπερ] supr. § 30. See on 1. 15; 4. 21. "and they seem to me to view them as people do a hail-storm, each hoping that it may not fall on themselves, but .." Comp. 18. 45.

γενέσθαι] the regular word in speaking of natural phenomena of this kind. Thuc. 2. 4; 2. 77 al.

οὐδεὶς] cf. 1. 19. The passage is obviously imitated by Sall. *Frag. Hist.* lib. 1, "Qui videmini intenta mala, quasi fulmen, optare ac quisque ne attingant, sed prohibere ne conari quidem."

§ 34. ἐφ' οἷς] 23. 106, 190, τὸ δ' ἐφ' οἷς ... πρᾶγμα ἀλυσιτελὲς ... πόλει κατεσκευάζετο ἐναντιοῦσθαι. "for the outrages he is doing to the H., but even on account of the wrongs each are personally suffering."

ἀμύνεται, ἀλλ' οὐδ' ὑπὲρ ὧν αὐτὸς ἕκαστος ἀδικεῖται· τοῦτο γὰρ ἤδη τοὔσχατον ἐστίν. οὐ Κορινθίων ἐπ' Ἀμβρακίαν ἐλήλυθε καὶ Λευκάδα; οὐκ Ἀχαιῶν Ναύπακτον ὀμώμοκεν Αἰτωλοῖς παραδώσειν; οὐχὶ Θηβαίων Ἐχῖνον ἀφῄρηται; 35. καὶ νῦν ἐπὶ Βυζαντίους πορεύεται συμμάχους ὄντας; οὐχ ἡμῶν, ἐῶ τἄλλα, ἀλλὰ Χερρονήσου τὴν μεγίστην ἔχει πόλιν Καρδίαν; ταῦτα τοίνυν πάσχοντες ἅπαντες μέλλομεν καὶ μαλακιζόμεθα καὶ πρὸς τοὺς πλησίον βλέπομεν, ἀπιστοῦντες ἀλλήλοις, οὐ τῷ πάντας ἡμᾶς ἀδικοῦντι. καίτοι τὸν ἅπασιν ἀσελγῶς οὕτω χρώμενον τί οἴεσθε, ἐπειδὰν καθ' ἕνα ἡμῶν ἑκάστου κύριος γένηται, τί ποιήσειν;

36. Τί οὖν αἴτιον τουτωνί; οὐ γὰρ ἄνευ λόγου καὶ δικαίας αἰτίας οὔτε τόθ' οὕτως εἶχον ἑτοίμως πρὸς ἐλευθερίαν οἱ Ἕλληνες, οὔτε νῦν πρὸς τὸ δουλεύειν. ἦν τι τότ', ἦν, ὦ

ὑπέρ] Isocr. 5. 125 (quoted by Redh.), ἡμεῖς δ' οὐδ' ὑπὲρ ὧν κακῶς ἐπάθομεν ἀμύνεσθαι τολμῶμεν αὐτούς. In the following sentence the genitives are put at the head of their sentences as illustrations of the assertion αὐτὸς ἕκαστος ἀδικεῖται. "has he not wronged the C. by marching against A. .... the Achaeans by swearing .... the Thebans by taking from them E.?" In this translation the sense is expressed rather than the strict construction, for grammatically Κορινθίων is of course a gen. of possession. His attack upon Ambracia is mentioned above, § 27.

Ἐχῖνον] Ἐχῖνος δὲ πόλις, Θηβαίων μὲν ἄποικος, πλησίον δὲ Θετταλίας, ἀπὸ Ἐχίνου ἑνὸς τῶν Σπαρτῶν. Schol.

§ 35. Βυζαντίους] supr. 17 and 27. Grote, 11. 627.

συμμάχους has been wrongly translated by Reiske and others "our allies." Cf. 18. 87, παρελθὼν ἐπὶ Θρᾴκην Βυζαντίους συμμάχους ὄντας αὑτῷ.

οὐχ ἡμῶν] "of ours, I omit the rest, but does he not.."

Καρδίαν] Grote, 11. 623.

For μαλακιζόμεθα Dind. has μαλκίομεν (which Schäfer also held to be the true reading), from μαλκίω, formed like μηρίω. Harpocr. s. v. μαλακίζομεν, i. e. μαλκίομεν, says, Δημοσθένης δ' Φιλιππικῶν φησὶ "μένομεν καὶ μαλκιόμεθα." ἐν ἐνίοις γράφεται μαλκίομεν, ὅπερ δηλοῖ τὸν ὄρρον φρίττειν. Αἰσχύλος Ἑλλάδιψ "κεκμῆτι μαλκίων ποδί." Cf. L. and S. s. v. μαλκίω. Redh. quotes Sall. Catil. c. 52. 28: "Sed inertiâ et mollitie animi alius alium exspectantes cunctamini."

τί οἴεσθε .. τί ποιήσειν] as 18. 240, τί ἂν οἴεσθε .. τί ποιεῖν ἂν ἢ λέγειν; Dind. omits the second τί here with F. "yet what do you think he who is treating all so insolently (4. 9)—what do you think he will do, when he becomes master of each of us separately?"

καθ' ἕνα .. ἑκάστου] cf. 2. 24.

§ 36. Τί .. αἴτιον] 3. 30.

εἶχον ἑτ. πρός] "were so eager for."

ἦν .. ἦν] l. 19.

ΚΑΤΑ ΦΙΛΙΠΠΟΥ Γ.

ἄνδρες Ἀθηναῖοι, ἐν ταῖς τῶν πολλῶν διανοίαις ὃ νῦν οὐκ ἔστιν, ὃ καὶ τοῦ Περσῶν ἐκράτησε πλούτου καὶ ἐλευθέραν ἦγε τὴν Ἑλλάδα καὶ οὔτε ναυμαχίας οὔτε πεζῆς μάχης οὐδεμιᾶς ἡττᾶτο, νῦν δ' ἀπολωλὸς ἅπαντα λελύμανται καὶ ἄνω καὶ κάτω πεποίηκε τὰ τῶν Ἑλλήνων πράγματα. 37. τί οὖν ἦν τοῦτο; τοὺς παρὰ τῶν ἄρχειν βουλομένων ἢ διαφθείρειν τὴν Ἑλλάδα χρήματα λαμβάνοντας ἅπαντες ἐμίσουν, καὶ χαλεπώτατον ἦν τὸ δωροδοκοῦντα ἐξελεγχθῆναι, καὶ τιμωρίᾳ μεγίστῃ τοῦτον ἐκόλαζον. 38. τὸν οὖν καιρὸν ἑκάστου τῶν πραγμάτων, ὃν ἡ τύχη πολλάκις παρασκευάζει, οὐκ ἦν πρίασθαι παρὰ τῶν λεγόντων οὐδὲ τῶν στρατηγούντων, οὐδὲ τὴν πρὸς ἀλλήλους ὁμόνοιαν, οὐδὲ τὴν πρὸς τοὺς τυράννους καὶ τοὺς βαρβάρους ἀπιστίαν, οὐδ' ὅλως τοιοῦτον οὐδέν. 39. νῦν δ' ἅπανθ' ὥσπερ ἐξ ἀγορᾶς ἐκπέπραται ταῦτα, ἀντεισῆκται δὲ ἀντὶ τού-

ἦγε] Cobet adopts Schäfer's conj. διῆγε, "faciebat ut G. libera maneret." There seems no reason for any change. "led H. in the possession (in a state) of freedom," "kept H. free."

μάχης ... ἡττᾶτο] "which triumphed over the wealth of P. ... and let itself be overcome by"—"quailed under no battle:" it was something all the gold of Persia could not corrupt or danger intimidate into submission. Whiston does injustice to a good scholar when he quotes Schäfer as saying "notanda locutio pro ἐν μάχῃ." What he says is "ἡττᾶσθαι μάχης notanda locutio." The construction is the same as in Thuc. 4. 37, ἡσσηθεῖεν τοῦ παρόντος δεινοῦ. μάχῃ would have been altogether inappropriate.

νῦν δ'] "but which now by its loss has ruined every thing, and turned the affairs of H. upside down." The Zurich Editors, Fr., West., and Redh. read πάντα τὰ πράγματα with S. The sense is the same, τὰ πρ. referring to τὴν Ἑλλάδα.

ἄνω κ. κάτω] 2. 16. On the participle after ἐξελέγχεσθαι, 4. 37. "and it was a most grievous thing for a man to be convicted of taking a bribe," as opposed to the ζῆλος, κ.τ.λ. below.

§ 37. τοῦτον] "such person." After ἡ τύχη Bekk. had καὶ τοῖς ἀμελοῦσι κατὰ τῶν προσεχόντων καὶ τοῖς μηδὲν ἐθέλουσι ποιεῖν κατὰ τῶν πάντα ἃ προσήκει πραττόντων. He now omits the words, with S pr. m. Dind. retains them.

§ 38. παρασκευάζει] 2. 3. "therefore the favourable moments for enterprises which F. often provides could not as they occurred (ἐκάστου) be bought from . . " as could be done in their own times. 19. 6; Aesch. 3. 94, καιροὶ πέπραται τηλικοῦτοι. This was one of the standing charges against public men at Athens, which Dem. himself did not escape: cf. Aesch. 3. 92. al.

τὴν πρὸς .. ἀπιστίαν] 6. 24. On τὴν πρὸς .. note to 6. 3, τὴν πρὸς ὑμᾶς..

§ 39. ἐκπέπραται] "but now all these principles have been sold off as if in open market (so that there are none now to be had), and those

70   ΔΗΜΟΣΘΕΝΟΤΣ   [9. 40

των ύφ' ων απόλωλε καὶ νενόσηκεν ἡ Ἑλλάς. ταῦτα δ'
ἐστὶ τί; ζῆλος, εἴ τις εἴληφέ τι, γέλως, ἂν ὁμολογῇ, μῖσος.
ἂν τούτοις τις ἐπιτιμᾷ, τἆλλα πάνθ' ὅσα ἐκ τοῦ δωροδοκεῖν
ἤρτηται. 40. ἐπεὶ τριήρεις γε καὶ σωμάτων πλῆθος καὶ
χρημάτων καὶ τῆς ἄλλης κατασκευῆς ἀφθονία, καὶ τἆλλα
οἷς ἄν τις ἰσχύειν τὰς πόλεις κρίνοι, νῦν ἅπασι καὶ
πλείω καὶ μείζω ἐστὶ τῶν τότε πολλῷ. ἀλλ' ἅπαντα
ταῦτ' ἄχρηστα ἄπρακτα ἀνόνητα ὑπὸ τῶν πωλούντων
γίγνεται.

41. Ὅτι δ' οὕτω ταῦτ' ἔχει, τὰ μὲν νῦν ὁρᾶτε δήπου καὶ
οὐδὲν ἐμοῦ προσδεῖσθε μάρτυρος· τὰ δ' ἐν τοῖς ἄνωθεν
χρόνοις ὅτι τἀναντία εἶχεν, ἐγὼ δηλώσω, οὐ λόγους ἐμαυτοῦ λέγων, ἀλλὰ γράμματα τῶν προγόνων τῶν ὑμετέρων,
ἃ 'κεῖνοι κατέθεντο εἰς στήλην χαλκῆν γράψαντες εἰς
ἀκρόπολιν. 42. Ἄρθμιος, φησίν, ὁ Πυθώνακτος Ζελείτης

imported in exchange for them by which Hellas has been ruined and made sick," "has been made sick unto death," by being brought into that state of νόσος so graphically described in 18, 45: cf. 6. 1.

ταῦτα .. τί] § 16.

ζῆλος] comp. what is said about Olynthus in 19. 265, and ib. 259.

τούτοις] neuter, "such doings."

ἤρτηται] "all the other concomitants, in short, of corrupt on." Observe the omission of καὶ before expressions, such as that here, by which enumerations are closed. 8. 25; Pa. Dem. 10. 10; 21. 136 al.

§ 40. ἐπεὶ .. γε] "Nam ni omnia a corruptelā penderent, melius de nobis ageretur, quum ..." (Fr.). cf. supr. § 29.

σωμάτων] "men." 18. 20, οὔτε χρήμασιν οὔτε σώμασιν.

κατασκευῆς] "materials," "munitions of war of all kinds," as arms, &c., the sense being determined by the context. 19. 89, κατασκευαῖς ὅπλων καὶ χόραι καὶ προσόδου, Thuc. 2. 14, and 97.

οἷς .. κρίνοι] 2. 15. "are generally considered to constitute the strength of states."

τῶν τότε] i. e. ἢ τοῖς τότε: 3. 32. Note the emphatic position of πολλῷ.

ὑπὸ .. γίγνεται] "are rendered .. by"—all these material advantages are rendered useless by the venality of οἱ λέγοντες καὶ οἱ στρατηγοῦντες § 18.

§ 41. Ὅτι] "for proof that." Madv. 192 b, r. Cobet, N. Lct. p. 367.

προσδεῖσθε] "need the addition of my testimony."

ἄνωθεν] 2. 10, κάτωθεν. "but that it was quite otherwise in former times .." δεικνύων, which he read after ὑμετέρων, Bekk. now omits with S pr. m. Dind. retains it. "not by words of my own, but by adducing an inscription." ἐκεῖνοι Dind.; ἃ κεῖνοι Bekk. and West. from S; cet. ἐκεῖνοι Cf. 4. 4.

κατέθεντο εἰς] Madv. 79. Thuc. 4. 57, καταθέσθαι ἐν ταῖς νήσοις. On the absence of the art. with ἀκρόπολιν, Madv. 8, r. 2 d.

εἰς στήλην] supr. 27.

§ 42. φησίν] sc. τὰ γράμματα. Aesch. 3. 110, γέγραπται γὰρ οὕτως

—44.] ΚΑΤΑ ΦΙΛΙΠΠΟΥ Γ. 71

ἄτιμος καὶ πολέμιος τοῦ δήμου τοῦ Ἀθηναίων καὶ τῶν συμμάχων αὐτὸς καὶ γένος. εἶθ᾽ ἡ αἰτία γέγραπται δι᾽ ἣν ταῦτ᾽ ἐγένετο· ὅτι τὸν χρυσὸν τὸν ἐκ Μήδων εἰς Πελοπόννησον ἤγαγεν. ταῦτ᾽ ἐστὶ τὰ γράμματα. 43. λογίζεσθε δὴ πρὸς θεῶν, τίς ἦν ποθ᾽ ἡ διάνοια τῶν Ἀθηναίων τῶν τότε ταῦτα ποιούντων, ἢ τί τὸ ἀξίωμα. ἐκεῖνοι Ζελείτην τινὰ Ἄρθμιον δοῦλον βασιλέως (ἡ γὰρ Ζέλειά ἐστι τῆς Ἀσίας), ὅτι τῷ δεσπότῃ διακονῶν χρυσίον ἤγαγεν εἰς Πελοπόννησον, οὐκ Ἀθήναζε, ἐχθρὸν αὐτῶν ἀνέγραψαν καὶ τῶν συμμάχων αὐτὸν καὶ γένος, καὶ ἀτίμους. 44. τοῦτο δ᾽ ἐστὶν οὐχ ἣν ἄν τις οὑτωσὶ φήσειεν ἀτιμίαν· τί γὰρ τῷ Ζελείτῃ, τῶν Ἀθηναίων κοινῶν εἰ μὴ μεθέξειν ἔμελλεν; ἀλλ᾽ ἐν τοῖς φονικοῖς γέγραπται νόμοις, ὑπὲρ ὧν ἂν μὴ διδῷ

ἐν τῇ ἀρᾷ Εἴ τις τάδε, φησί, παραβαίνῃ .. ἐναγὴς, φησίν, ἔστω .."
ἄτιμος] "an outlaw."
αὐτὸς καὶ γ.] "himself and his family." The young student should observe that τε is in such cases commonly omitted after αὐτός. Thuc. 2. 31, Ἀθηναῖοι πανδημεί, αὐτοὶ καὶ οἱ μέτοικοι: id. 4. 90 al. In 19. 271, where this inscription was read by the clerk of the court, Dem. says, ἀκούετε ... τῶν γραμμάτων λεγόντων Ἄρθμιον τὸν Πυθώνακτος τὸν Ζηλείτην ἐχθρὸν εἶναι καὶ πολέμιον τοῦ δήμου τοῦ Ἀ. καὶ τῶν συμμάχων καὶ γένος πᾶν.
ἡ αἰτία] According to Deinarchus (2, § 25) this was the only case in which the reason was assigned for the sentence of outlawry.
τὸν ἐκ Μ.] 1. 15.
§ 43. ἢ δ. ... ἀξίωμα] "what must have been the sentiment (infr. 53) ... or rather what the dignity ..." On ἀξίωμα and the difference between it and ἀξίωσις, Grote, 6. 233 note. Cf. Eth. Nic. 4, c. 7.
εἰς Π. οὐκ Ἀ.] So Deinarchus, quoted above. Dem. (19. 271) speaks more generally (εἰς τοὺς Ἕλληνας), and so Aeschines (3. 258), adding that though he was their proxenus they had nearly put him

to death, and ἐξεκήρυξαν. ἐκ τῆς πόλεως καὶ ἐξ ἁπάσης ἧς Ἀθηναῖοι ἄρχουσιν.
ἀνέγραψαν] "they wrote him up an enemy," "they recorded him as ..." Before Bekk.'s edition εἶναι was read after ἀτίμους. Comp. 23. 200, οὐκ ἐψηφίσαντο ἀγώγιμον, where after ἀγώγιμον Bekk. had εἶναι in brackets, but now omits the word altogether.
§ 44. On οὑτωσί see l. 20. "not the outlawry ordinarily understood by the name."
τί γάρ] Pl. Prot. 310 D, τί οὖν σοὶ τοῦτο; "for what did a man of Z. care for being condemned to exclusion from the rights of an Athenian citizen?" On the position of τῶν Ἀθ. κ. cf. 4. 29. The rights of an Athenian citizen are summed up by Lyc. c. Leocr. 142, ἀλλ᾽ ἥκει ἱερῶν θυσιῶν ἀγορᾶς νόμων πολιτείας μεθέξων. Cf. Dem. 23. 65. Before ἀλλ᾽ Bekk. had the words ἀλλ᾽ οὐ τοῦτο λέγει. He now omits them with S pr. m. The sense of them is conveyed by ἀλλ᾽. Dind. retains them.
ἐν τοῖς φ.... ν.] cf. 23. 51, Ὁ μὲν νόμος ἐστὶν οὗτος Δράκοντος .'. καὶ οἱ ἄλλοι δέ, ὅσους ἐκ τῶν φονικῶν νόμων παρεγραψάμην, where Weber

φόνου δικάσασθαι. "καὶ ἄτιμος" φησι "τεθνάτω." τοῦτο δὴ λέγει, καθαρὸν τὸν τούτων τινὰ ἀποκτείναντα εἶναι. 45. οὐκοῦν ἐνόμιζον ἐκεῖνοι τῆς πάντων τῶν Ἑλλήνων σωτηρίας αὑτοῖς ἐπιμελητέον εἶναι· οὐ γὰρ ἂν αὑτοῖς ἔμελεν εἴ τις ἐν Πελοποννήσῳ τινὰς ὠνεῖται καὶ ἑιαφθείρει, μὴ τοῦθ᾽ ὑπολαμβάνουσιν· ἐκόλαζον δ᾽ οὕτω καὶ ἐτιμωροῦντο οὓς αἴσθοιντο ὥστε καὶ στηλίτας ποιεῖν. ἐκ δὲ τούτων εἰκότως τὰ τῶν Ἑλλήνων ἦν τῷ βαρβάρῳ φοβερά, οὐχ ὁ βάρβαρος τοῖς Ἕλλησιν. 46. ἀλλ᾽ οὐ νῦν· οὐ γὰρ οὕτως

quotes Plut. *Sol.* c. 17, τοὺς δράκοντος ἀνεῖλε (Solon) πλὴν τῶν φονικῶν ἁπάντας, the φ. νόμοι being, as Thirl. (2, c. 11) remarks, "in fact customs hallowed by time and religion, and so retained, not introduced, by his predecessor."

ὑπὲρ ὧν] "in reference to those for whom he does not allow a prosecution for murder, he (the legislator) says 'let him die an outlaw.'" Harpocr. referring to this passage says, ἄτιμος. τοῦτο ἰδίως ἔταξε Δ. Φιλιππικοῖς, ἤγουν ὃν ἂν τις ἀποκτείνας οὐχ ὑπόκειται ἐπιτιμίῳ. The argument, whatever be its value, is plain: "the ἀτιμία to which Arthmius, declared an enemy of the Athenian people, was condemned, could not be an ordinary suspension of rights. What punishment would that have been to a man of Zelea? Rather he became ἄτιμος in the sense in which the word is used in the φονικοὶ νόμοι—out of the pale of all law—so that he could be slain with impunity"—whether we choose to suppose that the words of the law were ἄτιμος ἔστω καὶ νηποινὶ τεθνάτω, and that Dem., looking merely to the requirements of his argument, omitted the intervening words and joined ἄτιμος directly with τεθνάτω, or which is, I think, more probable, that ἄτιμος τεθνάτω is an interpretative equivalent for νηποινί τ.

λέγει] i. e. the legislator; "by this he means.."

καθαρόν] "clear of blood-guiltiness." 19. 66; Andoc. 1, § 95, ὁ κτείνας σε καθαρὸς τὰς χεῖρας ἔσται, κατά γε τὸν Σόλωνος νόμον.

τούτων] i. e. Arthmius or any of his family.

εἶναι] "shall be." Madv. 168 a, 1.

§ 45. ἐπιμ. εἶναι] "that they were bound to watch over.." On εἰ after ἔμελεν, Madv. 194 c.

ὠνεῖται καὶ δ.] "buying and (i. e. and so, cf. l. 3) corrupting people in the P." On ὠνεῖται after ἔμελεν, Madv. 132 b.

μὴ τοῦθ᾽ ὑ.] i. e. εἰ μὴ τοῦθ᾽ ὑπελάμβανον.

ἐκόλαζον... καὶ ἐτ.] Heind. (Pl. *Prot.* § 40) after quoting this passage and Arist. *Eth. Nic.* 3. 5 (κολάζουσι καὶ τιμωροῦνται τοὺς δρῶντας μοχθηρά), says, "in quibus τιμωρεῖσθαι ad poenam referre puto legibus debitam, κολάζειν ad castigationem emendationemque peccantium." Arist. *Rhet.* 1. 10. 17. Cf. Don. *Gr. Gr.* p. 449.

οὕτω] "so sharply as even to engrave their names as infamous on pillars." Andoc. 1. 51, ἀναγραφέντας ἐν στήλαις ὡς ὄντας ἀλιτηρίους τῶν θεῶν: Arist. *Rhet.* 2. 23. 25, κατηγορήσαντος Θρασυβούλου, ὅτι ἦν στηλίτης γεγονὼς ἐν τῇ ἀκροπόλει.

οὓς αἴσθοιντο] "any they noticed." Madv. 133.

ἐκ δέ] "the natural result of this was.."

τὰ τῶν Ἑ.] § 45.

—48.] ΚΑΤΑ ΦΙΛΙΠΠΟΥ Γ. 73

ἔχεθ᾽ ὑμεῖς οὔτε πρὸς τὰ τοιαῦτα οὔτε πρὸς τἆλλα, ἀλλὰ
πῶς ; εἴπω ; κελεύετε καὶ οὐκ ὀργιεῖσθε ;

ΕΚ ΤΟΥ ΓΡΑΜΜΑΤΕΙΟΥ ΑΝΑΓΙΓΝΩΣΚΕΙ.

47. Ἔστι τοίνυν τις εὐήθης λόγος παρὰ τῶν παραμυθεῖ-
σθαι βουλομένων τὴν πόλιν, ὡς ἄρα οὔπω Φίλιππός ἐστιν
οἷοί ποτ᾽ ἦσαν Λακεδαιμόνιοι, οἳ θαλάττης μὲν ἦρχον καὶ
γῆς ἁπάσης, βασιλέα δὲ σύμμαχον εἶχον, ὑφίστατο δ᾽ οὐδὲν
αὐτούς· ἀλλ᾽ ὅμως ἠμύνατο κἀκείνους ἡ πόλις καὶ οὐκ
ἀνηρπάσθη. ἐγὼ δὲ ἁπάντων ὡς ἔπος εἰπεῖν πολλὴν
εἰληφότων ἐπίδοσιν, καὶ οὐδὲν ὁμοίων ὄντων τῶν νῦν τοῖς
πρότερον, οὐδὲν ἡγοῦμαι πλέον ἢ τὰ τοῦ πολέμου κεκινῆσθαι
καὶ ἐπιδεδωκέναι. 48. πρῶτον μὲν γὰρ ἀκούω Λακεδαι-

§ 46. ἔχεθ᾽ . . πρός] "your feelings are not the same either with
regard to . . ." I have put the
note of interrogation after εἴπω,
"shall I tell you?" Bekk. st.
joins εἴπω κελεύετε, which I do not
understand. Dind. rightly, I think,
encloses the heading ἐκ τοῦ γραμμα-
τείου ἀναγιγνώσκει in brackets, as
it seems to have been inserted because the copyist did not see that
the answer to ἀλλὰ πῶς ; εἴπω ; is
given in § 70 sq. If the heading
had been genuine we ought surely to
have had λέξω and not εἴπω. Cf. 4
29 and 6. 28.
§ 47. Ἔστι τοίνυν] "there is
then . . ." Cf. 16. 11 ; 19. 187,
ἔστι τοίνυν τις πρόχειρος λόγος πᾶσι
τοῖς . . βουλομένοις : 20. 112 al. "a
foolish remark made by," "a foolish
saying of."
παρά] 18. 35, λόγοι παρὰ τούτου
ῥηθέντες : 19. 56, ταῖς παρ᾽ Αἰσχίνου
ῥηθείσαις ὑποσχέσεσι. Cf. 1. 10.
θ. . . καὶ γῆς ἁ.] 1. 9.
αὐτούς] "and nothing resisted
them." Cf. 3. 24.
ἀνηρπάσθη] "was not destroyed."
Ps. Dem. 10. 18 ; 21. 120, ἂν δ᾽
ἀνεξῆ ... διί με ἀνηρπάσθαι : and
the famous sentence in Aesch. 3.
133, Θῆβαι δέ, Θῆβαι πόλις ἀστυγεί-
των . . ἐκ μέσης τῆς Ἑλλάδος ἀνήρ-
πασται, "destroyed from off the
face of Hellas."
ἐγὼ δέ] in emphatic opposition to
those mentioned above. "but I
myself . ."
ὡς ἔπος εἰπεῖν] 6. 1.
εἰλ. ἐπίδοσιν] "have received
improvement." Isocr. 1. 1, μεγίστην διαφορὰν εἰλήφασιν : Id. 7.
6, πυκνοτάτας λαμβάνει τὰς μετα-
βολάς : Thuc. 1. 91, ὕψος λαμβάνει.
So Lucr. 5. 681, "cum sumant
augmina noctes."
κεκινῆσθαι] Isocr. 9. 7, τὰς ἐπι-
δόσεις ἰσμὲν γιγνομένας καὶ τῶν
τεχνῶν καὶ τῶν ἄλλων ἁπάντων οὐ
διὰ τοὺς ἐμμένοντας τοῖς καθιστῶσιν
ἀλλὰ διὰ τοὺς ἐπανορθοῦντας καὶ
τολμῶντας ἀεί τι κινεῖν τῶν μὴ
καλῶς ἐχόντων. Thuc. 1. 71. "I
do not think any thing has been so
changed (revolutionized) as the art
and practice of war."
§ 48. ἀκούω] 3. 21. "I am told
that in those times the L., as all the
rest, would for four or five months,
just (αὐτήν) the season, invade and
ravage . . ." This is illustrated by
Thuc. 2. 47, 57 ; 3. 1 al. With
τὴν ὥρ. comp. 4. 33 ; 8. 18 ; 56.
30, ταραχειμάζειν ἔδει καὶ περιμένειν
τὴν ὡραίαν.

ΔΗΜΟΣΘΕΝΟΥΣ [Θ. 49

μονίους τότε καὶ πάντας τοὺς ἄλλους τέτταρας μῆνας ἢ πέντε, τὴν ὡραίαν αὐτήν, ἐμβαλόντας ἂν καὶ κακώσαντας τὴν χώραν ὁπλίταις καὶ πολιτικοῖς στρατεύμασιν ἀναχωρεῖν ἐπ' οἴκου πάλιν· οὕτω δ' ἀρχαίως εἶχον, μᾶλλον δὲ πολιτικῶς, ὥστε οὐδὲ χρημάτων ὠνεῖσθαι παρ' οὐδενὸς οὐδέν, ἀλλ' εἶναι νόμιμόν τινα καὶ προφανῆ τὸν πόλεμον. 49. νυνὶ δ' ὁρᾶτε μὲν δήπου τὰ πλεῖστα τοὺς προδότας ἀπολωλεκότας, οὐδὲν δ' ἐκ παρατάξεως οὐδὲ μάχης γιγνόμενον ἀκούετε δὲ Φίλιππον οὐχὶ τῷ φάλαγγα ὁπλιτῶν ἄγειν βαδίζονθ' ὅποι βούλεται, ἀλλὰ τῷ ψιλοὺς ἱππέας τοξότας ξένους, τοιοῦτον ἐξηρτῆσθαι στρατόπεδον. 50. ἐπειδὰν δ' ἐπὶ τούτοις πρὸς νοσοῦντας ἐν αὑτοῖς προσπέσῃ καὶ μηδεὶς ὑπὲρ τῆς χώρας δι' ἀπιστίαν ἐξίῃ, μηχανήματ' ἐπιστήσας πολιορκεῖ. καὶ σιωπῶ θέρος καὶ χειμῶνα, ὡς οὐδὲν διαφέρει, οὐδ' ἐστὶν ἐξαίρετος ὥρα τις ἣν διαλείπει. 51. ταῦτα μέντοι πάντας εἰδότας καὶ λογιζομένους οὐ δεῖ προσέσθαι τὸν πόλε-

ἀναχωρεῖν] the Inf. of the imperfect. Madv. 117 b, r. 3.

ἀρχαίως εἶχον] "old-fashioned — primitive in their notions, or rather so sensible of their duties as citizens." Those were the days in which they had a due regard for the honour of the state and their duty as members of it. Cf. Arist. Nub. 915, φρονεῖς ἀρχαϊκά: cf. infr. 51, τὴν εὐήθειαν τὴν τοῦ τότε... πολέμου.

πολιτικῶς] "composed of citizens," not, as the fashion then was, of mercenaries. In Xen. Hell. 5. 3. 25, τὸ πολιτικόν is opposed to τοὺς συμμάχους. Eth. Nic. 3. 8. 9, πρῶτοι γὰρ φεύγουσι (οἱ στρατιῶται, "mercenaries," "professional soldiers") τὰ δὲ πολιτικά (the citizen troops) μένοντα ἀποθνῄσκει: Dem. 18. 237. On the dat. Madv. 42, r. 3.

ἀλλ' εἶναι] "theirs being a legitimate and open kind of war."

§ 49. δήπου] "you must see ..., and that nothing is done in fair field or battle.." Aesch. 3. 88, ἐκ παρατάξεως μάχη ἀρατή-

σαστες. Dem. 4. 23.

τῷ... ἐξηρτῆσθαι] "but by his having attached to him ... an army of this kind."

τοιοῦτον] see note to τούτῳ, 2. 6.

§ 50. ἐπὶ τούτοις] "at the head of these." Cf. 6. 12.

v. ἐν αὑτοῖς] "suffering from internal disorders." Cf. § 12.

μ. ἐπιστήσας] supr. § 17. θέρος depends on σιωπῶ, according to Madv. 191.

διαφέρει] sc. αὐτῷ. "and that there is no excepted season during which he rests." Comp. 2. 23. In 18. 235 he says that the soldiers of Philip τὰ ὅπλα εἶχον ἐν ταῖς χερσὶν ἀεί.

§ 51. ταῦτα] "reflecting on these notorious facts, you ought not to let the war come into the country, nor by looking at the simplicity of .. plunge head foremost into ruin." Xen. Cyrop. 1. 4. 8, ὁ ἵππος πίπτει εἰς γόνατα, καὶ μικροῦ κἀκεῖνον ἐξετραχήλισεν. Here in the metaphorical sense derived from this. Cf. 2. 9, ἀνεχαίτισε.

ΚΑΤΑ ΦΙΛΙΠΠΟΥ Γ.

μον εἰς τὴν χώραν, οὐδ' εἰς τὴν εὐήθειαν τὴν τοῦ τότε πρὸς Λακεδαιμονίους πολέμου βλέποντας ἐκτραχηλισθῆναι, ἀλλ' ὡς ἐκ πλείστου φυλάττεσθαι τοῖς πράγμασι καὶ ταῖς παρασκευαῖς, ὅπως οἴκοθεν μὴ κινήσεται σκοποῦντας, οὐχὶ συμπλακέντας διαγωνίζεσθαι. 52. πρὸς μὲν γὰρ πόλεμον πολλὰ φύσει πλεονεκτήμαθ' ἡμῖν ὑπάρχει, ἄν περ, ὦ ἄνδρες Ἀθηναῖοι, ποιεῖν ἐθέλωμεν ἃ δεῖ, ἡ φύσις τῆς ἐκείνου χώρας, ἧς ἄγειν καὶ φέρειν ἔστι πολλὴν καὶ κακῶς ποιεῖν, ἄλλα μυρία· εἰς δὲ ἀγῶνα ἄμεινον ἡμῶν ἐκεῖνος ἤσκηται.

53. Οὐ μόνον δὲ δεῖ ταῦτα γιγνώσκειν, οὐδὲ τοῖς ἔργοις ἐκεῖνον ἀμύνεσθαι τοῖς τοῦ πολέμου, ἀλλὰ καὶ τῷ λογισμῷ καὶ τῇ διανοίᾳ τοὺς παρ' ὑμῖν ὑπὲρ αὐτοῦ λέγοντας μισῆσαι, ἐνθυμουμένους ὅτι οὐκ ἔνεστι τῶν τῆς πόλεως ἐχθρῶν κρατῆσαι, πρὶν ἂν τοὺς ἐν αὐτῇ τῇ πόλει κολάσητε ὑπηρετοῦντας ἐκείνοις. 54. ὃ μὰ τὸν Δία καὶ τοὺς ἄλλους θεοὺς οὐ δυνήσεσθε ὑμεῖς ποιῆσαι, ἀλλ' εἰς τοῦτο ἀφῖχθε μωρίας ἢ παρανοίας ἢ οὐκ ἔχω τί λέγω (πολλάκις γὰρ ἔμοιγ'

ὡς ἐκ πλ.] "as long beforehand as possible .. by your measures and preparations." The "tiro" will observe that this is the regular position of ὡς (ὅτι): 18. 246, ὡς εἰς ἐλάχιστα: 23. 102, ὡς διὰ βραχυτάτου λόγου: Thuc. 3. 46, ὅτι ἐν βραχυτάτῳ. ὅπως with the fut. ind. as 1. 2, "that he does not..."

συμπλακέντας] 2. 21, "and not close with him in mortal struggle."

§ 52. γάρ] "because."

φύσει πλ.] "natural advantages." Comp. 4. 31.

ἄν περ] "if only."

ἧς ... πολλήν] 4. 16. Madv. 50 a, r. 3.

ἄλλα μ.] supr. 39. 1. 9, τἆλλα. Heind. Gorg. p. 517 D. He contrasts their resources for "a war" and "a battle" also in 14. 9, where he is speaking of their chance of success against Persia. For the change of preposition in πρὸς .. εἰς cf. 3. 1.

§ 53. Οὐ .. οὐδέ] "but it is not sufficient to adopt these resolutions or ...; you must also..." "Adverte Graecorum consuetudinem in talibus enuntiationibus adverbium μόνον soli priori membro sic tribuentium, ut etiam ad posterius pertineat" (Schäf.). Cf. 18. 2, τοῦτο δ' ἐστὶν οὐ μόνον τὸ προσεταγυσκέναι μηδέν, οὐδὲ τὸ ..;" ib. 107.

τῷ λ. καὶ τῇ θ.] i.e. both on rational and moral grounds, "on calculation, and on principle." Mr. K.

μισῆσαι] the ingressive aorist— "conceive a hatred of."

ἐν αὐτῇ τῇ π.] Comp. what he had just before said to them in θ. 61, cf. Livy, 3. 19, "Et vos ... prius in Clivum Capitolinum signa intulistis, quam hos hostes de foro tolleretis?"

§ 54. εἰς τοῦτο] 3. 3, εἰς πᾶν μ.

ἢ οὐκ ἔχω, κ.τ.λ.] "or—I know not what to call it; for often even the fearful thought has suggested itself to me, that some evil spirit is driving us to ruin." On this pas-

ἐπελήλυθε καὶ τοῦτο φοβεῖσθαι, μή τι δαιμόνιον τὰ πράγματα ἐλαύνῃ), ὥστε λοιδορίας φθόνου σκώμματος, ἧς τινὸς ἂν τύχητε ἕνεκ' αἰτίας ἀνθρώπους μισθωτούς, ὧν οὐδ' ἂν ἀρνηθεῖεν ἔνιοι ὡς οὐκ εἰσὶ τοιοῦτοι, λέγειν κελεύετε, καὶ γελᾶτε ἄν τισι λοιδορηθῶσιν. 55. καὶ οὐχί πω τοῦτο δεινόν, καίπερ ὂν δεινόν· ἀλλὰ καὶ μετὰ πλείονος ἀσφαλείας πολιτεύεσθαι δεδώκατε τούτοις ἢ τοῖς ὑπὲρ ὑμῶν λέγουσιν. καίτοι θεάσασθε ὅσας συμφορὰς παρασκευάζει τὸ τῶν τοιούτων ἐθέλειν ἀκροᾶσθαι. λέξω δ' ἔργα ἃ πάντες εἴσεσθε.

56. Ἦσαν ἐν Ὀλύνθῳ τῶν ἐν τοῖς πράγμασι τινὲς μὲν

sage Cobet (*Nov. Lect.* p. 228) remarks, "Mala manus addidit φοβεῖσθαι, et sic ἐλαύνῃ natum est. Dixerat orator, ut opinor, π. ἔμοιγ' ἐπελήλυθε καὶ τοῦτο· μή τι δ...," a sentence which, I venture to think, could not have been written by Dem. or any Greek author of repute. cf. 23. 145, θαυμάζειν ἐπελήλυθέ τί.. οὕτως ἐξηπάτησθε ῥᾳδίως. With this passage comp. Soph. *Antig.* 624; Xen. *Hell.* 6. 4. 2, ἡ δὲ ἐκκλησία (of the Spartans) ἀκούσασα ταῦτα δεινὸν μὲν φλυαρεῖν ἡγήσατο· ἤδη γάρ, ὡς ἔοικε, τὸ δαιμόνιον ἦγεν: Lys. 6. 32, ὑπὸ δαιμονίου τινὸς ἀγόμενος ἀνάγκῃ: Lyc. § 92; Aesch. 3. 117, 133; Dem. 24. 121.

ἧς τινὸς ἂν τ.] "for any cause whatever in short;" closing the enumeration, as 1. 13, πανθ'. With τύχητε Fr. &c. understand κελεύοντες. This explanation is highly improbable where the verb follows at such a distance as it does here. It is better to take it as a case of attraction. Thuc. 3. 43. πρὸς ὀργὴν ἥντινα τύχητ' ἔστιν ὅτε σφαλέντες ... ζημιοῦτε. Id. 8. 48, μεθ' ὁποτέρου ἂν τύχωσι τούτων ἐλευθέρους εἶναι. Cf. 1. 3. Comp. what he says in 18. 138, τῆς ἐπὶ ταῖς λοιδορίαις ἡδονῆς καὶ χάριτος τὸ τῆς πόλεως συμφέρον ἀνταλλαττόμενοι.

ἀρνηθεῖεν ... ὡς οὐκ] Thuc. 8.

24, οὐδ' αὐτοὺς ἀντιλέγοντας .. ὡς οὐ ... Madv. 210, r. 2, and 159, r. 3. He refers no doubt in particular to Aeschines and Philocrates.

γελᾶτε] as in the case of Philocrates, mentioned on 6. 30.

§ 55. καὶ .. δεινόν] "and bad as this is, it is not the worst. The worst is that you have also (besides bidding them speak) .." He no doubt alludes in particular to Aeschines, whom he had just before unsuccessfully impeached for misconduct as ambassador. 8. 30, καὶ τὸ .. εἶναι τοιούτους δεινὸν ὂν οὐ δεινόν ἐστιν. 21. 72; 23. 163, οὐ τοίνυν .. πω δῆλόν ἐσθ', οὕτω σαφῶς δῆλον δν .. ἀλλ'... Pl. *Lysis*, 204 D, καὶ ὃ μὲν καταλογάδην διηγεῖται δεινὰ ὄντα οὐ πάνυ τι δεινά ἐστιν ἀλλ' ἐπειδὰν ..

παρασκευάζει) "brings about," "causes," supr. 38. Observe the insertion of ἐθέλειν, which throws τῶν τοιούτων into greater prominence. Comp. § 53, τοὺς ἐν αὐτῇ τῇ πόλει κολάσητ' ὑπηρετοῦντας.

§ 56. Ἦσαν ... Φ.] "were the creatures of Philip," "were in his interest." Ocd. *Tyr.* 917; Livy, 21. 11, "adeo prope omnis Senatus Hannibalis erat." Madv. 47.

τῶν ἐν τοῖς πρ] "those engaged in the conduct of affairs," "public men." Thuc. 3. 28, γνόντες δ' οἱ ἐν τοῖς πράγμασιν. Supr. § 2 we have

—57.] ΚΑΤΑ ΦΙΛΙΠΠΟΥ Γ. 77

Φιλίππου καὶ πάνθ' ὑπηρετοῦντες ἐκείνῳ, τινὲς δὲ τοῦ βελτίστου καὶ ὅπως μὴ δουλεύσουσιν οἱ πολῖται πράττοντες. πότεροι δὴ τὴν πατρίδα ἐξώλεσαν; ἢ πότεροι τοὺς ἱππέας προύδοσαν, ὧν προδοθέντων Ὄλυνθος ἀπώλετο; οἱ τὰ Φιλίππου φρονοῦντες καὶ ὅτ' ἦν ἡ πόλις τοὺς τὰ βέλτιστα λέγοντας συκοφαντοῦντες καὶ διαβάλλοντες οὕτως ὥστε τὸν γ' Ἀπολλωνίδην καὶ ἐκβαλεῖν ὁ δῆμος ὁ τῶν Ὀλυνθίων ἐπείσθη.

57. Οὐ τοίνυν παρὰ τούτοις μόνοις τὸ ἔθος τοῦτο πάντα κακὰ εἰργάσατο, ἄλλοθι δ' οὐδαμοῦ ἀλλ' ἐν Ἐρετρίᾳ, ἐπειδὴ ἀπαλλαγέντος Πλουτάρχου καὶ τῶν ξένων ὁ δῆμος εἶχε τὴν πόλιν καὶ τὸν Πορθμόν, οἱ μὲν ἐφ' ὑμᾶς ἦγον τὰ πράγματα,

the more common phrase τοὺς ἐπὶ τοῖς πρ. ὄντας.
τοῦ β.] "on the patriotic side, and labouring to prevent." Cf. 1, 2.
τοὺς L] Thirl. 5. 316.
τὰ Φ φρ.] "the partisans of P., who while . ." Thuc. 6. 51, οἱ μὲν τὰ τῶν Συρακοσίων φρονοῦντες, al.
ἦν] "stood." 20. 22, ἄνπερ ἡ πόλις β. 8. 17; 18. 72, ζώντων Ἀθηναίων καὶ ὄντων.
τοὺς τὰ β. λ.] " the patriotic counsellors."
ἐκβαλεῖν] "so effectually that they induced," "till the people was induced even to expel *Apollonides*," well known to his hearers as the leader of the party favourable to them. The meaning of ἐκβαλεῖν is somewhat doubtful. Thirl. (5. 314) says, "We hear of a violent struggle between them and the friends of Athens, which ended in the expulsion or disgrace of one of their principal adversaries named A..," and in a note observes that "the word does not imply that he was obliged to seek his safety by flight from Olynthus," referring to 19. 337. ἐξεβάλετε αὐτόν, where its meaning is defined by ἐξεσυρίττετε ἐκ τῶν θεάτρων, and Aesch. 2. 4. αὐτὸν ἐπὶ τῆς αἰτίας ταύτης ἐξεβάλλετε, which simply means

that Dem. was stopped by an open expression of disapprobation. If we adopt this view, we must translate "disgraced." But γε and καὶ are without force unless we adopt the stronger meaning. The partisans of P. succeeded in alienating the people from their honest advisers in general, and even got the most prominent of them expelled. We cannot suppose that they still listened to the rest, but disgraced A. In particular, cf. Infr. 66, where the antithesis requires the stronger meaning.

§ 57. τοίνυν] continuative—"nor was it at Olynthus only . . ." supr. 27; 18. 288, καὶ οὐχ ὁ μὲν δῆμος οὕτως, οἱ δὲ πατέρες . . ἄλλως πως. Redh. compares Cic. *pro Mil.* § 84, "Neque in his corporibus . . . inest quiddam quod vigeat et sentiat, non est in naturae motu . ."
πάντα κακά] "utter ruin."
Πλουτάρχου] Thirl. 5. 261. Grote, 11. 474—477.
εἶχε τὴν π.] "was in possession of;" infr. 59.
ἐφ' . . ἦγον τὰ πρ.] 18. 151, ἐπὶ τὸν Φίλιππον εὐθὺς ἡγεμόνα ἦγον. So in Latin, Livy, 30. 23, "Princeps ejus factionis quae traxerat rem ad Poenos;" Id. 24, c. 2. Comp. the expression in Dem. 21. 116, ἐπειδὴ τοῦτο τὸ πρᾶγμα (the mur-

οἱ δ' ἐπὶ Φίλιππον. ἀκούοντες δὲ τούτων τὰ πολλὰ μᾶλλον οἱ ταλαίπωροι καὶ δυστυχεῖς Ἐρετριεῖς τελευτῶντες ἐπείσθησαν τοὺς ὑπὲρ αὑτῶν λέγοντας ἐκβαλεῖν. 58. καὶ γάρ τοι πέμψας Ἱππόνικον ὁ σύμμαχος αὐτοῖς Φίλιππος καὶ ξένους χιλίους, τὰ τείχη περιεῖλε τοῦ Πορθμοῦ καὶ τρεῖς κατέστησε τυράννους, Ἵππαρχον Αὐτομέδοντα Κλείταρχον· καὶ μετὰ ταῦτ' ἐξελήλακεν ἐκ τῆς χώρας δὶς ἤδη βουλομένους σώζεσθαι, τότε μὲν πέμψας τοὺς μετ' Εὐρυλόχου ξένους, πάλιν δὲ τοὺς μετὰ Παρμενίωνος.

59. Καὶ τί δεῖ τὰ πολλὰ λέγειν; ἀλλ' ἐν Ὠρεῷ Φιλιστίδης μὲν ἔπραττε Φιλίππῳ καὶ Μένιππος καὶ Σωκράτης καὶ Θόας καὶ Ἀγαπαῖος, οἵπερ νῦν ἔχουσι τὴν πόλιν (καὶ ταῦτ' ᾔδεσαν ἅπαντες), Εὐφραῖος δέ τις, ἄνθρωπος καὶ παρ' ἡμῖν ποτ' ἐνθάδε οἰκήσας, ὅπως ἐλεύθεροι καὶ μηδενὸς δοῦλοι ἔσονται. 60. οὗτος τὰ μὲν ἄλλα ὡς ὑβρίζετο καὶ προεπηλακίζετο ὑπὸ τοῦ δήμου, πολλὰ ἂν εἴη λέγειν· ἐνιαυτῷ δὲ πρότερον τῆς ἁλώσεως ἐνέδειξεν ὡς προδότην τὸν Φιλιστίδην καὶ τοὺς μετ' αὐτοῦ, αἰσθόμενος ἃ πράττουσιν. συστραφέντες δὲ ἄνθρωποι πολλοὶ καὶ χορηγὸν ἔχοντες

der) οὐδὲ καθ' ὃν οἷός τ' ἦν ἀγαγεῖν ἐπ' ἐμέ, "fasten on."

τούτων] i. e. the partisans of Philip. After μᾶλλον Bekk. had δὲ τὰ πάντα, which he now omits with S pr. m.

ἐκβαλεῖν] "disgrace" would suit the passage well enough. But the following sentence makes the stronger meaning more probable.

§ 58. αὐτοῖς] "their friend and ally as they thought him."

Πορθμοῦ] supr. 33. Hipparchus and Cleitarchus are mentioned in the list of traitors given in 18. 295.

β. σώζεσθαι] "attempting to deliver themselves," i. e. from the tyrants.

§ 59. Καὶ..ἀλλ'] supr. 25. So in Lat., *Pro Mil.* § 18, "Sed quid ego illa commemoro? Comprehensus est .. servus..;" *Tusc. Disp.* 2, § 28. "but what need of many words? At Oreus.."

ἐ. Φιλίππῳ] "was active for P." Thuc. 5: 76. With an acc. of the thing, 19. 77; 23. 11, Κερσοβλέπτῃ πράττων τὴν ἀρχήν. Grote, 11. 622. Harpocr. speaks of *Euphraeus* as having been a pupil of Plato. He was recommended by the philosopher to Perdiccas of Macedon, whose minister he was for some years. Thirl. 5. 165.

§ 60. τὰ μὲν ἄλλα] "how this person was in other ways insulted and ill-treated by the people would make a long story. But a year before the capture, perceiving what they were aiming at .."

συστραφέντες] 23. 170, συστραφέντων τοῦ τε Βηρισάδου καὶ τοῦ Ἀμαδόκου. "but a number of persons combining, having P. for a paymaster, and acting under his inspiration." Dind. is right, I

ΚΑΤΑ ΦΙΛΙΠΠΟΥ Γ.

Φίλιππον καὶ πρυτανευόμενοι ἀπάγουσι τὸν Εὐφραῖον εἰς τὸ δεσμωτήριον ὡς συνταράττοντα τὴν πόλιν. 61. ὁρῶν δὲ ταῦθ᾽ ὁ δῆμος ὁ τῶν Ὠρειτῶν, ἀντὶ τοῦ τῷ μὲν βοηθεῖν τοὺς δ᾽ ἀποτυμπανίσαι, τοῖς μὲν οὐκ ὠργίζετο, τὸν δ᾽ ἐπιτήδειον ταῦτα παθεῖν ἔφη καὶ ἐπέχαιρεν. μετὰ ταῦθ᾽ οἱ μὲν ἐπ᾽ ἐξουσίας ὁπόσης ἠβούλοντο ἔπραττον ὅπως ἡ πόλις ληφθήσεται, καὶ κατεσκευάζοντο τὴν πρᾶξιν τῶν δὲ πολλῶν εἴ τις αἴσθοιτο, ἐσίγα καὶ κατεπέπληκτο, τὸν Εὐφραῖον, οἷα ἔπαθε, μεμνημένοι. οὕτω δ᾽ ἀθλίως διέκειντο ὥστε οὐ πρότερον ἐτόλμησεν οὐδεὶς τοιούτου κακοῦ προσιόντος ῥῆξαι φωνήν, πρὶν διασκευασάμενοι πρὸς τὰ τείχη προσῇεσαν οἱ πολέμιοι· τηνικαῦτα δ᾽ οἱ μὲν ἠμύνοντο οἱ δὲ προυδίδοσαν. 62. τῆς δὲ πόλεως οὕτως ἁλούσης αἰσχρῶς καὶ κακῶς οἱ μὲν ἄρχουσι καὶ τυραννοῦσι, τοὺς τότε σώζοντας αὑτοὺς καὶ τὸν Εὐφραῖον ἑτοίμους ὁτιοῦν ποιεῖν ὄντας τοὺς μὲν ἐκβαλόντες τοὺς δὲ ἀποκτείναντες, ὁ δ᾽ Εὐφραῖος

think, in retaining παρ᾽ ἐκείνου after πρυτανευόμενοι. Bekk. st. omits the words, with S pr. m.

χορηγόν] here in the general sense of "one who finds the means for any thing." 19. 216, Φιλίππῳ χορηγῷ χρώμενοι. Aesch. 2. 79, where the speakers are said to make war χορηγὸν ταῖς καθ᾽ ἡμέραν δαπάναις.

ὡς] Madv. 175 d.

§ 61. ἀποτυμπανίσαι] "cudgel to death." Cf. Mr. Shill., De F. Leg. § 150.

ἐπιτήδειον . . . π.] i. e. ἄξιον. "sic latine idoneus pro dignus" (Schäf.). "deserved what he suffered." Madv. 149.

ἐπ᾽ ἐξουσίας] "with all the liberty of action . . ." 21. 138, ἐπ᾽ ἐξουσίας . . . πονηρὸν εἶναι.

τὴν πρᾶξιν] "the execution of the plot."

κατεπέπληκτο] "causam silentii indicat, tacebat attonitus" (Fr.). "were silent and intimidated" (Mr. K.).

τὸν Εὐ. . . . μεμνημένοι] εἴ τις being virtually plural: 2. 18. Madv.

99 d. Thuc. 2. 21, μεμνημένοι καὶ Πλειστοάνακτα . . ὅτι . ., "remembering the fate of."

ῥ. φωνήν] "rumpere vocem," "break silence." "Significanter dictum, loqui tanquam ruptis vinculis quibus timor vocem constrinxerat." Schäf.

διασκευασάμενοι] "prepared for action." Whiston adds, "i. e. having broken up their camp," a sense which would require ἀνασκευασάμενοι.

ἠμύνοντο] "were for resisting." Madv. 113, r. 1.

§ 62. ἄρχουσι καὶ τ.] the latter word defining the former: supr. 39. Perhaps this passage may remove Mr. Shilleto's hesitation in understanding 19. 366 (Bekk. 319), τὸν ἡγούμενον καὶ στρατηγοῦντα Ὀνόμαρχον in the same way. "Since the city was thus captured . . have been ruling as despots," "have been lords and masters."

τοὺς τότε . . τοὺς μὲν . . τοὺς δὲ] cf. 6. 11. "after banishing or putting to death those who . ." τότε, i. e. when Euphraeus laid an in-

ΔΗΜΟΣΘΕΝΟΤΣ [9. 63

ἐκεῖνος ἀπέσφαξεν ἑαυτόν, ἔργῳ μαρτυρήσας ὅτι καὶ δικαίως καὶ καθαρῶς ὑπὲρ τῶν πολιτῶν ἀνθειστήκει Φιλίππῳ.

63. Τί οὖν ποτ' αἴτιον, θαυμάζετ' ἴσως, τοῦ καὶ τοὺς Ὀλυνθίους καὶ τοὺς Ἐρετριεῖς καὶ τοὺς Ὠρείτας ἥδιον πρὸς τοὺς ὑπὲρ Φιλίππου λέγοντας ἔχειν ἢ τοὺς ὑπὲρ ἑαυτῶν; ὅπερ καὶ παρ' ὑμῖν, ὅτι τοῖς μὲν ὑπὲρ τοῦ βελτίστου λέγουσιν οὐδὲ βουλομένοις ἔνεστιν ἐνίοτε πρὸς χάριν οὐδὲν εἰπεῖν· τὰ γὰρ πράγματ' ἀνάγκη σκοπεῖν ὅπως σωθήσεται· οἱ δ' ἐν αὑτοῖς οἷς χαρίζονται Φιλίππῳ συμπράττουσιν. εἰσφέρειν ἐκέλευον, οἱ δ' οὐδὲν δεῖν ἔφασαν 64. πολεμεῖν καὶ μὴ πιστεύειν, οἱ δ' ἄγειν εἰρήνην, ἕως ἐγκατελήφθησαν. τἆλλα τὸν αὐτὸν τρόπον οἶμαι πάνθ', ἵνα μὴ καθ' ἕκαστα λέγω· οἱ μέν, ἐφ' οἷς χαριοῦνται, ταῦτ' ἔλεγον, οἱ δ' ἐξ ὧν ἔμελλον σωθήσεσθαι. πολλὰ δὲ καὶ τὰ τελευταῖα οὐχ

formation against them as traitors (§ 60).

καθαρῶς] "disinterestedly."

§ 63. Τί.. αἴτιον.. τοῦ] Bekk.; Dind., West., &c. read αἴτιον.. τό, with F S. In 8. 56 the same MSS. have τό.

ἔχειν] the inf. of the imperfect —"were more favourably inclined to.."

ἢ τοὺς] see note to § 2, παρ' ἐν..

ὅπερ] "the same as."

οὐδὲ β ἔνεστιν] "cannot even if they would."

τὰ.. πρ.] "how the interests of the state are to be." 6. 5.

ἐν... οἷς] "through the very things by which (supr. 2, ἐν οἷς) they make themselves agreeable they play into the hands of P."

ἐκέλευον] i. e. οἱ ὑπὲρ ἑαυτῶν λ., so that οἱ μέν is not omitted here as it is in some cases, e. g Xen. *Hell.* 1. 2. 14, ᾤχοντο δὲ Δεκέλειαν, οἱ δὲ ἐς Μέγαρα: "they (the patriots) called for a war-tax, the others said it was not required."

§ 64. **ἐγκατελήφθησαν**] "were caught in the net," "ensnared."

τἆλλα] Probably no verb is to be supplied: "and so, I suppose,

with every thing else, that I may not go into particulars." Redh. quotes Pl. *Crito*, 47 C, οὐκοῦν καὶ τἆλλα.. οὕτως, ἵνα μὴ πάντα διίωμεν. So *Gorg.* c. 30, Οὐκοῦν καὶ τἆλλα πάντα οὕτω, "and so with every thing else in the same way."

ἐφ' οἷς] Jelf, 634. 3. "proposed measures by which they would please (and with that view), the others those calculated to save them." Bekk. st. omits καὶ ἐλύπουν οὐδέν, which he read after ἔλεγον, with the note "καὶ ἐλύπουν οὐδέν in marg. Υ; μὴ λυποῦν (apposito in margine καὶ) Ω; ceteri om. ;"—and προσῆσαν δ' ἀνέχθειαι, which he had after σωθήσεσθαι. Dind. retains both.

πολλὰ.. καὶ τὰ τ.] "multa et quidem postrema (i. e. ea quae postremo prodiderunt)." Fr. "many things at last the people surrendered, not so much out of indulgence or through ignorance as from giving in as soon as they thought all was lost." "Γρο ἀλλὰ exspectes ὅτι. Sed ita saepius Graeci. Non multum differt οὐ μᾶλλον ἀλλὰ..." Schäf. Dind. quotes Prooem. 5.1, ἄξιον δ' οὐχ οὕτω τούτοις ἐπιτιμῆσαι .. ἀλλ' ὑμῶν.."

ΚΑΤΑ ΦΙΛΙΠΠΟΥ Γ.

οὕτως οὔτε πρὸς χάριν οὔτε δι᾽ ἄγνοιαν οἱ πολλοὶ προΐεντο, ἀλλ᾽ ὑποκατακλινόμενοι, ἐπειδὴ τοῖς ὅλοις ἡττᾶσθαι ἐνόμιζον. 65. ὃ νὴ τὸν Δία καὶ τὸν Ἀπόλλω δέδοικα ἐγὼ μὴ πάθητε ὑμεῖς, ἐπειδὰν ἴδητε ἐκλογιζόμενοι μηδὲν ὑμῖν ἐνόν. καίτοι μὴ γένοιτο μὲν τὰ πράγματ᾽ ἐν τούτῳ· τεθνάναι δὲ μυριάκις κρεῖττον ἢ κολακείᾳ τι ποιῆσαι Φιλίππου. 66. καλὴν γ᾽ οἱ πολλοὶ νῦν ἀπειλήφασιν Ὠρειτῶν χάριν, ὅτι τοῖς Φιλίππου φίλοις ἐπέτρεψαν αὑτούς, τὸν δ᾽ Εὐφραῖον ἠώθουν· καλὴν γ᾽ ὁ δῆμος ὁ Ἐρετριέων, ὅτι τοὺς μὲν ὑμετέρους πρέσβεις ἀπήλασε, Κλειτάρχῳ δ᾽ ἐνέδωκεν αὑτόν· δουλεύουσί γε μαστιγούμενοι καὶ σφαττόμενοι. καλῶς Ὀλυνθίων ἐφείσατο τῶν τὸν μὲν Λασθένη ἵππαρχον χειροτονησάντων, τὸν δὲ Ἀπολλωνίδην ἐκβαλόντων. 67. μωρία καὶ κακία τοιαῦτα ἐλπίζειν, καὶ κακῶς βουλευομένους καὶ μηδὲν ὧν προσήκει ποιεῖν ἐθέλοντας, ἀλλὰ τῶν ὑπὲρ τῶν ἐχθρῶν λεγόντων ἀκροωμένους, τηλικαύτην ἡγεῖσθαι πόλιν οἰκεῖν τὸ μέγεθος 68. ὥστε μηδέν, μηδ᾽ ἂν ὁτιοῦν ᾖ, δεινὸν πείσεσθαι. καὶ

τοῖς ἄλοις] 1. 3.

§ 65. πάθητε ὑμεῖς] "will be your feeling."

μηδὲν .. ἐνόν] "that you can do nothing."

καίτοι, κ.τ.λ.] "but I pray things may never come to this; if they should (δέ), it were better to die a thousand deaths than to do any thing out of base submission to (to ingratiate yourselves with) Philip." Bekk. had Φιλίππῳ, "to do any thing to please Philip out of .." He now reads Φιλίππου with S pr. m.

κολακείᾳ] Madv. 41.

§ 66. καλήν] "a fine return truly." For the ironical use of γε cf. 18. 266, ἀγαθῇ γ᾽, οὐχ ὁρᾷς; τύχῃ ..." 19. 253; 23. 122. Eur. Med. 514, καλόν γ᾽ ὄνειδος.

Κλειτάρχῳ] supr. § 58.

γε] "yes, they are slaves..."

Λασθένη] § 56, πότεροι τοὺς ἱππέας προὔδοσαν. 6. 21. When Demades afterwards moved that Euthycrates should be made a proxenus of Athens, Hyperides proposed

a decree ironically setting forth his claims to the honour: δεδόχθαι γὰρ φησὶ πρόξενον αὐτὸν εἶναι, ὅτι τὰ Φιλίππου συμφέροντα καὶ πράττει καὶ λέγει, ὅτι γενόμενος ἵππαρχοι τοὺς Ὀλυνθίων ἱππέας προὔδωκε Φιλίππῳ, ὅτι τοῦτο πρᾶξαι αἴτιος τοῦ Χαλκιδέων ὑπῆρξεν ὀλέθρου, ὅτι ἁλούσης Ὀλύνθου τιμητὴς ἐγένετο τῶν αἰχμαλώτων ... Hyper. frag. 80. Cf. 18. 47 sq.

§ 67. μωρία] "it is sheer folly and cowardice to entertain such hopes, and while ... those who speak in the interest of your enemies." The sentence, though general, applies, of course, in particular to themselves. Cf. infr. 73.

§ 68. ὥστε .. πείσεσθαι] Madv. 171 a, r. 2.

μηδ᾽ ἂν ὁτιοῦν ᾖ] "that come what will," "in any event." 19. 324, ὑποσχήσονται ἐξ ἂν μηδ᾽ ἂν ὁτιοῦν ᾖ κινηθήσονται. Comp. also 18. 168, ὡς οὐδ᾽ ἂν εἴ τι γένοιτ᾽ ..

μηδὲν ... δεινόν] Bekker has ὥστε μηδ᾽ ἂν ὁτιοῦν ᾖ δεινὸν πείσ. But the Greeks did not say ποσὰ τινα

G

μὴν κἀκεῖνο αἰσχρόν, ὕστερόν ποτ' εἰπεῖν " τίς γὰρ ἂν ᾠήθη ταῦτα γενέσθαι ; νὴ τὸν Δία, ἔδει γὰρ τὸ καὶ τὸ ποιῆσαι καὶ τὸ μὴ ποιῆσαι." πολλὰ ἂν εἰπεῖν ἔχοιεν Ὀλύνθιοι νῦν, ἃ τότ' εἰ προείδοντο, οὐκ ἂν ἀπώλοντο· πόλλ' ἂν Ὠρεῖται, πολλὰ Φωκεῖς, πολλὰ τῶν ἀπολωλότων ἕκαστοι. 69. ἀλλὰ τί τούτων ὄφελος αὐτοῖς ; ἕως ἂν σώζηται τὸ σκάφος, ἄν τε μεῖζον ἄν τ' ἔλαττον ᾖ, τότε χρὴ καὶ ναύτην καὶ κυβερνήτην καὶ πάντ' ἄνδρα ἑξῆς προθύμους εἶναι, καὶ ὅπως μήθ' ἑκὼν μήτ' ἄκων μηδεὶς ἀνατρέψει, τοῦτο σκοπεῖσθαι· ἐπειδὰν δὲ ἡ θάλαττα ὑπέρσχῃ, μάταιος ἡ σπουδή. 70. καὶ ἡμεῖς τοίνυν, ὦ ἄνδρες Ἀθηναῖοι, ἕως ἐσμὲν σῷοι, πόλιν μεγίστην ἔχοντες, ἀφορμὰς πλείστας, ἀξίωμα κάλλιστον,—τί ποιῶμεν ; πάλαι τις ἡδέως ἂν ἴσως ἐρωτήσων κάθηται. ἐγὼ νὴ Δι' ἐρῶ, καὶ

βίαιον, ἔννομον &c., but βίαια, ἔννομα, δεινά, or βίαιόν τι &c., and therefore πάσχω βίαια, δεινά, or βίαιόν τι, δεινόν τι &c. Seager feeling this proposed to read ὥστε μηδέν, ἂν ὁτιοῦν ᾖ, δεινὸν πείσεσθαι, which however is hardly Greek, or ὥστε μηδέν, μηδ'..., which last conj. is adopted by Dind., whom I have followed. Dobree proposed ὥστε, μηδ' ἂν ὁτιοῦν ᾖ, μηδέν·, quoting 20. 105, περὶ τοῦ μηδενὶ θεῖν μηδὲν διδόναι μηδ' ἂν ὁτιοῦν πράξῃ. ibid. 5, ἐκ τοῦ μηδενὶ μηδὲν μηδ' ἂν ἄξιοι ᾖ διδόναι.

τίς γάρ] "really who would have thought it !" Cf. 4. 10.

νὴ τὸν Δία ... γάρ] cf. 6. 13.

τὸ καὶ τό] "this or that." Cf. Mr. Shill., De F. Leg. § 83, διὰ τὸ καὶ τὸ ἰσώθησαν οἱ Φωκεῖς. 18. 243. Lys. 19. 59, καί μοι κάλει τὸν καὶ τὸν ... "Malim καὶ τὸ καὶ τὸ μὴ ποιῆσαι." Schäf. By the insertion of καί the sentence would gain in symmetry at the expense of taste. With the repetition of πολλά here comp. 18. 81, πολλὰ μὲν ἂν ... πολλὰ δὲ ... πολλὰ δί. Note the emphatic position of τότ'. Cf. 4. 29, τοῦτ' ἂν γένηται, "which if foreseen at the time would have saved them from destruction."

§ 69.] σώζηται = σῶν ᾖ, as in the application of the simile ἕως ἐσμὲν σῷοι. "is still safe."

ἄνδρα] "every man on board."

μήθ' ἑκὼν μήτ' ἄκων] "either designedly or by accident," a familiar form of words. Soph. Phil. 770, ἑφίεμαι ἑκόντα μήτ' ἄκοντα μηδέ τῳ τέχνῃ κείνοις μεθεῖναι ταῦτα.

ἀνατρέψει] Bekk. st. ; Bekk. ἀνατρέψῃ. See the note to 1. 2, βοηθήσετε.

The middle σωσεῖσθαι must be noticed : Don. p. 438. " carefully watch that .."

μ. ἡ σπουδή] "their exertions are vain." μάταιος is of two terminations also in 1. 17. On the omission of the copula, 6. 25.

§ 70. καὶ ἡμεῖς] 1. 11.

σῷοι] Bekk. ; σῷ Dind. Cf. I. Dind. Xen. Anab. Praef. p. ix; Colbet, Nov. Lect. p. 436.

ἀφορμάς πλ.] cf. 4. 40 ; 1. 19.

ἀξίωμα] "reputation."

τί π.] "what must we do?" Madv. 121. How much more effective in a rhetorical point of view this sudden question is than a formal application of the simile which the hearer would at once supply, is obvious.

ἂν ... ἐρωτήσων] Bekk. ; Dind. ἐρωτήσας. Fr. and Redh. follow Herm., who says "recte ponitur

ΚΑΤΑ ΦΙΛΙΠΠΟΥ Γ.

γράψω δέ, ὥστε ἂν βούλησθε χειροτονήσετε. αὐτοὶ πρῶτον ἀμυνόμενοι καὶ παρασκευαζόμενοι, τριήρεσι καὶ χρήμασι καὶ στρατιώταις λέγω (καὶ γὰρ ἂν ἅπαντες δήπου δουλεύειν συγχωρήσωσιν οἱ ἄλλοι, ἡμῖν γ' ὑπὲρ τῆς ἐλευθερίας ἀγωνιστέον), 71. ταῦτα δὴ πάντα αὐτοὶ παρασκευασάμενοι καὶ ποιήσαντες φανερὰ τοῖς ἄλλοις ἤδη παρακαλῶμεν, καὶ τοὺς ταῦτα διδάξοντας ἐκπέμπωμεν πρέσβεις, ἵν' ἐὰν μὲν πείσητε, κοινωνοὺς ἔχητε καὶ τῶν κινδύνων καὶ τῶν ἀναλωμάτων, ἂν τι δέῃ, εἰ δὲ μή, χρόνους γε ἐμποιῆτε τοῖς πράγμασιν. 72. ἐπειδὴ γάρ ἐστι πρὸς ἄνδρα καὶ οὐχὶ συνεστώσης πόλεως ἰσχὺν ὁ πόλεμος, οὐδὲ τοῦτ' ἄχρηστον, οὐδ' αἱ

ἄν, quod simulatque interpungas apparet, πάλαι τις, ἤδίως ἂν ἴσως, ἐρωτήσων κάθηται. Supplendum est enim ἐρωτῶν sive τοῦτο ποιῶν." Redh. quotes in support of this view Aesch. 2. 6, ἐγὼ δ' ἐπ' αὐτῷ τούτῳ, δικαίως ἄν, ὑπολαμβάνω . . σωθήσεσθαι, where however Bekk. reads σώζεσθαι, with which ἂν is joined. If ἐρωτήσων be retained, ἂν must go with it, the construction being not uncommon. Cf. 19. 342. Pl. Apol. c. 17, ἐμοῦ οὐκ ἂν ποιήσοντος ἄλλα: Lys. 31. 21, ἂν ποιήσοντα (Cob. ποιήσαντα): Isocr. 6. 62, ἐνιστάμαι . . . Ἀθηναίους . . . ἂν ποιήσοντας: Thuc. 5. 15, ἂν ἐνδεξομένους: Id. 6. 20, ἂν . . προσδεξομένας (Bekk., Poppo, &c. προσδεξαμένας): Isocr. 8. 81, μάλιστ' ἂν ὑμᾶς λυπήσοντα: Xen. Mem. 2. 2. 3. (In 18. 168 Bekker still reads ἂν . . . συμπεισθέντων, a form justly condemned by Cobet, Nov. Lect. p. 171, as "barbarum"). Cf. on the other hand Cobet, Nov. Lect. p. 693, where he strenuously denies the legitimacy of the construction, in which Madv. (184, r.) agrees with him: "some of my hearers (6. 4) perhaps have long been anxious to ask."

καὶ . . δὲ] 3. 15. "and will move a resolution too."

χειροτονήσετε] Bekk. st. from S and other MSS.; Bekk. χειροτονή- σατε. S has the fut. ind. also in 4. 30, where Bekk. st. reads χειροτονήσατε. Cf. 6. 6, προσθήσεσθε.

λέγω] 1. 27. "with ships I mean, and . . for of course should all . . we must fight for . . When I say we have made all these preparations ourselves . . let us then . ." For παρασκευασάμενοι (so also Dind.) West., Fr., and Redh. read παρασκευασμένοι with S, a combination of the perf. and aor. which often occurs. Cf. 19. 18, 72, 207.

§ 71. τοὺς τ. δ.] 1. 2; 2. 11. "to make this known," i. e. that we are ready to take the field. After πρέσβεις Bekk. had, from all his MSS. except S pr. m., the words πανταχοῖ, εἰς Πελοπόννησον, εἰς Ῥόδον, εἰς Χίον, ὡς Βασιλέα λέγω (οὐδὲ γὰρ τῶν ἐκείνῳ συμφερόντων ἀφίστηκε τὸ μὴ τοῦτον ἐᾶσαι πάντα καταστρέψασθαι) . . Dind. retains them.

χρ. γε ἐμποιῆτε] "you may at least delay operations," or simply "gain time." Thuc. 3. 38, χρόνον διατριβὴν ἐμποιησάντων. Dem. 23. 93. Comp. 19. 324, χρόνος ἐγγίγνεται τοῖς πράγμασιν.

§ 72. πρὸς ἄνδρα] "against an individual man (to whom something may happen at any time), and not against the strength of an established (permanent) state, even this . . .," l. e. χρόνους ἐμπ. τοῖς πρ.

πέρυσι πρεσβεῖαι περὶ τὴν Πελοπόννησον ἐκεῖναι καὶ κατηγορίαι, ἃς ἐγὼ καὶ Πολύευκτος ὁ βέλτιστος ἐκεινοσὶ καὶ Ἡγήσιππος καὶ οἱ ἄλλοι πρέσβεις περιήλθομεν, καὶ ἐποιήσαμεν ἐπισχεῖν ἐκεῖνον καὶ μήτ' ἐπ' Ἀμβρακίαν ἐλθεῖν μήτ' ἐς Πελοπόννησον ὁρμῆσαι. 73. οὐ μέντοι λέγω μηδὲν αὐτοὺς ὑπὲρ αὐτῶν ἀναγκαῖον ἐθέλοντας ποιεῖν τοὺς ἄλλους παρακαλεῖν· καὶ γὰρ εὔηθες τὰ οἰκεῖα αὐτοὺς προεμένους τῶν ἀλλοτρίων φάσκειν κήδεσθαι, καὶ τὰ παρόντα περιορῶντας ὑπὲρ τῶν μελλόντων τοὺς ἄλλους φοβεῖν. οὐ λέγω ταῦτα, ἀλλὰ τοῖς μὲν ἐν Χερρονήσῳ χρήματ' ἀποστέλλειν φημὶ δεῖν καὶ τἆλλα ὅσα ἀξιοῦσι ποιεῖν, αὐτοὺς δὲ παρασκευάζεσθαι, τοὺς δ' ἄλλους Ἕλληνας συγκαλεῖν συνάγειν διδάσκειν νουθετεῖν· ταῦτ' ἐστὶ πόλεως ἀξίωμα ἐχούσης ἡλίκον ὑμῖν ὑπάρχει. 74. εἰ δ' οἴεσθε Χαλκιδέας τὴν Ἑλλάδα σώσειν

ἃs is referred by Schäf. to αἱ πέρυσι πρεσβεῖαι, to which κατηγορίαι is subordinate. Compare, with Westermann, Hom. *Odyss.* 2. 283, θάνατον καὶ κῆρα μέλαιναν, δε δὴ σφ. σχιδόν ἐστιν: Dem. 47. 77, ἀνάγνωθί μοι τὸν νόμον καὶ τὴν μαρτυρίαν, δε κελεύει... It seems more correct to say that ἅs refers to both ; κατηγορίαι ἃs περιήλθομεν becoming a possible expression by its combination with πρεσβεῖαι. cf. 1. 3, and 6. 32, note to λόγον... τοιήσω. On the accusative Madv. 26, and Lob. Soph. *Aj.* 290. " nor were those missions of last year or the changes with which I and my excellent friend P. there... went about the P." Cf. 8. 37, τί οὖν πρεσβεύεσθε καὶ κατηγορεῖτε ... a passage which, as Thirl. (vi. p. 18, note) observes, sufficiently defends the present reading against Winiewski's proposal to substitute Ἀκαρνανίαν for κατηγορίαι, though the embassy to Acarnania is attested by Aesch. 3. 97. On these missions see Thirl. l. c. ; Dem. 18. 79. *Polyeuctus*, of the deme Sphettus, a political friend of Dem., afterwards accused along with him of taking bribes from Harpalus. cf. Deinarch. c. Dem. § 100; *Gr. and R. Dict. of Biogr.* s. v.

καὶ ἐποιήσαμεν] " and by which we made him." Madv. 104 a.

§ 73. οὐ .. λέγω] " I do not however recommend that you should invite the rest, if you are not willing to take any measure necessary for your defence ... whilst you are sacrificing your own interests to profess ... "

τοὺς .. ἐν X.] supr. 20.

συγκαλεῖν, κ.τ.λ.] "summon, bring together, instruct, warn the rest." 8. 76. The words fall into two pairs. Comp. with Redh. 39. 34, ἂν δ' ἐπιβουλεύῃς διακῇς, φθονῇς βλασφημῇς: 23. 185, πολίτης εὐεργέτης στέφανος δωρεαί: Cic. *Phil.* 7. 26, "excitati erecti, parati armati ;" 14. 8, "pestem vastitatem, cruciatus tormenta ;" *Catil.* 3, § 1. *Hegesippus*, another political friend of Dem., and author of the speech περὶ Ἀλοννήσου.

ταῦτ'] "this is the part that should be played by a city possessing such a reputation as ours."

§ 74. X. ἢ M.] "that Ch. or M.," people of their calibre. Possibly

ΚΑΤΑ ΦΙΛΙΠΠΟΥ Γ.

ἢ Μεγαρέας, ὑμεῖς δ' ἀποδράσεσθαι τὰ πράγματα, οὐκ ὀρθῶς οἴεσθε· ἀγαπητὸν γὰρ ἂν αὐτοὶ σώζωνται τούτων ἕκαστοι. ἀλλ' ὑμῖν τοῦτο πρακτέον· ὑμῖν οἱ πρόγονοι τοῦτο τὸ γέρας ἐκτήσαντο καὶ κατέλιπον μετὰ πολλῶν καὶ μεγάλων κινδύνων. 75. εἰ δ' ὃ βούλεται ζητῶν ἕκαστος καθεδεῖται, καὶ ὅπως μηδὲν αὐτὸς ποιήσει σκοπῶν, πρῶτον μὲν οὐδὲ μὴ ποθ' εὕρῃ τοὺς ποιήσοντας, ἔπειτα δέδοικα ὅπως μὴ πάνθ' ἅμα, ὅσα οὐ βουλόμεθα, ποιεῖν ἡμῖν ἀνάγκη γενήσεται.

76. Ἐγὼ μὲν δὴ ταῦτα λέγω, ταῦτα γράφω· καὶ οἴομαι καὶ νῦν ἔτι ἐπανορθωθῆναι ἂν τὰ πράγματα τούτων γιγνομένων. εἰ δέ τις ἔχει τούτων τι βέλτιον, λεγέτω καὶ συμβουλευέτω. ὅ τι δ' ὑμῖν δόξει, τοῦτ', ὦ πάντες θεοί, συνενέγκοι.

this refers to the project of a league among all the cities of Euboea for the maintenance of their independence, set on foot by Callias of Chalcis, and the great promises he made of assistance in men and money from Achaea, Megara, and Euboea. Aesch. 3. 94 sq.

τὰ πρ.] "the work," "the task."

ἀγαπητὸν ... ἂν] "may be thankful if." supr. 17; 8. 18. Note the emphasis on ὑμῖν: "no! *you* must .."

γέρας] i. e. the privilege of saving Hellas and being the champions of its liberties: cf. 4. 3. "to *you* your ancestors bequeathed this privilege won by many .."

μετά] 3. 36.

§ 75. ὃ βούλεται] "his pleasure (and not his duty), and looking how he shall escape doing any thing himself .."

πρ. μὲν .. ἔπειτα] supr. 9. "besides that there is no chance of his finding any to do it (3. 35), I fear .."

οὐδὲ μὴ ποθ' εὕρῃ] 4. 44.

δέδοικα ὅπως μή] Madv. 124 *b*. Xen. *Mem.* 2. 9. 2, εἰ μὴ φοβοίμην ὅπως μὴ ἐπ' αὐτόν με τράποιτο. Pl. *Phaed.* p. 84 B, οὐδὲν δεινὸν μὴ φοβηθῇ ... ὅπως μὴ ... οἴχηται.

ὅσα οὐ β.] referring to the definite duties they could not bring themselves to perform—"all we do not wish." 1. 15.

ποιεῖν .. ἀνάγκη] 1. 15.

§ 76. ἐπανορθωθῆναι ἂν] 4. 13; ἀπαλλάξαι ἄν.

γιγνομένων] i. e. ἐὰν γίγνηται. Madv. 135 *c*, r. 1 *a*. "and I believe that even now our fortunes might be retrieved if this be done."

τούτων τι β.] Bekk.; Dind. reads τι τούτων β.; West. omits τι with S. Without τι the words cannot give the meaning required here: cf. supr. 68, δεινὸν τι ἐσεσθαι.

λ. καὶ σ.] "let him come forward and give it."

συνενέγκοι] compare the conclusions of the third and fourth speeches.

ΚΑΤΑ ΦΙΛΙΠΠΟΥ Δ.

ΥΠΟΘΕΣΙΣ. Καὶ οὗτος τὴν αὐτὴν ὑπόθεσιν ἔχει τῷ φθάνοντι καὶ πλέον οὐδὲν οὐδὲ ἴδιον, πλὴν τὸ περὶ τῆς ὁμονοίας πολίτευμα· διαφερομένων γὰρ τῶν πλουσίων πρὸς τοὺς πένητας, ὁ Δημοσθένης καταπαύειν πειρᾶται τὴν στάσιν, τῷ μὲν δήμῳ παραινῶν μὴ δημεύειν τὰς τῶν πλουσίων οὐσίας, τοῖς δὲ πλουσίοις μὴ φθονεῖν τοῖς ἀπόροις τοῦ δημοσίου λήμματος. πείθει δὲ τοὺς Ἀθηναίους καὶ πρὸς τὸν Περσῶν βασιλέα περὶ συμμαχίας πρεσβεύεσθαι.

1. Καὶ σπουδαῖα νομίζων, ὦ ἄνδρες Ἀθηναῖοι, περὶ ὧν βουλεύεσθε, καὶ ἀναγκαῖα τῇ πόλει, πειράσομαι περὶ αὐτῶν εἰπεῖν ἃ νομίζω συμφέρειν. οὐκ ὀλίγων δ᾽ ὄντων ἁμαρτημάτων οὐδ᾽ ἐκ μικροῦ χρόνου συνειλεγμένων, ἐξ ὧν φαύλως ταῦτ᾽ ἔχει, οὐδέν ἐστιν, ὦ ἄνδρες Ἀθηναῖοι, τῶν πάντων δυσκολώτερον εἰς τὸ παρὸν ἢ ὅτι ταῖς γνώμαις ὑμεῖς

ARGUMENT.—τῷ φθάνοντι] "the preceding," i. e. the 9th. A great deal is borrowed from the 8th, as will be seen from the references in the notes.

τὸ ... πολίτευμα] "the advice:" § 35 sq.

δημεύειν] §§ 44, 45.

πρὸς τὸν Π. β.] § 31 sq.

Note.—Though reckoned by Dionysius Halic. among the genuine speeches of Demosthenes, and referred to without any misgiving by Aristeides, Hermogenes, and other rhetors, the fourth Philippic has by nearly all critics been condemned as spurious. Few students of Demosthenes will doubt the correctness of their judgment. The various points in the speech upon which this conclusion is founded are noticed in their several places. Those who look upon the speech as genuine refer it to B.C. 341.

§ 1. σπουδαῖα] "important," = the σπουδῆς ἄξια of Isocr. 8. 1, who refers to such exordia as this: ἅπαντες μὲν εἰώθασιν οἱ παριόντες ἐνθάδε ταῦτα μέγιστα φάσκειν εἶναι καὶ μάλιστα σπουδῆς ἄξια τῇ πόλει περὶ ὧν ἂν αὐτοὶ μέλλωσι συμβουλεύειν. Dem. 24. 4 uses language very similar to this.

ἀναγκαῖα] "of pressing consequence to."

οὐδ᾽ ἐκ, κ.τ.λ.] "the accumulation of no inconsiderable time."

ἐξ ὧν. κ.τ.λ.] "which have brought things to..."

ταῖς γν... ἀφ] cf. 4. 12, ἀπηρτημένοι ... ταῖς γνώμαις: 9. 19. 'the worst fault of all is your indifference to the public business.'

ΚΑΤΑ ΦΙΛΙΠΠΟΤ Δ. 87

ἀφεστήκατε τῶν πραγμάτων, καὶ τοσοῦτον χρόνον σπουδάζετε ὅσον ἂν κάθησθε ἀκούοντες, ἢν προσαγγελθῇ τι νεώτερον, εἶτ' ἀπελθὼν ἕκαστος ὑμῶν οὐ μόνον οὐδὲν φροντίζει περὶ αὐτῶν, ἀλλ' οὐδὲ μέμνηται. 2. ἡ μὲν οὖν ἀσέλγεια καὶ πλεονεξία, ᾗ πρὸς ἅπαντας ἀνθρώπους Φίλιππος χρῆται, τοσαύτη τὸ πλῆθος ὅσην ἀκούετε· ὅτι δ' οὐκ ἔνι ταύτης ἐκείνων ἐπισχεῖν ἐκ λόγου καὶ δημηγορίας, οὐδεὶς ἀγνοεῖ δήπου. καὶ γὰρ εἰ μηδ' ἀφ' ἑνὸς τῶν ἄλλων τοῦτο μαθεῖν δύναταί τις, ὡδὶ λογισάσθω. ἡμεῖς οὐδαμοῦ πώποτε, ὅπου περὶ τῶν δικαίων εἰπεῖν ἐδέησεν, ἡττήθημεν οὐδ' ἀδικεῖν ἐδόξαμεν, ἀλλὰ πάντων πανταχοῦ κρατοῦμεν καὶ περίεσμεν τῷ λόγῳ. 3. ἆρ' οὖν διὰ τοῦτ' ἐκείνῳ φαύλως ἔχει τὰ πράγματα ἢ τῇ πόλει καλῶς; πολλοῦ γε καὶ δεῖ· ἐπειδὰν γὰρ ὁ μὲν λαβὼν μετὰ ταῦτα βαδίζῃ τὰ ὅπλα, πᾶσι τοῖς οὖσιν ἑτοίμως κινδυνεύσων, ἡμεῖς δὲ καθώμεθα εἰρηκότες τὰ

σπουδάζετε] "you are interested," "give your attention."

ἢν προσαγγελθῇ] Bekk.; Dind. ἢ πρ., with F S T: "you give your attention to it just while you are listening to some news that may be reported, then you go away each of you, and so far from caring any thing about it, forget it altogether (do not so much as remember it)." This is the character of the people given, according to Dem. 19. 136, by Aeschines to Philip— ὁ μὲν ἦλθεν, ὁ δ' ἀπῆλθεν, μέλει δ' οὐδενὶ τῶν κοινῶν, οὐδὲ μέμνηται.

προσαγγελθῇ] 4. 36.

§ 2. οὖν] l. 2.

ἀσέλγεια] comp. the opening words of 21. 1, τὴν μὲν ἀσέλγειαν ... καὶ τὴν ὕβριν, ᾗ πρὸς ἅπαντας ἀεὶ χρῆται Μειδίας. Cf. 9. 35, "the overbearing and ambitious spirit P. exhibits—shows in his conduct towards all." The Schol. supposes that the speech was delivered without preparation, on the receipt of an alarming despatch from *Thrace*, and in this way explains the introduction of so many passages from other speeches. This is one of the passages from which he infers that such a despatch was received; but in quoting it he omits the words ᾗ πρὸς ἅπαντας ἀνθρώπους Φίλιππος χρῆται.

τὸ πλῆθος] here, as frequently, "extent."

ἀκούετε] l. e. from preceding speakers.

ἐκ.. δημηγορίας] "by talk and declamation."

οὐδεὶς ... δήπου] 9. 29, where Bekk. had οὐδεὶς ἀγνοεῖ δήπου, as here.

περὶ τῶν δ.] 6. 1.

ἐδέησεν] "we had to," "were called upon to."

πάντων π.] cf. 2. 24, "we beat and get the better of all every where in argument." 6. 3 and 18. 244.

§ 3. πολλοῦ .. δεῖ] 9. 18.

ἐπειδὰν] "for when he after this marches arms in hand, ready and willing to risk his all (9. 18), while we sit still the arguers and hearers of these claims.." οἱ μὲν is read before εἰρηκότες in F T Ω. 18. 121, νόμους μετατιθῶμεν, τῶν δ' ἀφαιρῶν μέρη. 19. 180.

[ΔΗΜΟΣΘΕΝΟΥΣ] [10. 4

δίκαια, οἳ δ' ἀκηκοότες, εἰκότως οἶμαι τοὺς λόγους τὰ ἔργα παρέρχεται, καὶ προσέχουσιν ἅπαντες οὐχ οἷς εἴπομέν ποθ' ἡμεῖς δικαίοις ἢ νῦν ἂν εἴποιμεν, ἀλλ' οἷς ποιοῦμεν. ἔστι δὲ ταῦτα οὐδένα τῶν ἀδικουμένων σώζειν δυνάμενα· οὐδὲν γὰρ δεῖ πλείω περὶ αὐτῶν λέγειν. 4. τοιγάρτοι διεστηκότων εἰς δύο ταῦτα τῶν ἐν ταῖς πόλεσι, τῶν μὲν εἰς τὸ μήτε ἄρχειν βίᾳ βούλεσθαι μηδενὸς μήτε δουλεύειν ἄλλῳ, ἀλλ' ἐν ἐλευθερίᾳ καὶ νόμοις ἐξ ἴσου πολιτεύεσθαι, τῶν δ' εἰς τὸ ἄρχειν μὲν τῶν πολιτῶν ἐπιθυμεῖν, ἑτέρῳ δ' ὑπακούειν, δι' ὅτου ποτ' ἂν οἴωνται τοῦτο δυνήσεσθαι ποιῆσαι, οἱ τῆς ἐκείνου προαιρέσεως, οἱ τυραννίδων καὶ δυναστειῶν ἐπιθυμοῦντες, κεκρατήκασι πανταχοῦ, καὶ πόλις δημοκρατουμένη βεβαίως οὐκ οἶδ' εἴ τίς ἐστι τῶν πασῶν λοιπὴ πλὴν ἡ ἡμετέρα. 5. καὶ κεκρατήκασιν οἱ δι' ἐκείνου τὰς πολιτείας ποιούμενοι πᾶσιν ὅσοις πράγματα πράττεται, πρώτῳ μὲν

οὐχ οἷς] "claims we once advanced or might now advance."
ἔστι . . . δυνάμενα] J. 25, and infr. § 14.
γάρ] "so it is useless to say . ."
§ 4. διεστηκότων] Instances of this division of parties are given in 9. 59 sq. : "as the several states are split into the two parties (cf. infr. 51, εἰς δύο ταῦτα διῄρηται, and 53 ; Pl. *Rep*. 5. 470 D, διαστῇ πόλις) of those who wish (i. e. διεστηκότων εἰς τὸ . . . βούλεσθαι) . . . but to live in freedom and under laws on terms of equality, and of those who long to govern their fellow-citizens and be subject to any external power by whose help they think they will be able . . ."
On νόμοις cf. 6. 25. As the words δι' ὅτου ἂν show that if Philip is specially meant others are included, ἐκείνου must necessarily be taken with Schäfer as a neuter referring to τὸ ἄρχειν . . ἐπιθυμεῖν, "the men of these views,"—προαίρεσις being often used in a political sense, e. g. 18. 59, πολλῶν προαιρέσεων οὐσῶν τῆς πολιτείας.
δυναστειῶν, as distinguished from τυραννίδων, must mean an ἀρχεῖν τῶν πολιτῶν divided among several persons. Cf. Thuc. 3. 62, which will also serve to illustrate νόμοις: ἡμῶν . . ἡ πόλις τότε ἐτύγχανεν οὔτε κατ' ὀλιγαρχίαν ἰσόνομον πολιτεύουσα, οὔτε κατὰ δημοκρατίαν ὅπερ δέ ἐστι νόμοις μὲν καὶ τῷ σωφρονεστάτῳ ἐναντιώτατον, ἐγγυτάτω δὲ τυράννου, δυναστεία ὀλίγων ἀνδρῶν εἶχε τὰ πράγματα. "tyrannies and despotic authorities." Iufr. 53.
πόλις δ.] "and I question whether among them all there is a state left, except your own, under a firmly established democracy."
§ 5. οἱ δι' ἐ. τὰς π. π.] "this party" (τὰς π. π. being of course the resolution of πολιτευόμενοι "qui illâ ratione ac consilio agunt in republicâ administrandâ," Redh.) : "this party has gained the upper hand by all the means with which affairs are managed, first and mainly because those who . . a person to give it in their interest (i. e. of those who wish to make themselves despots)." Dind. and the Zurich editors read βουλομένοις, which makes the sense clearer.

—7.] ΚΑΤΑ ΦΙΛΙΠΠΟΥ Δ. 89

πάντων καὶ πλείστῳ τῷ τοὺς βουλομένους χρήματα λαμβάνειν ἔχειν τὸν δώσοντα ὑπὲρ αὐτῶν, δευτέρῳ δὲ καὶ οὐδὲν ἐλάττονι τούτου τῷ δύναμιν τὴν καταστρεφομένην τοῖς ἐναντιουμένους αὐτοῖς ἐν οἷς ἂν αἰτήσωσι χρόνοις παρεῖναι. 6. ἡμεῖς δ' οὐ μόνον τούτοις ὑπολειπόμεθα, ὦ ἄνδρες Ἀθηναῖοι, ἀλλ' οὐδ' ἀνεγερθῆναι δυνάμεθα, ἀλλὰ μανδραγόραν πεπωκόσιν ἤ τι φάρμακον ἄλλο τοιοῦτον ἐοίκαμεν ἀνθρώποις· εἶτ', οἶμαι, (δεῖ γάρ, ὡς ἐγὼ κρίνω, λέγειν τἀληθῆ) οὕτω διαβεβλήμεθα καὶ καταπεφρονήμεθα ἐκ τούτων ὥστε τῶν ἐν αὐτῷ τῷ κινδυνεύειν ὄντων οἱ μὲν ὑπὲρ τῆς ἡγεμονίας ἡμῖν ἀντιλέγουσιν, οἱ δ' ὑπὲρ τοῦ ποῦ συνεδρεύσουσι, τινὲς δὲ καθ' ἑαυτοὺς ἀμύνεσθαι μᾶλλον ἢ μεθ' ἡμῶν ἐγνώκασιν.

7. Τοῦ χάριν δὴ ταῦτα λέγω καὶ διεξέρχομαι; οὐ γὰρ ἀπεχθάνεσθαι μὰ τὸν Δία καὶ πάντας τοὺς θεοὺς προαιροῦμαι. ἵν' ὑμῶν ἕκαστος, ὦ ἄνδρες Ἀθηναῖοι, τοῦτο γνῷ καὶ ἴδῃ, ὅτι ἡ καθ' ἡμέραν ῥᾳστώνη καὶ ῥᾳθυμία, ὥσπερ τοῖς ἰδίοις βίοις, οὕτω καὶ ταῖς πόλεσιν οὐκ ἐφ' ἑκάστου τῶν ἀμελουμένων ποιεῖ τὴν αἴσθησιν εὐθέως, ἀλλ' ἐπὶ τῷ

αὐτοῖς .. παρεῖναι] "is at their command."

§ 6. τούτοις] "in these respects." Madv. 40.

ἀλλ' οὐδ'] "we are not even able to rouse ourselves."

μανδραγόραν] Xen. Symp. 2. 24, τῷ γὰρ ὄντι ὁ οἶνος ἄρδων τὰς ψυχὰς τὰς μὲν λύπας ὥσπερ ὁ μανδραγόρας κοιμίζει. Pl. Rep. 6. 488 c; Othello, act 3, sc. 3.

εἶτ', οἶμαι] "the natural result is ..."

διαβεβλ.] "discredited," "in bad repute."

ἐκ τούτων] Madv. 39, 1.

ἐν αὐτῷ τῷ κ.] "in actual danger."

οἱ μέν] Wolff refers this to the Spartans. It more probably refers to the Thebans.

ποῦ σ.] "the place of congress," "the place where the congress shall be held." The people of Chalcis are probably meant: cf. Thirl. 5. 44.

καθ' ἑαυτούς] we might refer this to the Byzantines: cf. 8. 14 sq.

§ 7. λέγω καὶ διεξέρχομαι] 9. 7. λέγω καὶ διορίζομαι. 18. 22, ἐδίδαξα καὶ διεξῆλθον. 18. 21, ἀκριβολογοῦμαι καὶ διεξέρχομαι ... " with what object do I enter into this detail?"

γνῷ καὶ ἴδῃ] 4. 3.

ἡ καθ' ἡμέραν ῥᾳστώνη] "that habitual indolence and indifference do not make themselves felt by states any more than by individuals in private life on the occasion of each instance of neglect (ἐπί, cf. 2. 1), but come upon them in the general result." cf. 1. 11.

π. τὴν αἴσθησιν] Thuc. 2. 61, τὸ λυποῦν ἔχει ἤδη τὴν αἴσθησιν ἑκάστῳ.

90   [ΔΗΜΟΣΘΕΝΟΥΣ]   [10. 8

κεφαλαίῳ τῶν πραγμάτων ἅπαντα. 8. ὁρᾶτε Σέρριον καὶ Δορίσκον· ταῦτα γὰρ πρῶτον ὠλιγωρήθη μετὰ τὴν εἰρήνην, ἃ πολλοῖς ὑμῶν οὐδὲ γνώριμά ἐστιν ἴσως. ταῦτα μέντοι ἐαθέντα καὶ παροφθέντα ἀπώλεσε Θρᾴκην καὶ Κερσοβλέπτην, σύμμαχον ὄντα ὑμῶν. πάλιν ταῦτ' ἀμελούμενα ἰδὼν καὶ οὐδεμιᾶς βοηθείας τυγχάνοντα παρ' ὑμῶν κατέσκαπτε Πορθμόν, καὶ τυραννίδα ἀπαντικρὺ τῆς Ἀττικῆς ἐπετείχισεν ὑμῖν ἐν τῇ Εὐβοίᾳ. 9. ταύτης ὀλιγωρουμένης Μέγαρα ἑάλω παρὰ μικρόν. οὐδὲν ἐφροντίσατε οὐδ' ἐπεστράφητε ἐπ' οὐδενὶ τούτων, οὐδ' ἐνεδείξασθε τοῦθ', ὅτι οὐκ ἐπιτρέψετε ταῦτα ποιεῖν αὐτῷ· Ἀντρῶνας ἐπρίατο καὶ μετ' οὐ πολὺν χρόνον τὰ ἐν Ὠρεῷ πράγματ' εἰλήφει. 10. πολλὰ δὲ καὶ παραλείπω, Φεράς, τὴν ἐπ' Ἀμβρακίαν ὁδόν, τὰς ἐν Ἤλιδι σφαγάς, ἄλλα μυρία· οὐ γὰρ ἵν' ἐξαριθμήσωμαι τοὺς βεβιασμένους καὶ τοὺς ἠδικημένους ὑπὸ Φιλίππου, ταῦτα διεξῆλθον, ἀλλ' ἵνα τοῦθ' ὑμῖν δείξω, ὅτι οὐ στήσεται πάντας ἀνθρώπους ἀδικῶν, τὰ δ' ὑφ' αὑτῷ ποιούμενος Φίλιππος, εἰ μή τις αὐτὸν κωλύσει.

§ 8. Σέρριον, κ.τ.λ.] note to 9. 15.
οὐδὲ γ] "places which I dare say many of you never even heard of," "not even known by name."
ταῦτα, κ.τ.λ.] "yet your abandonment and disregard . . ." cf. Grote, 11. 557.
Πορθμόν] 9. 58.
ἐπετείχισεν] "and he established a tyranny over against A. in Euboea as a fortress against you," 9. 58. 19. 326, ἀντὶ δὲ τοῦ τὴν Εὔβοιαν ἀντ' Ἀμφιπόλεως ὑμῖν παραδοθῆναι ὁρμητήρια ἐφ' ὑμᾶς ἐν Εὐβοίᾳ Φ. προσπαρασκευάζεται καὶ Γεραιστῷ καὶ Μεγάροις ἐπιβουλεύων διατελεῖ.
§ 9. παρὰ μικρόν] "very nearly." Thuc. 7. 71, καὶ παρ' ὀλίγον ἢ διέφευγον ἢ ἀπώλλυντο. Id. 8. 76. Aesch. 3. 258, παρ' οὐδὲν μὲν ἦλθον ἀποκτεῖναι. Madv. 75 f.
ἐπεστράφητε ἐπ' οὐδενί] Bekk.; οὐδὲν τούτων F S T. Dind. Cobet, Nov. Lect. p. 628, conj. οὐδὲ τούτων: cf. Mr. Shill., de F. Leg. § 349. "you did not trouble yourselves at (about) . ."
ἐπιτρέψετε] Madv. 132 b.
Ἀντρῶνας] πόλις ἐν Θετταλίᾳ (Harpocr.). The subject here referred to does not seem to be mentioned elsewhere.
τὰ . . εἰλήφει] "had made himself master of Oreus:" cf. 6. 7, κύριος . . τῶν ἐν Φ. πραγμάτων. 1. 21; 9. 12, 33.
§ 10. Φεράς] 9. 12.
ἐπ' Ἀμβρ.] 9. 27, 72.
τὰς . . σφαγάς] 9. 27.
ἄλλα μ.] 9. 39.
ἐξαριθμήσωμαι] The word is used by Dem. only in the active voice, 27. 58 and 52. 7. "give a complete (ἐξ) catalogue of."
στήσεται] 4. 43; Infr. 36. "will not desist from wronging all people or reducing them under his power, unless some one interferes to stop him."
πάντας . . ἀδικῶν] from 9. 6, 35. τὰ μὲν omitted, as οἱ μὲν in § 3.

—13.] ΚΑΤΑ ΦΙΛΙΠΠΟΤ Δ. 91

11. Εἰσὶ δέ τινες οἳ πρὶν ἀκοῦσαι τοὺς ὑπὲρ τῶν πραγμάτων λόγους εὐθέως εἰώθασιν ἐρωτᾶν "τί οὖν χρὴ ποιεῖν;" οὐχ ἵνα ἀκούσαντες ποιήσωσι (χρησιμώτατοι γὰρ ἂν ἦσαν ἁπάντων) ἀλλ' ἵνα τοῦ λέγοντος ἀπαλλαγῶσιν. δεῖ δ' ὅμως εἰπεῖν ὅ τι χρὴ ποιεῖν. πρῶτον μέν, ὦ ἄνδρες Ἀθηναῖοι, τοῦτο παρ' ὑμῖν αὐτοῖς βεβαίως γνῶναι, ὅτι τῇ πόλει Φίλιππος πολεμεῖ καὶ τὴν εἰρήνην λέλυκε, καὶ κακόνους μέν ἐστι καὶ ἐχθρὸς ὅλῃ τῇ πόλει καὶ τῷ τῆς πόλεως ἐδάφει, προσθήσω δὲ καὶ τοῖς ἐν τῇ πόλει θεοῖς, οἵπερ αὐτὸν ἐξολέσειαν, 12. οὐδενὶ μέντοι μᾶλλον ἢ τῇ πολιτείᾳ πολεμεῖ οὐδ' ἐπιβουλεύει, καὶ σκοπεῖ μᾶλλον οὐδὲν τῶν πάντων ἢ πῶς ταύτην καταλύσει. καὶ τοῦτ' ἐξ ἀνάγκης τρόπον τινὰ νῦν γε δὴ ποιεῖ· λογίζεσθε γάρ. ἄρχειν βούλεται, τούτου δ' ἀνταγωνιστὰς μόνους ὑπείληφεν ὑμᾶς. ἀδικεῖ πολὺν ἤδη χρόνον, καὶ τοῦτ' αὐτὸς ἄριστα σύνοιδεν ἑαυτῷ· οἷς γὰρ οὖσιν ὑμετέροις ἔχει χρῆσθαι, τούτοις ἅπαντα τἆλλα βεβαίως κέκτηται· εἰ γὰρ Ἀμφίπολιν καὶ Ποτίδαιαν προεῖτο, οὐδ' ἂν ἐν Μακεδονίᾳ μένειν ἀσφαλῶς ἐδύνατο. 13. ἀμφότερα οὖν οἶδε, καὶ αὐτὸν ὑμῖν ἐπιβουλεύοντα καὶ ὑμᾶς αἰσθανομένους. εὖ φρονεῖν δ' ὑμᾶς ὑπολαμβάνων μισεῖν αὐτὸν ἡγεῖται. πρὸς δὲ τούτοις τοσούτοις οὖσιν,

§ 11.] §§ 11—16 are taken with some changes from the speech on the Chersonese, §§ 38—45.
πρὶν ἀκοῦσαι] "without waiting to hear the speeches about the subject of debate.."
ἂν ἦσαν] If they did so listen "they would be the most serviceable of men." Madv. 117.
γνῶναι] "you must be firmly convinced of this in your minds, that.. and to its soil, nay, I will add, to the gods in it. May they destroy him!" For τοῖς ... θεοῖς we have in 8. 40 τοῖς ἐν τῇ πόλει πᾶσιν ἀνθρώποις.
ἐδάφει] Ps. Dem. 26. 11, τῆς πόλεως ὑπὲρ αὐτῶν τῶν ἐδάφων εἰς κίνδυνον.. καταπλεκομένης. Aesch. 3. 134, ἤδη περὶ τοῦ τῆς πατρίδος ἐδάφους (ἀγωνίζεται).

§ 12.] Much of this and part of the following section is taken almost verbatim from 6. §§ 17, 18. The eighth speech comes in again at οἶδεν ἀκριβῶς.
οὐδενὶ] neuter.
πῶς] Madv. 198 b; cf. 9. 75.
καὶ τοῦτ'] "and this he now at least is in a manner forced to do." 8. 41 has καὶ τοῦτ' εἰκότως τρ. τινὰ πράττει: cf. 6. 17. For ἐν Μακεδονίᾳ Dem. has οἴκοι.
§ 13. πρὸς δέ] "and in addition to these so important considerations ...; but should ever any reverse happen to him—and many may happen to the man.." In 8, l. c. the remark is general—ἃ πολλὰ γένοιτ' ἂν ἀνθρώπῳ. Cobet, Nov. Lect. p. 605, says, "in cod. S scriptum est γένοιτο ἀνθρώπῳ, quae

[ΔΗΜΟΣΘΕΝΟΥΣ] [10. 14

οἶδεν ἀκριβῶς ὅτι οὐδ' ἂν ἁπάντων τῶν ἄλλων γένηται κύριος, οὐδὲν ἔστ' αὐτῷ βεβαίως ἔχειν ἕως ἂν ὑμεῖς δημοκρατῆσθε, ἀλλ' ἐάν ποτε συμβῇ τι πταῖσμα (πολλὰ δ' ἂν γένοιτο τἀνθρώπῳ), ἥξει πάντα τὰ νῦν βεβιασμένα καὶ καταφεύξεται πρὸς ὑμᾶς 14 ἐστὲ γὰρ ὑμεῖς οὐκ αὐτοὶ πλεονεκτῆσαι καὶ κατασχεῖν ἀρχὴν εὖ πεφυκότες, ἀλλ' ἕτερον λαβεῖν κωλῦσαι καὶ ἔχοντ' ἀφελέσθαι καὶ ὅλως ἐνοχλῆσαι τοῖς ἄρχειν βουλομένοις καὶ πάντας ἀνθρώπους εἰς ἐλευθερίαν ἐξελέσθαι δεινοί. οὔκουν βούλεται τοῖς αὑτοῦ καιροῖς τὴν παρ' ὑμῶν ἐλευθερίαν ἐφεδρεύειν, οὐ κακῶς οὐδ ἀργῶς ταῦτα λογιζόμενος. 15. πρῶτον μὲν δὴ τοῦτο δεῖ, ἐχθρὸν ὑπειληφέναι τῆς πολιτείας καὶ τῆς δημοκρατίας ἀδιάλλακτον ἐκεῖνον, δεύτερον δὲ εἰδέναι σαφῶς ὅτι πάνθ' ὅσα πραγματεύεται καὶ κατασκευάζεται νῦν, ἐπὶ τὴν ἡμετέραν πόλιν παρασκευάζεται. οὐ γὰρ οὕτως εὐήθης ὑμῶν ἐστὶν οὐδεὶς ὥσθ' ὑπολαμβάνειν τὸν Φίλιππον τῶν

non est vera lectio, sed verae proxima ; legendum enim γένοιτ' ἀνθρώπῳ." Dind. has γένοιτο ἀνθρώπῳ, a very improbable hiatus. In Bekker's reading, the words are, of course, a remark on the part of the speaker.

πάντα] 1. 12; 4. 8. "all those who are now kept down by force will come and seek your protection," "take refuge with you." In 8. 41 we have the more forcible expression τὰ νῦν συμβεβιασμένα, i. e. the various elements of Philip's dominion had been brought into a σύστημα, and were kept so by force.

§ 14. ἐστὲ ... εὖ πεφ.] 3. 33. "for it is not your nature yourselves to be grasping and to seize on dominion, but for preventing others from getting it, and taking it from them when they have it—in a word, for giving trouble to aspirants to empire and vindicating the liberty of all men, you are famous"—"you have a natural capacity." On κατασχεῖν see the excellent note of Mr. Shill., de F. Lg. § 165.

εἰς ἐλ. ἐξελέσθαι] Lys. 23. 9, ὅτι εἴη αὐτῷ ἀδελφὸς ὃς ἐξαιρήσοιτο εἰς ἐλευθερίαν. S has here ἀφελέσθαι, as Isocr. 12, § 97, τοῖς παρὰ τῶν ἄλλων τοὺς οἰκέτας εἰς ἐλευθερίαν ἀφαιρουμένοις. Harpocr., ἀφαίρεσις ἰδίως λέγεται ἡ εἰς ἐλευθερίαν. 'Υπερίδης ἐν τῷ κατ' Ἀρισταγόρας.

δεινοί] 1. 3.

τοῖς αὑτοῦ α.] cf. 3. 7.

τὴν παρ' ὑ. ἐλ.] "a free spirit emanating from you," "your liberty:" 1. 12. Isaeus, 1. 39. ἡ παρ' ὑμῶν αἰσχύνη. Lyc. § 32, ὁ . . παρὰ τῶν πολιτῶν φόβος.

ἐφεδρεύειν] 3. 7: comp. Lys. 1. 49, ὑπὸ τῶν νόμων ἐφεδρεύεσθαι.

§ 15.] τοῦτο is explained by the following sentence: "In the first place then you must assume him to be . . . that all his present operations and schemes are directed against our city," "that in all his . . . he is making preparations for attacking . . ."

ὥσθ'] after εὐήθης instead of the ὅτι of 8. 44.

—18.]   ΚΑΤΑ ΦΙΛΙΠΠΟΥ Δ.   93

μὲν ἐν Θρᾴκῃ κακῶν (τί γὰρ ἂν ἄλλο τις εἴποι Δρογγί- λον καὶ Καβύλην καὶ Μάστειραν καὶ ἃ νῦν φασὶν αὐτὸν ἔχειν) τούτων μὲν ἐπιθυμεῖν καὶ ὑπὲρ τοῦ ταῦτα λαβεῖν καὶ πόνους καὶ χειμῶνας καὶ τοὺς ἐσχάτους κινδύνους ὑπομένειν, 16. τῶν δ' Ἀθηναίων λιμένων καὶ νεωρίων καὶ τριήρων καὶ τῶν ἔργων τῶν ἀργυρείων καὶ τοσού- των προσόδων καὶ τόπου καὶ δόξης, ὧν μήτ' ἐκείνῳ μήτ' ἄλλῳ γένοιτο μηδενὶ χειρωσαμένῳ τὴν πόλιν τὴν ἡμετέραν κυριεῦσαι, οὐκ ἐπιθυμεῖν, ἀλλὰ ταῦτα μὲν ὑμᾶς ἐάσειν ἔχειν, ὑπὲρ δὲ τῶν μελινῶν καὶ τῶν ὀλυρῶν τῶν ἐν τοῖς Θρᾳκίοις σιροῖς ἐν τῷ βαράθρῳ χειμάζειν. 17. οὐκ ἔστι ταῦτα, ἀλλὰ κἀκεῖνα ὑπὲρ τοῦ τούτων γίγνεσθαι κύριος καὶ τἆλλα πάντα πραγματεύεται. ταῦτα τοίνυν ἕκαστον εἰδότα καὶ γιγνώσκοντα παρ' αὑτῷ δεῖ μὰ Δί' οὐ γράψαι κελεύειν πόλεμον τὸν τὰ βέλτιστα ἐπὶ πᾶσι δικαίοις συμ- βουλεύοντα· τοῦτο μὲν γάρ ἐστι λαβεῖν ὅτῳ πολεμήσετε βου- λομένων, οὐχ ἃ τῇ πόλει συμφέρει πράττειν. 18. ὁρᾶτε γάρ.

τούτων μέν] on account of the parenthesis. "no one among you is so silly as to suppose that P. covets the miseries in T. ... that I say he covets *these*.." Observe the feeble ἃ νῦν φασὶν αὐτὸν ἔχειν in place of the ἃ νῦν ἐξαιρεῖ καὶ κατα- σκευάζεται of 8. 44.

§ 16. τῶν ἔργων τῶν ἀργ.] at Laurium. The words καὶ τόπου καὶ δόξης are not in B. 45.

ἐν . . κυριεῦσαι] "but does not covet the harbours of Athens ... (may neither he nor any one else become master of them by the sub- jugation of our city).."

κυριεῦσαι] an ingressive aorist: 1. 13.

σιροῖς] Varro, *de Re Rusticâ*, 1. 57 (quoted by Redh.), "Quidam granaria habent sub terris speluncas quas vocant *σιρούς*, ut in Cappa- docia et Thraciâ." "store-pits." Lord Brougham.

ἐν τῷ β.] Bekk. *Anecd.* p. 219, βάραθρον Ἀθήνησι ἦν ὄρυγμά τι ἐν Κειριαδῶν δήμῳ τῆς Οἰνηΐδος φυλῆς,

εἰς ὃ τοὺς ἐπὶ θανάτῳ καταγνωσθέν- τας ἐσέβαλον. Called ὄρυγμα by Dein. *c. Dem.* §62. Harpocr. s. v., Δημοσθένης δὲ ἐν Φιλιππικοῖς οὐ κυ- ρίως αὐτὸ λέγει ἀλλ' ἐκ μεταφορᾶς, οἷον ἐν τῷ ὀλέθρῳ. "in the midst of horrors," Mr. K.

§ 17. οὐκ . . ἀλλά] "no! no! the object of these as of all his other ..."

παρ' αὑτῷ] cf. § 11. "you ought not therefore, persuaded each of you and convinced of this in your own minds .."

οὐ γράψαι] because this might expose him to danger: cf. 8. 68.

μὰ π. θ.] "In all honesty." 8. 9, εἴπερ ὡς ἀληθῶς ἐπὶ πᾶσι θ. ταῦτα συμβουλεύουσι. 4. 51, ἐπ' ἀθλίοις.

ἔστι . . βουλομένων] "is the part of people who wish ..," "would indicate a wish on your part to get some one to fight with." Madv. 113, r. cf. § 19.

§ 18. ὁρᾶτε γάρ .. ἔ.] supr. 12, λογ. γὰρ. ἄρχειν ... "only see: if for Philip's first violation of the

[ΔΗΜΟΣΘΕΝΟΥΣ] [10. 19

εἰ δι' ἃ πρῶτα παρεσπόνδησε Φίλιππος ἡ δευτέρα ἡ τρίτα (πολλὰ γάρ ἐστιν ἐφεξῆς) ἔγραψέ τις αὐτῷ πολεμεῖν, ὃ δ' ὁμοίως ὥσπερ νῦν, οὐ γράφοντος οὐδενὸς πόλεμον, Καρδιανοῖς ἐβοήθει, οὐκ ἂν ἀνηρπασμένος ἦν ὁ γράψας καὶ διὰ τοῦτο πάντες ᾐτιῶντο Καρδιανοῖς βεβοηθηκέναι; 19. μὴ τοίνυν ζητεῖτε ὅντινα, ἀνθ' ὧν Φίλιππος ἐξαμαρτάνει, μισήσετε καὶ τοῖς παρ' ἐκείνου μισθαρνοῦσι διασπάσασθαι παραβαλεῖτε μηδ' αὐτοὶ χειροτονήσαντες πόλεμον βούλεσθε παρ' αὐτοῖς ἡμῖν ἐρίζειν εἰ δέον ἢ μὴ δέον ὑμᾶς τοῦτο πεποιηκέναι· ἀλλ' ὃν ἐκεῖνος πολεμεῖ τρόπον, τοῦτον μιμεῖσθε, τοῖς μὲν ἀμυνομένοις ἤδη χρήματα καὶ τἆλλα ὅσων δέονται διδόντες, αὐτοὶ δ' εἰσφέροντες, ὦ ἄνδρες Ἀθηναῖοι, καὶ κατασκευαζόμενοι στράτευμα, τριήρεις ταχείας, ἵππους, ἱππαγωγούς, τἆλλα ὅσα εἰς πόλεμον, 20. ἐπεὶ νῦν γε γέλως ἐστὶν ὡς χρώμεθα τοῖς πράγμασι, καὶ Φίλιππον δ' ἂν αὐτὸν οὐδὲν ἄλλο οἶμαι μὰ τοὺς θεοὺς εὔξασθαι ποιεῖν τὴν πόλιν ἢ ταῦτα· ὑστερίζετε, ἀναλίσκετε, ὅτῳ παραδώσετε τὰ πράγ-

treaty... for there is a long series of them, any one had made a motion to go to war with him, and he, just as he is now doing without any one having made such motion, had helped... would not the mover have been destroyed, as having provoked a war?" cf. 8. 57, 5§. From πρὶν ἂν ὥσπερ νῦν αὐτὰ παρῇ τὰ πρ. (§ 39), and K. ἐβοήθει, the Schol. draws another argument in confirmation of his opinion that a despatch had been received announcing that P. was assisting the Cardians. The compiler of the speech is employing a passage from 8. 5§, and evidently thinking only of the situation at that time.
ἀνηρπασμένος] 9. 47.
§ 19. [ζητεῖτε] 3. 11.
δ. παραβαλεῖτε] "don't therefore look for a person to make a scapegoat of for Philip's offences, and fling to his hirelings to be torn in pieces." On the inf. see Don. 607 α; Madv. 153. cf. 5. 5, and 8. 20.

εἰ δ. ἢ μὴ δ.] "whether you ought or ought not to have done so." For the omission of the subst. verb comp. Hyper. Fun. Or. 1. 205, ἀλλ', εἰ δέον εἰπεῖν, καὶ μείζω.
ὃν.. τρόπον] i. e. with acts of hostility, but without openly declaring war. cf. 9. 8.
τοῖς μὲν ἀμυνομένοις] 9. 20 and 73.
τἆλλα, κ.τ.λ.] "all the other requisites for a war." 9. 39, τἆλλα πάνθ'.
§ 20. γέλως ἐστίν] This sentence is from 4. 25.
ἂν.. εὔξασθαι] 8. 20. ἢ ταῦτα ἃ νῦν ποιεῖτε· ὅτῳ π. τὰ πράγματα [ζητεῖτε], δυσχεραίνετε ... Bekk. The words ἃ νῦν π. he now omits, with S pr. m. and other MSS. Dind. retains them and reads ζητεῖτε with S m. sec. in mrg. If Bekker's present reading is retained we must understand it to mean "you raise difficulties about the person to whom you are to commit.."
ἀναλίσκετε] "throw away mo-

ΚΑΤΑ ΦΙΛΙΠΠΟΥ Δ.

μάτα δυσχεραίνετε, ἀλλήλους αἰτιᾶσθε. ἀφ' ὅτου δὲ ταῦτα γίγνεται, ἐγὼ διδάξω, καὶ ὅπως παύσεται, λέξω. 21. οὐδὲν πώποτε, ὦ ἄνδρες Ἀθηναῖοι, τῶν πραγμάτων ἐξ ἀρχῆς ἐνεστήσασθε οὐδὲ κατεσκευάσασθε ὀρθῶς, ἀλλὰ τὸ συμβαῖνον ἀεὶ διώκετε, εἶτ' ἐπειδὰν ὑστερίσητε παύεσθε· ἕτερον πάλιν ἐὰν συμβῇ τι, παρασκευάζεσθε καὶ θορυβεῖσθε. 22. τὸ δ' οὐχ οὕτως ἔχει· οὐκ ἔνεστι βοηθείαις χρωμένους οὐδὲν τῶν δεόντων ποτὲ πρᾶξαι, ἀλλὰ κατασκευάσαντας δεῖ δύναμιν, καὶ τροφὴν ταύτῃ πορίσαντας καὶ ταμίας καὶ δημοσίους, καὶ ὅπως ἔνι τὴν τῶν χρημάτων φυλακὴν ἀκριβεστάτην γενέσθαι οὕτω ποιήσαντας, τὸν μὲν τῶν χρημάτων λόγον παρὰ τούτων λαμβάνειν, τὸν δὲ τῶν ἔργων παρὰ τοῦ στρατηγοῦ, καὶ μηδεμίαν πρόφασιν τοῦ πλεῖν ἄλλοσε ἢ πράττειν ἄλλο τι τῷ στρατηγῷ καταλείπειν. 23. ἂν οὕτω ποιήσητε καὶ τοῦτο ἐθελήσητε ὡς ἀληθῶς, ἄγειν εἰρήνην δικαίαν καὶ μένειν ἐπὶ τῆς αὑτοῦ Φίλιππον

ncy." For ἀφ' ὅτου Dind. has ἀφ' οὗ.

§ 21. ἐξ ἀρχῆς] 4. 1.

ἐνεστήσασθε] 18. 193, ὅτι οὐ καλὰ καὶ τῆι πόλεωι ἄξια πράγματα ἐνεστησάμην. "in no instance have you set on foot or contrived your measures rightly in the beginning."

τὸ σ. ἀεὶ δ.] 4. 39. Observe the prominence of ἕτερον. 4. 29, τοῦτ' ἂν γένηται.

θορυβεῖσθε] 8. 11.

§ 22. τὸ δ'] "quum tamen..." Madv. 188, r. 7; Heind. Theaet. § 37. Pl. Alcib. 1, § 15, τὸ δ' ᾠδί πως εἶχεν· Ἔμαθον ἐγὼ.., and so frequently. Sometimes we have the fuller expression τὸ δ' ἀληθές, as Rep. 4. 443 D, τὸ δέ γε ἀληθές, τοιοῦτόν μέν τι ἦν . . ἡ δικαιοσύνη . . Mr. K. conveys the sense very well by his translation, "but that is not the way of proceeding." The passage from οὐκ ἔνεστι to the end of § 27 is taken from 8. 47 sq.

βοηθείαις] 4. 32. "it is not possible as long as you employ hasty levies to accomplish any good result; you must organize a standing force.."

ταμίας] 4. 33.

δημοσίους] "officials." 2. 19.

οὕτω π.] i. e. τὴν φυλακήν. "and take measures to secure the strictest care possible of your funds."

πρόφασιν] 4. 25.

πλεῖν] "sailing elsewhere (i. e. than to the seat of war, as Chares had done 4. 24; also 2. 28) on engaging in any other enterprise.."

§ 23.] For ἂν Dem. l. c. has κἂν.

ὡς ἀληθῶς] "in earnest," 6. 10. note to ὡς ἑτέρως. The Zurich editors omit ὡς with S, which however has the word in 8. 47. If this reading could be adopted καὶ must be omitted before μένειν, as it is by S in 8. l. c., ἀληθῶς going with what follows.

μ. ἐπὶ τῆς αὑτοῦ] Thuc. 4. 118, ἐπὶ τῆς αὑτῶν μένειν ἑκατέρους, ἔχοντας ἅπερ νῦν ἔχομεν. "keep at home," "confine himself to his own country;" cf. 4. 9.

96   [ΔΗΜΟΣΘΕΝΟΥΣ]   [10. 24

ἀναγκάσετε, ἢ πολεμήσετε ἐξ ἴσου καὶ ἴσως ἄν, ἴσως, ὦ ἄνδρες Ἀθηναῖοι, ὥσπερ νῦν ὑμεῖς πυνθάνεσθε τί ποιεῖ Φίλιππος καὶ ποῖ πορεύεται, οὕτως ἂν ἐκεῖνος φροντίσαι ποῖ ποτὲ ἡ τῆς πόλεως ἀπῆρκε δύναμις καὶ ποῦ φανήσεται.

24. Εἰ δέ τῳ δοκεῖ ταῦτα καὶ δαπάνης πολλῆς καὶ πόνων πολλῶν καὶ πραγματείας εἶναι, καὶ μάλα ὀρθῶς δοκεῖ. ἀλλ᾽ ἐὰν λογίσηται τὰ τῇ πόλει μετὰ ταῦτα γενησόμενα ἐὰν ταῦτα μὴ ἐθέλῃ ποιεῖν, εὑρήσει λυσιτελοῦν τὸ ἑκόντας ποιεῖν τὰ δέοντα. εἰ μὲν γάρ ἐστί τις ἐγγυητὴς ὑμῖν θεῶν (οὐ γὰρ ἀνθρώπων γε οὐδεὶς ἂν γένοιτο ἀξιόχρεως τηλικούτου πράγματος) ὡς ἐὰν ἄγηθ᾽ ἡσυχίαν καὶ πάντα προῆσθε, οὐκ ἐπ᾽ αὐτοὺς ὑμᾶς τελευτῶν ἐκεῖνος ἥξει, 25. αἰσχρὸν μὲν νὴ τὸν Δία καὶ πάντας θεοὺς καὶ ἀνάξιον ὑμῶν καὶ τῶν ὑπαρχόντων τῇ πόλει καὶ πεπραγμένων τοῖς προγόνοις, τῆς ἰδίας ῥαθυμίας ἕνεκα τοὺς ἄλλους ἅπαντας Ἕλληνας εἰς δουλείαν προέσθαι, καὶ ἔγωγ᾽ αὐτὸς μὲν τεθνάναι μᾶλλον ἂν ἢ ταῦτ᾽ εἰρηκέναι βουλοίμην 26. οὐ μὴν ἀλλ᾽ εἴ τις ἄλλος λέγει καὶ ὑμᾶς πείθει, ἔστω, μὴ ἀμύνεσθε, ἅπαντα πρόεσθε. εἰ δὲ μηδενὶ τοῦτο δοκεῖ, τοὐναντίον δὲ πρόισμεν ἅπαντες, ὅτι ὅσῳ ἂν πλειόνων ἐάσωμεν ἐκεῖνον γενέσθαι κύριον, τοσούτῳ

πυνθάνεσθε] "haec fortasse ex *De F. Leg.* (19. 288), νῦν δ᾽ ἤδη περιερχόμεθ᾽ ἡμεῖς... ὑπακουστοῦντες .. τοῦ τάφροισι Φ., (ᾗ ἡ τίθηκεν. Dobree, cf. 4. 10. "may be anxious to learn the destination of our force, and where it will make its appearance."

§ 24.] Sections 24—28 are taken almost verbatim from 8. 48—52.

δαπάνης πολλῆς .. εἶναι] Madv. 54 *b*. Dem. 8. 48 has δ. μεγάλης. "are affairs of..," "will entail both great expense and trouble." For the form of argument comp. 2. 22.

καί in καὶ μάλα is *epitatic*. cf. 3. 2.

τὰ .. γ.] "what the consequences will be to us."

λυσιτελοῦν] Madv. 178 *a*. "that it is our interest."

εἰ μέν] "for if some god is surety to you (for certainly of men no one could be an adequate surety for a thing so important), that, if you keep quiet and sacrifice every thing, he will not attack yourselves at last, though it would be disgraceful .. and the antecedents of the city and the achievements .. to abandon the rest of the K. to subjection, and though I .., still .,'' μέν in both cases referring to οὐ μὴν ἀλλ᾽.

ἀξιόχρεως] Dem. 40. 61, μάρτυρας ἀξιόχρεως, "credible witnesses." Lat. "testis locuples." Pl. *Apol.* 38 B, ἐγγυηταὶ δ᾽ ὑμῖν ἔσονται τοῦ ἀργυρίου οὗτοι ἀξιόχρεῳ. With ὑπαρχ. τῇ πόλει comp. with Redh. Dem. 60. 31, δεῖν οὖν ἡγήσαντο ἢ ζῆν ἀξίως τῶν ὑπαρχόντων ἢ τεθνάναι καλῶς. infr. 73.

ΚΑΤΑ ΦΙΛΙΠΠΟΥ Δ.

χαλεπωτέρῳ καὶ ἰσχυροτέρῳ χρησόμεθα ἐχθρῷ, ποῖ ἀναδυόμεθα, ἢ τί μέλλομεν; ἢ πότε, ὦ ἄνδρες Ἀθηναῖοι, τὰ δέοντα ποιεῖν ἐθελήσομεν; ὅταν νὴ Δί᾽ ἀναγκαῖον ᾖ. 27. ἀλλ᾽ ἢν μὲν ἄν τις ἐλευθέρων ἀνθρώπων ἀνάγκην εἴποι, οὐ μόνον ἤδη πάρεστιν ἀλλὰ καὶ πάλαι παρελήλυθε, τὴν δὲ τῶν δούλων ὑπεύχεσθαι δήπου μὴ γενέσθαι δεῖ. διαφέρει δὲ τί; ὅτι ἐστὶν ἐλευθέρῳ μὲν ἀνθρώπῳ μεγίστη ἀνάγκη ἡ ὑπὲρ τῶν γιγνομένων αἰσχύνη, καὶ μείζω ταύτης οὐκ οἶδα ἥντινα ἂν εἴποι τις, δούλῳ δὲ πληγαὶ καὶ ὁ τοῦ σώματος αἰκισμός· ὃ μήτε γένοιτο οὔτε λέγειν ἄξιον.

28. Τὸ μὲν τοίνυν, ὦ ἄνδρες Ἀθηναῖοι, πρὸς τὰ τοιαῦτα ὀκνηρῶς διακεῖσθαι ἃ δεῖ τοῖς σώμασι καὶ ταῖς οὐσίαις λειτουργῆσαι ἕκαστον, ἐστὶ μὲν οὐκ ὀρθῶς ἔχον, οὐδὲ πολλοῦ δεῖ, οὐ μὴν ἀλλ᾽ ἔχει τινὰ πρόφασιν ὅμως· τὸ δὲ μηδ᾽ ὅσα ἀκοῦσαι δεῖ μηδ᾽ ὅσα βουλεύσασθαι προσήκει, μηδὲ ταῦτ᾽ ἐθέλειν ἀκούειν, τοῦτ᾽ ἤδη πᾶσαν ἐπιδέχεται κατηγορίαν.

§ 26. χρησόμεθα] "shall find him." 1. 9.

ποῖ ἀναδυόμεθα] "how long do we mean to hang back?" ὅμοιον τῷ ποῖ μενεῖς ῥάθυμοι (Soph. *El.* 958, where Wolff quotes Arist. *Lysistr.* 526, ποῖ χρῆν ἀναμεῖναι) ἀντὶ τοῦ μέχρι τίνος. Schol. ἀπὸ μεταφορᾶς τῶν ὑποζυγίων τῶν ἀναδυομένων καὶ φευγόντων ὑποδῦναι τὸν ζυγόν. Schol. ib. cf. 8. 77, ἐὰν δὲ δέῃ τι ποιεῖν ἀναδυόμενοι.

ὅταν νὴ Δί᾽] 4. 10, ἐπειδὰν νὴ Δί᾽ ἀνάγκη ᾖ.

§ 27. ἢν ... ἄν τις .... εἴποι] "what one may call." 9. 40, ἂν κρίνοι. On μὴ after ἀπεύχομαι, Madv. 210.

ἡ ὑπὲρ] "shame for what is happening.." 4. 10, τὴν ὑπὲρ τῶν πραγμάτων αἰσχύνην.

οὐκ οἶδα] "and I don't know what greater could be named."

ὃ μήτε γ. οὔτε] infr. 68, οὔτ᾽ εἰμὶ μήτε γενοίμην. 21. 209, ὃ μὴ γένοιτο οὐδ᾽ ἔσται. 25. 86, οὔτε γὰρ ἔστι μήτε γένοιτο ταῦτα. "a state of things which I pray may never be, and which is not fit to be mentioned." Don. *Gr.* p. 553. With οὔτε λ. ἄξιον comp. 18. 195.

§ 28. ἃ δεῖ] "such public services as each is liable to in person and property." σώμασι, i. e. by serving as a soldier. 16. 12, καὶ χρήματ᾽ εἰσφέρειν καὶ τοῖς σώμασι κινδυνεύειν, and 9. 40.

ἐστὶ .. ἔχον] cf. 2. 26.
οὐδὲ π. δεῖ] 9. 23.

πρόφασιν] "excuse."

τὸ δέ] "but to be unwilling even to hear what it is necessary you should hear and proper you should consider .. to be unwilling to listen even to these things does indeed justify the strongest censure." ἤδη, i. e. there we come to something which admits of no excuse, but is simply and purely οὐκ ὀρθῶς ἔχον: cf. 19. 19. So οὐκέτι in negative sentences. *Jam* is similarly used in Latin: cf. Lucr. 1. 436, with Mr. Munro's note.

ἐπιδέχεται] Aesch. 1. 48, ὥστε μὴ ἐπιδέχεσθαι δόξαν αἰτίας πονηρᾶς.

[ΔΗΜΟΣΘΕΝΟΥΣ] [10. 29

29. ὑμεῖς τοίνυν οὐκ ἀκούειν πρὶν ἂν ὥσπερ νῦν αὐτὰ παρῇ τὰ πράγματα, οὐδὲ βουλεύεσθαι περὶ οὐδενὸς εἰώθατε ἐφ' ἡσυχίας· ἀλλ' ὅταν μὲν ἐκεῖνος παρασκευάζηται, ἀμελήσαντες τοῦ ποιεῖν ταὐτὸ καὶ ἀντιπαρασκευάζεσθαι ῥᾳθυμεῖτε, καὶ ἐάν τι λέγῃ τις, ἐκβάλλετε, ἐπειδὰν δ' ἀπολωλὸς ἢ πολιορκούμενόν τι πύθησθε, ἀκροᾶσθε καὶ παρασκευάζεσθε. 30. ἦν δ' ἀκηκοέναι μὲν καὶ βεβουλεῦσθαι τότε καιρὸς ὅθ' ὑμεῖς οὐκ ἠθέλετε, πράττειν δὲ καὶ χρῆσθαι τοῖς παρεσκευασμένοις νῦν, ἡνίκ' ἀκούετε. τοιγαροῦν ἐκ τῶν τοιούτων ἐθῶν μόνοι τῶν πάντων ἀνθρώπων ὑμεῖς τοῖς ἄλλοις τοὐναντίον ποιεῖτε· οἱ μὲν γὰρ ἄλλοι πρὸ τῶν πραγμάτων εἰώθασι χρῆσθαι τῷ βουλεύεσθαι, ὑμεῖς δὲ μετὰ τὰ πράγματα.

31. Ὃ δὴ λοιπόν ἐστι, καὶ πάλαι μὲν ἔδει, διαφεύγει δ' οὐδὲ νῦν, τοῦτ' ἐρῶ. οὐδενὸς τῶν πάντων οὕτως ὡς χρημάτων δεῖ τῇ πόλει πρὸς τὰ νῦν ἐπιόντα πράγματα. συμβέβηκε δ' εὐτυχήματα ἀπὸ ταὐτομάτου, οἷς ἂν χρησώμεθα

§ 29. **αὐτά**] "actually."
The phrase **ἐφ' ἡσυχίας** seems only to occur once in the genuine speeches of Dem.: 45. 14, ὅσαις δὲ τούτων μηδείν, λογισμὸς δ' ἐφ' ἡσυχίας τοῦ συμφέροντος. Elsewhere we have μεθ' ἡσυχίας, 8. 13, or καθ' ἡσυχίαν, 8. 12, or ἐν ἡσυχίᾳ. We find ἐφ' ἡσυχίας again in Ps. Dem. 13. 8, ἐπὶ πολλῆς μὲν ἡσυχίας καὶ ἠρεμίας ὑμῶν.
ἐκβάλλετε] 9. 36. Isocr. 8. 3, εἰώθατε πάντας τοὺς ἄλλους ἐκβάλλειν πλὴν τοὺς συναγορεύοντας ταῖς ὑμετέραις ἐπιθυμίαις. Aristoph. (*Eq.* 525) says of the poet Magnes, ἐξεβλήθη πρεσβύτης ὤν.
ἐπειδὰν ... παρασκευάζεσθε] cf. 8. 11.
§ 30. **ἀκηκοέναι**] "but the proper time to have heard and taken your resolution was when..." cf. 4. 19.
ἐκ] "in consequence of:" 6. 27.
μόνοι τῶν πάντων] "you, unlike every one else, exactly reverse the practice of other people. They..." "you, singular in the practice, reverse the course usually followed.

Every other people .." 30. 62, εἴ τινες μόνοι τῶν ἄλλων μετοίκων μὴ χορηγοῖεν. 23. 185, οὗτος εἷς ἁπάντων τῶν ἄλλων μόνος. The words οἱ μὲν .. πράγματα are taken from 5. 2, where however after ἄλλοι we find πάντες ἄνθρωποι.
§ 31. Ὃ δὴ λοιπόν, κ.τ.λ.] i. e. the applying to Persia for assistance.
διαφεύγει] Aesch. 3. 249, τῆς δημοκρατίας ἐπιμελήθητε ἤδη διαφευγούσης ὑμᾶς—"which though it ought to have been done long ago, is not even yet slipping from your hands," "is not even yet too late." Mr. K. Redh. takes it in the sense of "slipping from the memory," as in Isocr. 4. 187, πολλά με διαπέφευγεν ἂν διενοήθην. But both ἔδει and διαφεύγει refer to ὃ λ. ἐστι, the course left for them deliberating now, as ever, μετὰ τὰ πράγματα.
ἀπὸ ταὐτομάτου] S has εὐτύχημα ἀπ' αὐτομάτου. Accordingly the Zurich editors read ἀπ' αὐτομάτου, though the article cannot possibly be dispensed with, as it might be

ΚΑΤΑ ΦΙΛΙΠΠΟΥ Δ.

ὀρθῶς, ἴσως ἂν γένοιτο τὰ δέοντα. πρῶτον μὲν γάρ. οἷς βασιλεὺς πιστεύει καὶ εὐεργέτας ὑπείληφεν αὐτοῦ, οὗτοι μισοῦσι καὶ πολεμοῦσι Φιλίππῳ. 32. ἐπειδ' ὁ πράττων καὶ συνειδὼς ἅπανθ' ὅσα Φίλιππος κατὰ βασιλέως παρασκευάζεται, οὗτος ἀνάσπαστος γέγονε, καὶ πάσας τὰς πράξεις βασιλεὺς οὐχ ἡμῶν κατηγορούντων ἀκούσεται, οἷς ὑπὲρ τοῦ συμφέροντος ἂν ἡγήσαιτο τοῦ ἰδίου λέγειν, ἀλλὰ τοῦ πράξαντος αὐτοῦ καὶ διοικοῦντος, ὥστ' εἶναι πιστάς, καὶ λοιπὸν λόγον εἶναι τοῖς παρ' ἡμῶν πρέσβεσιν ὃν βασιλεὺς ἥδιστα ἂν ἀκούσαι, 33. ὡς τὸν ἀμφοτέρους ἀδικοῦντα κοινῇ τιμωρήσασθαι δεῖ, καὶ ὅτι πολὺ τῷ βασιλεῖ φοβερώτερος ἔσθ' ὁ Φίλιππος ἂν προτέροις ἡμῖν ἐπιθῆται· εἰ γὰρ ἐγκαταλειπόμενοί τι πεισόμεθα ἡμεῖς, ἀδεῶς ἐπ' ἐκεῖνον ἤδη πορεύσεται. ὑπὲρ δὴ τούτων ἁπάντων οἴομαι δεῖν ὑμᾶς πρεσβείαν ἐκπέμπειν ἥτις τῷ βασιλεῖ διαλέξεται, καὶ τὴν ἀβελτερίαν

with τύχη, the nom. being τὸ αὐτόματον. This will be clear from Arist. p. 195, b 31, πολλὰ καὶ εἶναι [λέγεται] καὶ γίνεσθαι διὰ τύχην καὶ διὰ τὸ αὐτόματον. "have happened providentially, by a right employment of which . ." For the consir., 3. 33. ἐὰν . . χρήσησθε, ἴσως ἂν . . κτήσαισθε.

καὶ (οὓς) εὐεργέτας] see note 3. 24. The Thracians are supposed to be meant, who for services rendered to Darius when returning from his invasion of Scythia, were regarded as benefactors of Persia. But could the king on any supposition be said πιστεύειν Teres and the Odrysae? Böhnecke is more probably right in referring the passage to Mentor and Memnon (Thirl. 6. 143; Grote, 11. 609), though in this case πολεμοῦσι can hardly be understood strictly— at least there is no direct evidence of the fact.

Φιλίππῳ] Bekk. and Dind.; Vöm. and the Zur. editors Φίλιππον from S. The acc. might legitimately stand here, the case being accommodated to μισοῦσι, as Lys. 6. 31, ἐπιτιμᾷ καὶ ἀποδοκιμάζει τῶν ἀρχόντων τισί. But we also find passages where πολεμεῖν standing alone takes the acc., as 23. 165, μῆνας ἑπτὰ διήγαγεν ἡμᾶς πολεμῶν.

§ 32. ὁ πράττων] "the person who conducted and was in the secret of . ." The allusion is to Hermias, the despot of Atarneus and friend of Aristotle, who married his sister. cf. Grote, l. c.

ἀνάσπαστος] a word often used by Herod. of the inhabitants of cities carried off into farther Asia. Here of Hermias, who was seized by Mentor and sent up to Susa, where he was put to death.

καὶ πάσας] "and the king will hear of all the intrigues . . whom he might conceive to be speaking . . (Thuc. 1. 68, τῶν λεγόντων . . ὑπενοεῖτε δι' ἔχθραν τῶν αὐτοῖς ἰδίᾳ διαφόρων λέγουσι), but from the very person who conducted and managed them; so that the charges will be credible, and the only argument left for our a. will be one which . ."

§ 33. τι πεισόμεθα] 9. 20. διαλέξεται] 2. 6: for the fut. ind. 1. 2, ἐρεῖ.

[ΔΗΜΟΣΘΕΝΟΥΣ] [10. 34

ἀποθέσθαι δι' ἥν πολλάκις ἠλαττώθητε, "ὁ δὴ βάρβαρος" καὶ "ὁ κοινὸς ἅπασιν ἐχθρός" καὶ πάντα τὰ τοιαῦτα. 34. ἐγὼ γὰρ ὅταν τιν' ἴδω τὸν μὲν ἐν Σούσοις καὶ Ἐκβατάνοις δεδοικότα καὶ κακόνουν εἶναι τῇ πόλει φάσκοντα, ὃς καὶ πρότερον συνεπηνώρθωσε τὰ τῆς πόλεως πράγματα καὶ νῦν ἐπηγγέλλετο (εἰ δὲ μὴ ἐδέχεσθ' ὑμεῖς ἀλλ' ἀπεψηφίζεσθε, οὐ τὰ ἐκείνου αἴτια), ὑπὲρ δὲ τοῦ ἐπὶ ταῖς θύραις ἐγγὺς οὑτωσὶ ἐν μέσῃ τῇ Ἑλλάδι αὐξανομένου λῃστοῦ τῶν Ἑλλήνων ἄλλο τι λέγοντα, θαυμάζω, καὶ δέδοικα τοῦτον, ὅστις ἂν ᾖ ποτ', ἔγωγ', ἐπειδὴ οὐχ οὗτος Φίλιππον.

35. Ἔστι τοίνυν τι πρᾶγμα καὶ ἄλλο, ὃ λυμαίνεται τὴν πόλιν ὑπὸ βλασφημίας ἀδίκου καὶ λόγων οὐ προσηκόντων διαβεβλημένον, εἶτα τοῖς μηδὲν τῶν ἐν τῇ πολιτείᾳ δικαίων βουλομένοις ποιεῖν πρόφασιν παρέχει· καὶ πάντων ὅσα ἐκλείπει, δέον παρά του γίγνεσθαι, ἐπὶ τοῦθ' εὑρήσετε τὴν αἰτίαν ἀναφερομένην. περὶ οὗ πάνυ μὲν φοβοῦμαι, οὐ μὴν ἀλλ' ἐρῶ· 36. οἶμαι γὰρ ἕξειν καὶ ὑπὲρ τῶν ἀπόρων τὰ δίκαια ἐπὶ τῷ συμφέροντι τῆς πόλεως εἰπεῖν πρὸς τοὺς

ὁ δὴ β.] Schäf. says, "sine cunctatione scribendum ὁ δὲ βάρβαρος. Et videtur δέ in ipso καὶ latere. Cf. 21. 209, τὸν δὲ βάσκανον . . τὸν δὲ ὄλεθρον." There is no need for any change. δή is due to the speaker, and is ironical. Pl. Apol. 27 A, ἆρα γνώσεται Σωκράτης, ὁ σοφὸς δή. "the barbarian forsooth !" and "the common enemy of Hellas," and the like.

§ 34. πρότερον] i. e. in the time of Conon, B.C. 393. "helped to re-establish the fortunes of our city, and lately offered to do so."

τὰ ἐκείνου] Bekk. st. with S.

τὰ ἐ.] Bekk. st. "the fault was not his." But Dind. is, I think, right in retaining γε in his last edition, in spite of the authority of MS. S.

λῃστοῦ] "but holds different language of him who close to our doors is thus growing up in the midst of Hellas as a robber of . . ." af. 6. 6. With λῃστοῦ comp. 9. 22.

ἔγωγ'] "and fear him, whoever he is, myself, because he . ."

§ 35. Ἔστι τοίνυν] cf. 9. 47. It seems vain to attempt to reconcile the view here taken of the Theoric Fund with that put forward in the Olynthiac Orations, or with the tone and spirit of the attack in 3. 21 sq. on the policy of Eubulus and his party, by whom the Fund was upheld. The discrepancy has justly furnished critics with one of their strongest arguments against the genuineness of the speech.

διαβεβλημένον] "in invidiam vocata." "the attacking of which."

εἶτα] "and so." l. 12.

τῶν . . δ.] "public duties."

καὶ πάντων] "and you will find that the reason of every failure on the part of any citizen to do his duty is still referred to this,"—this is the standing excuse.

δέον] Madv. 182: cf. 3. 18.

§ 36. τὰ δ. . . . εἰπεῖν] "make out a case for the advantage."

ΚΑΤΑ ΦΙΛΙΠΠΟΥ Δ.

εὐπόρους καὶ ὑπὲρ τῶν κεκτημένων τὰς οὐσίας πρὸς τοὺς ἐπιδεεῖς, εἰ ἀνέλοιμεν ἐκ μέσου καὶ τὰς βλασφημίας ἃς ἐπὶ τῷ θεωρικῷ ποιοῦνταί τινες οὐχὶ δικαίως, καὶ τὸν φόβον ὡς οὐ στήσεται τοῦτο ἄνευ μεγάλου τινὸς κακοῦ· οὗ οὐδὲν ἂν εἰς τὰ πράγματα μεῖζον εἰσενεγκαίμεθα, οὐδ᾽ ὅ τι κοινῇ μᾶλλον ἂν ὅλην ἐπιρρώσειε τὴν πόλιν. 37. οὑτωσὶ δὲ σκοπεῖτε· ἐρῶ δ᾽ ὑπὲρ τῶν ἐν χρείᾳ δοκούντων εἶναι πρότερον. ἦν ποτ᾽ οὐ πάλαι παρ᾽ ἡμῖν ὅτ᾽ οὐ προσῄει τῇ πόλει τάλαντα ὑπὲρ τριάκοντα καὶ ἑκατόν· καὶ οὐδείς ἐστι τῶν τριηραρχεῖν δυναμένων οὐδὲ τῶν εἰσφέρειν ὅστις οὐκ ἠξίου τὰ καθήκοντα ἐφ᾽ ἑαυτὸν ποιεῖν ὅτι χρήματα οὐ περιῆν, ἀλλὰ καὶ τριήρεις ἔπλεον καὶ χρήματα ἐγίγνετο καὶ πάντα ἐποιοῦμεν τὰ δέοντα. 38. μετὰ ταῦτα ἡ τύχη, καλῶς ποιοῦσα, πολλὰ πεποίηκε τὰ κοινά, καὶ τετρακόσια ἀντὶ τῶν ἑκατὸν ταλάντων προσέρχεται, οὐδενὸς οὐδὲν ζημιουμένου τῶν τὰς οὐσίας ἐχόντων, ἀλλὰ καὶ προσλαμβάνοντος· οἱ γὰρ εὔποροι πάντες ἔρχονται

α. τὰς οὐσίας] cf. § 38. Lys. 29. 4. διιρὸν εἰ οἱ μὲν τὰς οὐσίας ἔχοντες ὀλοφυροῦνται τριηραρχοῦντες. Isocr. 6. 67. Thuc. 1. 7, οἱ τὰ μείζω κεκτημένοι. "people of property."

εἰ ἀνέλοιμεν] "could we remove out of the way (clear away) both the abuse which some direct against . . ., and the fear expressed that it (i. e. the Theoric Fund) cannot stand (be maintained) without . . ." With φ. ὡς στήσεται comp. 14. 25, οἱ λέγοντες φοβοῖεν ὡς ἥξει βασιλεύς: Soph. *El.* 1426.

στήσεται] 4. 43; supr. 10.

οὗ, κ. τ. λ.] "no greater service to our affairs could we contribute, or one more likely to strengthen the whole commonwealth (i. e. than removing the dissatisfaction about the Theoric Fund)."

§ 37. ἦν] "there was a time, not long ago (cf. 4. 3, ἐξ οὗ χρόνος οὐ πολύς), when there did not come in to the state . . (when our yearly revenue was . .)."

προσῄει] in the next section προσέρχεται: Thuc. 2. 13, προσιόντων. See Böckh's remarks on this passage in his *Publ. Econ.* bk. 3, c. 19.

οὐκ ἠξίου] "demurred to perform," "claimed to be exempt from." The οὐ is to be explained by the note to 6. 33.

τὰ κ.] "the duties that devolved on him because there was not a surplus." Xen. *Cyrop.* 1. 2, 5, ὅπως καὶ οὗτοι τὰ καθήκοντα ἀποτελῶσιν. The word gained greater currency afterwards as a term of the Stoical Ethics. Cf. Ritter and Preller, § 404.

ἐγίγνετο] "was forthcoming." Mr. K.

§ 38. καλῶς π.] 1. 28. "happily."

τῶν ἑκατόν] l. e. the 130 talents mentioned in § 37.

προσλ.] absolutely, "gaining."

μεθέξοντες τούτου, καὶ καλῶς ποιοῦσιν. 39. τί οὖν μαθόντες τοῦτο ὀνειδίζομεν ἀλλήλοις καὶ προφάσει χρώμεθα τοῦ μηδὲν ποιεῖν, πλὴν εἰ τῇ παρὰ τῆς τύχης βοηθείᾳ γεγοννίᾳ τοῖς ἀπόροις φθονοῦμεν; οὓς οὔτ' ἂν αἰτιασαίμην ἔγωγε οὔτ' ἀξιῶ. 40. οὐδὲ γὰρ ἐν ταῖς ἰδίαις οἰκίαις ὁρῶ τὸν ἐν ἡλικίᾳ πρὸς τοὺς πρεσβυτέρους οὕτω διακείμενον οὐδ' οὕτως ἀγνώμονα οὐδ' ἄτοπον τῶν ὄντων οὐδένα ὥστε, εἰ μὴ ποιήσουσιν ἅπαντες ὅσ' ἂν αὐτός, οὐ φάσκοντα ποιήσειν οὐδὲν οὐδ' αὐτόν· καὶ γὰρ ἂν τοῖς τῆς κακώσεως εἴη νόμοις οὗτός γε ἔνοχος· δεῖ γάρ, οἶμαι, τοῖς γονεῦσι τὸν ὡρισμένον ἐξ ἀμφοτέρων ἔρανον, καὶ παρὰ τῆς φύσεως καὶ παρὰ τοῦ νόμου, δικαίως φέρειν καὶ ἑκόντα ὑποτελεῖν. 41. ὥσπερ τοίνυν ἑνὸς ἡμῶν ἑκάστου τίς ἐστι γονεύς, οὕτω συμπάσης τῆς

τούτου] i. e. the surplus, the Theoric Fund.

κ. ποιοῦσιν] "as they have perfect right." 21. 212, εἰσὶ . . . . εἰς τὰ μάλιστα αὐτοὶ πλούσιοι καὶ καλῶς ποιοῦσι, where see Spalding's note.

§ 39. **τί . . μαθόντες**] Madv. 176 b, r.; Don. p. 382. "what then makes us reproach one another with this, and employ it as an excuse for . . ?"

πλὴν εἰ] 3. 18. μή, which Bekk. had after εἰ, he now omits with S.

φθονῶ has here a dat. of the thing, as in Isocr. 8. 124, οὐκ ἀγανακτοῦμεν, οὐδὲ φθονοῦμεν ταῖς εὐπραγίαις αὐτῶν. Id. 5. 131. "unless we grudge the relief which has been given by fortune to the needy."

οὔτ' ἀξιῶ] "nor do I think it right." sc. αἰτιάσασθαι. 8. 46, χρήματα δ' εἰσφέρειν καὶ τοὺς συμμάχους ἀξιοῦν. 19. 98, and ib., ἀφίημι Αἰσχίνην καὶ ὑμᾶς συμβουλεύω.

§ 40. **ὥστε . . . οὐ φάσκοντα**] a not uncommon syntax: cf. 3. 1. Redh. quotes Isae. 9. 16, ἐπιδείξω . . οὕτω σφόδρα . . μισοῦντα τοῦτον, ὥστε πολὺ δὴ θᾶττον διατιθέμενον. "for neither in private families do I find the grown-up son behaving so . . or any one in the world so wanting in right feeling or so unreasonable as to declare that unless all will do just what he does, he will do nothing himself." τῶν ὄντων, sc. ἀνθρώπων. So Whiston, who yet tr. "consistent with his position."

τῆς κακώσεως] cf. Gr. and Rom. Ant. The ἀγὼν being τιμητός, the penalty might be fixed at death: cf. Lys. 13. 91.

ἔρανον] "for a man ought, I take it, to bring dutifully to his p. the contribution assigned both by nature and by the law, and pay it cheerfully." On the Ἔρανος in general see Böckh, Publ. Econ. p. 345, Engl. Tr.; Gr. and Rom. Ant. s. v.; cf. Ps. Dem. 25. 21; 21. 101, with Buttmann's note.

§ 41. **ἑνὸς . . τίς**] "as then each of us has a parent, so ought we to look upon the collective people as the common parent of the state (and therefore entitled to all due maintenance), and so far from depriving them of any part of what the state gives them, we ought, if even there were none of these resources, to look out for other means of preventing . . "

ΚΑΤΑ ΦΙΛΙΠΠΟΥ Δ.

πόλεως κοινοὺς δεῖ γονέας τοὺς σύμπαντας ἡγεῖσθαι, καὶ προσήκει τούτους οὐχ ὅπως ὧν ἡ πόλις δίδωσιν ἀφελέσθαι τι, ἀλλ᾽ εἰ καὶ μηδὲν ἦν τούτων, ἄλλοθεν σκοπεῖν ὅπως μηδενὸς ὄντες ἐνδεεῖς περιοφθήσονται. 42. τοὺς μὲν τοίνυν εὐπόρους ταύτῃ χρωμένους τῇ γνώμῃ οὐ μόνον ἡγοῦμαι τὰ δίκαια ποιεῖν ἄν, ἀλλὰ καὶ τὰ λυσιτελῆ· τὸ γὰρ τῶν ἀναγκαίων τινὰ ἀποστερεῖν κοινῇ κακόνους ἐστὶ ποιεῖν πολλοὺς ἀνθρώπους τοῖς πράγμασιν· τοῖς δ᾽ ἐν ἐνδείᾳ. δι᾽ ὃ δυσχεραίνουσι τὸ πρᾶγμα οἱ τὰς οὐσίας ἔχοντες καὶ κατηγοροῦσι δικαίως, τοῦτ᾽ ἀφελεῖν ἂν συμβουλεύσαιμι. 43. δίειμι δέ, ὥσπερ ἄρτι, τὸν αὐτὸν τρόπον καὶ ὑπὲρ τῶν εὐπόρων, οὐ κατοκνήσας εἰπεῖν τἀληθῆ. ἐμοὶ γὰρ οὐδεὶς οὕτως ἄθλιος οὐδ᾽ ὠμὸς εἶναι δοκεῖ τὴν γνώμην, οὔκουν Ἀθηναίων γε, ὥστε λυπεῖσθαι ταῦτα λαμβάνοντας ὁρῶν τοὺς ἀπόρους καὶ τῶν ἀναγκαίων ἐνδεεῖς ὄντας. 44. ἀλλὰ ποῦ συντρίβεται τὸ πρᾶγμα καὶ ποῦ δυσχεραίνεται; ὅταν τὸ ἀπὸ τῶν κοινῶν ἔθος ἐπὶ τὰ

οὐχ ὅπως... ἀλλ᾽] cf. 6. 9.
§ 42. χρ. τῇ γν.] 4. 6.
ποιεῖν ἄν] Bekk. He now omits ἄν with S, and so Dind. It seems to be required by the argument,— "the wealthy then (as the result of the preceding argument) if they adopt this principle will, I think, not only do what is.." Bekker's present reading can only mean "in adopting.. are doing.." But this was just what he was urging them to do. I therefore retain ἄν.
κοινῇ] Mr. K. well tr. "is to unite them in disaffection to the commonwealth."
δι᾽ ὅ] "which makes."
§ 43. δίειμι] "state the case in the same way on behalf of.."
ἄθλιος] 3. 21. "such a wretch, or so hardhearted."
οὔκουν.. γε] "at any rate among ourselves." Soph. Phil. 907, οὔκουν ἐν οἷς γε ὁρᾷς. Ant. 993.
τοὺς ἀ. καὶ] a description of one and the same class. "the needy, who are in want of the necessaries of life."

§ 44. ποῦ συντρίβεται) "what is it in the thing that gives offence?" "where lies the grievance?" "Simile ductum de curribus in stadio currentibus, ad metam adhaerentibus, aut inter se complicatis eoque confractis." Reiske.
ὅταν τό] "when they see persons transferring the practice followed in regard to the public funds to private." The next section determines the sense of the passage. The rich were discontented on account of the confiscation to which their property was at any moment liable (cf. Böckh, Publ. Econ. bk. 3, c. 14). τὸν λέγοντα is then the popular speaker who, in the interest of the people as he professed, proposed such appropriation of the estates of the rich, and was a favourite accordingly. Cf. 8. 69. ὅστις μὲν... παριδὼν ἃ συνοίσει τῇ πόλει, κρίνει δημεύει, δίδωσι κατηγορεῖ... Schäf. understands τὸν λέγοντα to mean the "dives coram populo causam agens."

[ΔΗΜΟΣΘΕΝΟΥΣ] [10. 45

ἴδια μεταβιβάζοντας ὁρῶσί τινας, καὶ μέγαν μὲν ὄντα παρ᾽ ὑμῖν εὐθέως τὸν λέγοντα, ἀθάνατον δ᾽ ἕνεκ᾽ ἀσφαλείας, ἑτέραν δὲ τὴν κρύβδην ψῆφον τοῦ φανερῶς θορύβου. 45. ταῦτ᾽ ἀπιστίαν, ταῦτ᾽ ὀργὴν ἔχει. δεῖ γάρ, ὦ ἄνδρες Ἀθηναῖοι, δικαίως ἀλλήλοις τῆς πολιτείας κοινωνεῖν, τοὺς μὲν εὐπόρους εἰς μὲν τὸν βίον τὸν ἑαυτῶν ἀσφαλῶς ἔχειν νομίζοντας καὶ ὑπὲρ τούτων μὴ δεδοικότας, εἰς δὲ τοὺς κινδύνους κοινὰ ὑπὲρ τῆς σωτηρίας τὰ ὄντα τῇ πατρίδι παρέχοντας, τοὺς δὲ λοιποὺς τὰ μὲν κοινὰ κοινὰ νομίζοντας καὶ μετέχοντας τὸ μέρος, τὰ δὲ ἑκάστου ἴδια τοῦ κεκτημένου. οὕτω καὶ μικρὰ πόλις μεγάλη γίγνεται καὶ μεγάλη σώζεται. ὡς μὲν οὖν εἴποι τις ἄν, ἃ παρ᾽ ἑκατέρων εἶναι δεῖ, ταῦτ᾽ ἴσως ἐστίν· ὡς δὲ καὶ γένοιτ᾽ ἂν ἐν νόμῳ, διορθώσασθαι δεῖ.

46. Τῶν δὲ παρόντων πραγμάτων καὶ τῆς ταραχῆς πολλὰ πόρρωθέν ἐστι τὰ αἴτια· ἃ εἰ βουλομένοις ὑμῖν ἀκούειν ἐστίν,

ἕνεκ᾽ ἀσφ.] 3. 14.
ἑτέραν] "contradicts your openly expressed applause," which last words Schäf. explains to mean, "plausum coronae manifestum, qui divitem causam agentem nihil non sperare jubeat, quam spem post frustretur ἡ κρύβδην ψῆφος." Dobree understands the passage otherwise: "quum videant suasorem gratiâ florere poenae securum, quippe qui judicum suffragiis absolvatur, etsi clamore condemnetur. Alludit ad παρανόμων γραφάς." But this does not seem to agree with the context.
§ 45. ἔχει] "breed," "produce." 2. 3; supr. 28; infr. 46.
δικαίως] cf. Don. N'ew Cratyl: § 290.
τοὺς μέν, κ.τ.λ.] "the wealthy believing themselves secure in regard to their fortunes, and without apprehension on that score (τούτων referring in a general way to τὸν βίον, 2. 3), and yet in times of danger putting their property at the service of the state for.." cf. 14. 25 sq.
κοινά] 2. 30.

μ. τὸ μέρος] "receiving their share." Madv. 37 a, note.
ἴδια] "and private property as (exclusively) belonging to its owner." Cic. de Off. 1. 7, "justitiae primum munus est ... ut communibus utatur, privatis ut suis."
ὡς ... εἴποι τις ἄν] cf. 6. 3. The meaning is, "this is perhaps a fair statement of the duties of each class; measures should be taken for securing the performance of them under the provisions of a law."
ἐν] "according to," "in conformity with." Thuc. 1. 77. Pl. Crit. 121 B, ἐν τοῖς νόμοις βασιλεύειν. Pl. Legg. 9. 874 C, καθαρὸς ἔστω ἐν τῷ νόμῳ "lege."
§ 46. πόρρωθεν] "of long standing:" cf. § 1.
βουλομένοις .. ἐθέλω] 1. 1. On the dat. Madv. 38 d. "saepius dicitur κατ᾽ ἔλλειψιν infinitivi (ἀκούειν)." Schäf. I rather think the full expression is the more common in Dem. Cf. 18. 11; 21. 130, and other passages collected by Weber, Aristocr. § 18.

ἐθέλω λέγειν. ἐξέστητε, ὦ ἄνδρες Ἀθηναῖοι, τῆς ὑποθέσεως ἐφ' ἧς ὑμᾶς οἱ πρόγονοι κατέλιπον, καὶ τὸ μὲν προΐστασθαι τῶν Ἑλλήνων καὶ δύναμιν συνεστηκυῖαν ἔχοντας πᾶσι τοῖς ἀδικουμένοις βοηθεῖν περίεργον ἐπείσθητε εἶναι καὶ μάταιον ἀνάλωμα ὑπὸ τῶν ταῦτα πολιτευομένων, τὸ δ' ἐν ἡσυχίᾳ διάγειν καὶ μηδὲν τῶν δεόντων πράττειν, ἀλλὰ προϊεμένους καθ' ἓν ἕκαστον πάντα ἑτέροις ἐᾶσαι λαβεῖν, θαυμαστὴν εὐδαιμονίαν καὶ πολλὴν ἀσφάλειαν ἔχειν ᾤεσθε. 47. ἐκ δὲ τούτων παρελθὼν ἐπὶ τὴν τάξιν ἐφ' ἧς ὑμῖν τετάχθαι προσῆκεν ἕτερος, οὗτος εὐδαίμων καὶ μέγας καὶ πολλῶν κύριος γέγονεν, εἰκότως· πρᾶγμα γὰρ ἔντιμον καὶ μέγα καὶ λαμπρόν, καὶ περὶ οὗ πάντα τὸν χρόνον αἱ μέγισται τῶν πόλεων πρὸς αὑτὰς διεφέροντο, Λακεδαιμονίων μὲν ἠτυχηκότων, Θηβαίων δὲ ἀσχόλων διὰ τὸν Φωκικὸν πόλεμον γενομένων, ἡμῶν δὲ ἀμελούντων ἔρημον ἀνείλετο. 48. τοιγάρτοι τὸ μὲν φοβεῖσθαι τοῖς ἄλλοις, τὸ δὲ συμμάχους πολλοὺς ἔχειν καὶ δύναμιν μεγάλην ἐκείνῳ περιγέγονε, καὶ τοσαῦτα πράγματα καὶ τοιαῦτα ἤδη περιέστηκε τοὺς Ἕλληνας ἅπαντας ὥστε μηδ' ὅ τι χρὴ συμβουλεύειν εὔπορον εἶναι.

49. Ὄντων δ', ὦ ἄνδρες Ἀθηναῖοι, τῶν παρόντων πραγμάτων, ὡς ἐγὼ κρίνω, φοβερῶν οὐδένες ἐν μείζονι κινδύνῳ τῶν

ὑποθέσεως] "the principle," the subjective side of the τάξις of the next section. S γρ. has τάξεως here.

προΐστασθαι] cf. 4. 3, note to προστάτως.

συνεστηκυῖαν] 8. 46. "standing."

ἐπείσθητε] "have let yourselves be persuaded."

τῶν ταῦτα π.] "by the politicians of these views," "of this school;" the party referred to in 3. 22 sq. With the expression comp. 3. 29.

καθ' ἓν ἕ.] "one after another." cf. 1. 14.

ἔχειν] "carries with it." supr. 44.

§ 47. ἕτερος] "but in consequence of these things another (a stranger) has stepped forward into the position you ought to have filled and become . ." cf. 8. 67.

καὶ περὶ οὗ] 9. 22, where however the subject is differently treated. The ἔντιμον καὶ μέγα καὶ λαμπρόν here is the honour of being the recognized προστάτης of Hellas, which Philip is here supposed to have gained at the end of the war, but which Dem. would never have admitted.

Λ. μὲν ἠτυχ., κ.τ.λ.] borrowed from 3. 27.

ἔρημον] "uncontested.". 3, l. c.

§ 48. περιγέγονε] "the result to others is alarm, to himself the possession of many allies and great power; and difficulties so many and various encompass the Hellenes, that it is not even easy to know what advice to give."

§ 49. οὐδένες] 1. 14.

[ΔΗΜΟΣΘΕΝΟΥΣ] [10. 50

πάντων εἰσὶν ὑμῶν, οὐ μόνον τῷ μάλιστα ὑμῖν ἐπιβουλεύειν
Φίλιππον, ἀλλὰ καὶ τῷ πάντων ἀργότατα αὐτοὶ διακεῖσθαι.
εἰ τοίνυν τὸ τῶν ὠνίων πλῆθος ὁρῶντες καὶ τὴν εὐετηρίαν τὴν
κατὰ τὴν ἀγορὰν, τούτοις κεκήλησθε ὡς ἐν οὐδενὶ δεινῷ τῆς
πόλεως οὔσης, οὔτε προσηκόντως οὔτ' ὀρθῶς τὸ πρᾶγμα
κρίνετε· 50. ἀγορὰν μὲν γὰρ ἄν τις καὶ πανήγυριν ἐκ
τούτων ἢ φαύλως ἢ καλῶς κατεσκευάσθαι κρίνοι· πόλιν δ'
ἣν ὑπείληφεν, ὃς ἂν τῶν Ἑλλήνων ἄρχειν ἀεὶ βούληται,
μόνην ἂν ἐναντιωθῆναι καὶ τῆς πάντων ἐλευθερίας προστῆ-
ναι, οὐ μὰ Δί' ἐκ τῶν ὠνίων, εἰ καλῶς ἔχει, δοκιμάζειν δεῖ,
ἀλλ' εἰ συμμάχων εὐνοίᾳ πιστεύει καὶ τοῖς ὅπλοις ἰσχύει,
ταῦθ' ὑπὲρ τῆς πόλεως δεῖ σκοπεῖν ἃ σφαλερῶς ὑμῖν καὶ οὐ
καλῶς ἅπαντα ἔχει. 51. γνοίητε δ' ἄν, εἰ σκέψαισθε ἐκείνως.
πότε μάλιστα ἐν ταραχῇ τὰ τῶν Ἑλλήνων γέγονε πράγματα; οὐδένα γὰρ χρόνον ἄλλον ἢ τὸν νυνὶ παρόντα οὐδ'
ἂν εἷς εἴποι. τὸν μὲν γὰρ ἄλλον ἅπαντα εἰς δύο ταῦτα
διῄρητο τὰ τῶν Ἑλλήνων, Λακεδαιμονίους καὶ ἡμᾶς, τῶν δ'
ἄλλων Ἑλλήνων οἱ μὲν ἡμῖν οἱ δὲ ἐκείνοις ὑπήκουον. βασιλεὺς δὲ καθ' αὑτὸν μὲν ὁμοίως ἅπασιν ἄπιστος ἦν, τοὺς δὲ

τῷ ... ἐπιβ] supr. § 11 sq.
ἀργ... B.] 6. 3.
τό.. πλῆθος] Benseler omits τό
with S. The omission is obviously
due to the following τῶν. The art.
cannot be dispensed with.
εὐετηρίαν.. ἀγοράν] "pretiorum
salubritatem." Reiske. cf. Thuc.
2. 38; Isocr. 4. 42, ἐμπόριον γὰρ
ἐν μέσῳ τῆς Ἑλλάδος τὸν Πειραιᾶ
κατεσκευάσατο, τοσαύτην ἔχονθ'
ὑπερβολήν, ὥσθ' ἃ παρὰ τῶν ἄλλων
ἐν παρ' ἑκάστων χαλεπόν ἐστι λαβεῖν, ταῦθ' ἅπαντα παρ' αὑτῆς ῥᾴδιον
εἶναι πορίσασθαι.
κεκήλησθε ὡς] "have let yourselves be beguiled into thinking."
Madv. 181, r. 2.
§ 50. πανήγυριν] "fair." cf. Bekker's *Charicles*, p. 227, Engl. tr.
πόλιν δ'] "but for a city which
every successive aspirant to dominion over Hellas (9. 37) has deemed
could alone oppose him, and stand
forward in defence of the liberty of
all, its prosperity assuredly ought
not to be tested by the abundance
of its market wares, but whether
..., these, I say, are the questions
one ought to consider in regard to
such a city, and these .." cf. 6. 10.
καὶ οὐ καλῶς ἅπαντα ἔχει] Bekk.
st. from F T Ω; Bekk. καὶ οὐδαμῶς
ἅπαντα κ. ἔχει, and so Vöm. and
Dind. S pr. m. has καὶ οὐδαμῶς
ἅπαντα ἔχει, obviously a distortion
of the reading in F T Ω.
§ 51. γνοίητε, κ.τ.λ] Madv. 135.
οὐδένα γάρ] "certainly no one
could name any other than .."
εἰς δ. ταῦτα διῄρητο] S omits εἰς
δ. ταῦτα and has διῃρεῖτο: it omits
also δ' after τῶν. "was divided
into the two parties of the L. and
ourselves." Thuc. 1. 1; Id. 3. 82
init.
δύο ταῦτα] cf. § 4.
καθ' αὑτόν] "upon his own account."

—53.] ΚΑΤΑ ΦΙΛΙΠΠΟΥ Δ. 107

κρατουμένους τῷ πολέμῳ προσλαμβάνων, ἄχρι οὗ τοῖς ἑτέροις ἐξ ἴσου ποιήσαι, διεπιστεύετο, ἔπειτ᾽ οὐχ ἧττον αὐτὸν ἐμίσουν οὓς σώσειε τῶν ὑπαρχόντων ἐχθρῶν ἐξ ἀρχῆς. 52. νῦν δὲ πρῶτον μὲν βασιλεὺς ἅπασι τοῖς Ἕλλησιν οἰκείως ἔχει, καὶ πάντων δὴ ἥκιστα ἡμῖν, ἂν τι μὴ νῦν ἐπανορθωσώμεθα· ἔπειτα προστασίαι πολλαὶ καὶ πανταχόθεν γίγνονται, καὶ τοῦ πρωτεύειν ἀντιποιοῦνται μὲν πάντες, ἀφεστᾶσι δ᾽ ἔνιοι καὶ φθονοῦσι καὶ ἀπιστοῦσιν ἑαυτοῖς, οὐχ ὡς ἔδει, καὶ γεγόνασι καθ᾽ αὑτοὺς ἕκαστοι, Ἀργεῖοι Θηβαῖοι Λακεδαιμόνιοι Κορίνθιοι Ἀρκάδες ἡμεῖς. 53. ἀλλ᾽ ὅμως εἰς τοσαῦτα μέρη καὶ τοσαύτας δυναστείας διῃρημένων τῶν Ἑλληνικῶν πραγμάτων, εἰ δεῖ τἀληθῆ μετὰ παρρησίας εἰπεῖν, τὰ παρ᾽ οὐδέσι τούτων ἀρχεῖα καὶ βουλευτήρια ἐρημότερα ἄν τις ἴδοι τῶν Ἑλληνικῶν πραγμάτων ἢ τὰ παρ᾽ ἡμῖν, εἰκότως· οὔτε γὰρ φιλῶν οὔτε πιστεύων οὔτε

προσλαμβάνων] "he used to take to him (take up the cause of) those who were getting worsted in war, and retain their confidence till he put them on an equality with . . "

ἄχρι οὗ .. τ.] Madv. 114 c, τ. 1. Vöm. and Benseler read ἄχρις, to avoid the hiatus.

οὓς σώσειε] 9. 43, οὓς αἴσθοιντο.

τῶν ὑ. ἐχ. ἐξ ἀρχῆς] Mr. K. inadvertently tr. "*his* original enemies." The meaning clearly is the "original enemies" of the parties succoured.

§ 52. καὶ πάντων] "exspectes ἀλλὰ πάντων. Sed Graeci scriptores enuntiationes negantes, quarum de genere nostra est, alientibus persaepe jungunt per copulativam καί." Schäf. The meaning is, "the king is on friendly terms with all the H. and therefore with us; but with us least of all, unless we do something to put things on a better footing." καὶ therefore may be tr. "though."

προστασίαι] Instead of Athens being acknowledged as the champion of Hellas, "protectorates are starting up in great numbers on all sides." On all sides states were aspiring προΐστασθαι τῶν Ἑ., but on condition that they had the hegemony. supr. 6, οἱ μὲν ὑπὲρ τῆς ἡ. ἡμῖν ἀντιλέγουσιν.

ἀφεστᾶσι] "have seceded," "hold themselves aloof."

ἑαυτοῖς] "one another." cf. 4. 10.

οὐχ ὡς ἔδει] "secus quam oportebat." 18. 271, φοράν τινα τῶν πραγμάτων χαλεπὴν καὶ οὐχ οἵαν ἔδει. On οὐχ cf. 3. 1; 4. 38, ὡς οὐκ ἔδει.

§ 53. δυναστείας, used in § 4 in a more strictly political sense, here as referring to the states just mentioned means "powers," "leaderships." cf. Isocr. 4. 22, where the word is used as = ἡγεμονία.

διῃρ. τῶν Ἑ. πρ.] "the politics of H.," or simply "Hellas:" cf. Thuc. 1. 110 in.

οὐδέσι] 1. 19. "there are none whose town-halls and council-chambers one would see more deserted by H. politics . ."

ἴδοι τῶν Ἑ. πρ.] cf. 18. 59; 3. 25.

φιλῶν] "from love."

[ΔΗΜΟΣΘΕΝΟΥΣ]   [10. 54

φοβούμενος οὐδεὶς ἡμῖν διαλέγεται. 54. αἴτιον δὲ τούτων οὐχ ἕν, ὦ ἄνδρες Ἀθηναῖοι, (ῥᾴδιον γὰρ ἂν ἦν ὑμῖν μεταθεῖναι), ἀλλὰ πολλὰ καὶ παντοδαπὰ ἐκ παντὸς ἡμαρτημένα τοῦ χρόνου, ὧν τὸ καθ' ἕκαστον ἐάσας, εἰς ὃ πάντα συντείνει λέξω, δεηθεὶς ὑμῶν, ἂν λέγω τἀληθῆ μετὰ παρρησίας, μηδὲν ἀχθεσθῆναί μοι. πέπραται τὰ συμφέροντα ἐφ' ἑκάστου τῶν καιρῶν, καὶ μετειλήφατε ὑμεῖς μὲν τὴν σχολὴν καὶ τὴν ἡσυχίαν, ἐφ' ὧν κεκηλημένοι τοῖς ἀδικοῦσιν οὐ πικρῶς ἔχετε, ἕτεροι δὲ τὰς τιμὰς ἔχουσιν. 55. καὶ τὰ μὲν περὶ τἆλλα οὐκ ἄξιον ἐξετάσαι νῦν· ἀλλ' ἐπειδάν τι τῶν πρὸς Φίλιππον ἐμπέσῃ, εὐθὺς ἀναστάς τις λέγει ὡς οὐ δεῖ ληρεῖν οὐδὲ γράφειν πόλεμον, παραθεὶς εὐθέως ἑξῆς τὸ τὴν εἰρήνην ἄγειν ὡς ἀγαθὸν καὶ τὸ τρέφειν μεγάλην δύναμιν ὡς χαλεπόν, καὶ "διαρπάζειν τινὲς τὰ χρήματα βούλονται," καὶ ἄλλους λόγους ὡς οἷόν τε ἀληθεστάτους λέγουσιν. 56. ἀλλὰ δεῖ δήπου τὴν μὲν εἰρήνην ἄγειν οὐχ ὑμᾶς πείθειν,

διαλέγεται] 2. 6.
§ 54. αἴτιον δέ] cf. 9. 2. "and this state of things comes not from a single cause, but from errors many and various committed throughout times gone by."
ἐκ π. . . τοῦ χρ.] 4. 1.
ὧν . . ἐάσας] "waiving an enumeration."
μηδὲν ἀχθ.] cf. 9. 3.
ἐφ' ἑ. τῶν κ.] "on the occasion of each of your . ." "upon every opportunity." 9. 38. Benseler reads ἀφ' from S—a mere clerical error elevated to the dignity of a new reading.
μετειλήφατε] "have received as your share." Madv. 57, note.
τὴν σχολήν] 8. 53, ἐκ δὲ τούτων περιγίγνεται ὑμῖν μὲν ἡ σχολὴ καὶ τὸ μηδὲν ἤδη ποιεῖν. . τούτοις δὲ αἱ χάριτες καὶ ὁ μισθὸς ὁ τούτων.
κεκηλημένοι] supr. 49.
ἕτεροι] "intelligendi sunt proditores a Philippo corrupti." Schäf.
τὰς τ.] "while others get the rewards," = the ὁ μισθός of the pass. just quoted.

§ 55. καὶ . . ἀλλ'] cf. 9. 59.
τὰ . . περὶ τἆλλα] "the circumstances of the other cases." 8. 52.
τι τῶν πρὸς Φ.] "any of the questions between us and P." 14. 2, ὡς γνώμης ἔχω περὶ τῶν πρὸς βασιλέα, and ib. § 6.
ἐμπέσῃ] "comes up," "is started." Pl. Rep. 1. 354 B, λόγου ἐμπεσόντος ὅτι . . Also of the speaker, 18. 42, ἀλλὰ γὰρ ἐμπέπτωκα εἰς λόγους.
τις] one of the peace-at-any-price party.
γράφειν π.] supr. § 18.
παραθεὶς . . ἑξῆς] "going on immediately to say 'what a blessing it is to be at peace. . .'" For τὸ τὴν εἰρ. Bens. had τῷ . . from S.
ὡς οἷόν τε ἀληθεστάτους] Bekk. at. from S ; ὡς οἴονται ἀλ. Bekk.
§ 56. ἀλλὰ δεῖ] "but surely it is not you that need to be persuaded to keep the peace—you that sit persuaded already—but the person who is committing hostilities." For οἵ Bekk. had οἷ γε. He now omits γε, with S.

οἱ πεπεισμένοι κάθησθε, ἀλλὰ τὸν τὰ τοῦ πολέμου πράττοντα· ἂν γὰρ ἐκεῖνος πεισθῇ, τά γε ἀφ' ὑμῶν ὑπάρχει· νομίζειν δ' εἶναι χαλεπὰ οὐχ ὅσα ἂν εἰς σωτηρίαν δαπανῶμεν, ἀλλ' ἃ πεισόμεθ' ἂν μὴ ταῦτ' ἐθέλωμεν ποιεῖν, καὶ τὸ διαρπασθήσεσθαι τὰ χρήματα τῷ φυλακὴν εὑρεῖν δι' ἧς σωθήσεται κωλύειν, οὐχὶ τῷ τοῦ συμφέροντος ἀποστῆναι. 57. καίτοι ἔγωγε ἀγανακτῶ καὶ τοῦτο, εἰ τὰ μὲν χρήματα λυπεῖ τινὰς ὑμῶν εἰ διαρπασθήσεται, ἃ καὶ φυλάττειν καὶ κολάζειν τοὺς ἁρπάζοντας ἐφ' ὑμῖν ἐστί, τὴν δὲ Ἑλλάδα πᾶσαν ἐφεξῆς οὑτωσὶ Φίλιππος ἁρπάζων οὐ λυπεῖ, καὶ ταῦτ' ἐφ' ὑμᾶς ἁρπάζων. 58. τί ποτ' οὖν, ὦ ἄνδρες Ἀθηναῖοι, τὸν μὲν οὕτω φανερῶς ἀδικοῦντα καὶ πόλεις καταλαμβάνοντα οὐδεὶς πώποτε τοῦτον εἶπεν ὡς ἀδικεῖ καὶ πόλεμον ποιεῖ, τοὺς δὲ μὴ ἐπιτρέπειν μηδὲ προΐεσθαι ταῦτα συμβουλεύοντας, τούτους πόλεμον ποιεῖν φασίν; ὅτι τὴν αἰτίαν τῶν ἐκ τοῦ πολέμου συμβησομένων δυσχερῶν (ἀνάγκη γάρ, ἀνάγκη πολλὰ λυπηρὰ ἐκ τοῦ πολέμου γίγνεσθαι) τοῖς ὑπὲρ ὑμῶν τὰ βέλτιστα λέγειν οἰομένοις ἀναθεῖναι βούλονται. 59. ἡγοῦνται γάρ, ἐὰν μὲν ὑμεῖς ὁμοθυμαδὸν ἐκ μιᾶς γνώμης Φίλιππον ἀμύνησθε, κἀκείνου κρατήσειν ὑμᾶς καὶ αὐτοῖς οὐκ ἔσεσθαι μισθαρνεῖν, ἂν δ' ἀπὸ τῶν πρώτων

τά γε ἀφ' ὑμ. ὑπ.] 8. 5, τά γε ἀφ' ὑμῶν ἕτοιμα ὑπάρχοντα ὁρῶ. "quae quidem a vobis praestanda ;" "*your part,*" "you are quite ready on your part."

καὶ τό] "and prevent that 'plundering the treasury' they talk of (supr. 55) by devising means for its safe keeping, not by withdrawing from our interest." cf. 8. 53, 54.

§ 57.] ἀγ. . . τοῦτο] Madv. 27; Heind. Pl. *Phaed.* § 21. "yet this too moves my indignation that some of you are pained at the possible embezzlement . . (on εἰ δ. Madv. 132 *d*), but are not pained to see P. plundering all H. in detail in the way he is doing, and plundering it moreover in order to attack you."

For καὶ τοῦτο Dem. has (8. 55) καὶ αὐτὸ τοῦτο, and so Bekk. He now omits αὐτό, with F S and pr. T.

οὑτωσί] 1. 20; supr. 34. Observe the οὐ which legitimately follows εἰ, "that." Madv. 194 *c*, and 202, r., and note to 1. 34.

§ 58. τί ποτ'] "why then, I ask, is it that of the man . . has said that . ."

ὡς ἀδικεῖ] Madv. 159, r. 3.

πόλ. ποιεῖ] Bekk. ; πολεμοποιεῖ Dind., as Xen. *Hell.* 5. 2. 30, λαμβάνω τουτονὶ Ἰσμήνιον ὡς πολεμοποιεῖ.

ἀναθεῖναι] "cast upon." 18. 17, τὰ πεπραγμένα . . ἀνατιθεὶς ἐμοί.

§ 59. ὁμ. ἐκ μιᾶς γν.] cf. on 3. 6. "heartily out of one mind," "with one heart and mind." Dind. encloses ἐκ μ. γνώμης in brackets.

ἀπὸ . . θ.] "If on the first alarm

[ΔΗΜΟΣΘΕΝΟΥΣ] [10. 60

θορύβων αἰτιασάμενοί τινας πρὸς τὸ κρίνειν τράπησθε, αὐτοὶ μὲν τούτων κατηγοροῦντες ἀμφότερ' ἕξειν, καὶ παρ' ὑμῖν εὐδοκιμήσειν καὶ παρ' ἐκείνου χρήματα λήψεσθαι, ὑμᾶς δ' ὑπὲρ ὧν δεῖ παρὰ τούτων δίκην λαβεῖν, παρὰ τῶν ὑπὲρ ὑμῶν εἰρηκότων λήψεσθαι. 60. αἱ μὲν ἐλπίδες αἱ τούτων αὗται, καὶ τὸ κατασκεύασμα τὸ τῶν αἰτιῶν, ὡς ἄρα βούλονταί τινες πόλεμον ποιῆσαι· ἐγὼ δ' οἶδα ἀκριβῶς ὅτι οὐ γράψαντος Ἀθηναίων οὐδενὸς πόλεμον πολλὰ Φίλιππος ἔχει τῶν τῆς πόλεως καὶ νῦν εἰς Καρδίαν πέπομφε βοήθειαν. εἰ μέντοι βουλόμεθ' ἡμεῖς μὴ προσποιεῖσθαι πολεμεῖν ἡμῖν ἐκεῖνον, ἀνοητότατος πάντων ἂν εἴη εἰ τοῦτ' ἐξελέγχοι· ὅταν γὰρ οἱ ἀδικούμενοι ἀρνῶνται, τί τῷ ἀδικοῦντι προσήκει; 61. ἀλλ' ἐπειδὰν ἐφ' ἡμᾶς αὐτοὺς ἴῃ, τί φήσομεν τότε; ἐκεῖνος μὲν γὰρ οὐ πολεμεῖν, ὥσπερ οὐδὲ Ὠρείταις τῶν στρατιωτῶν ὄντων ἐν τῇ χώρᾳ, οὐδὲ Φεραίοις πρότερον, πρὸς τὰ τείχη προσβάλλων αὐτῶν, οὐδ' Ὀλυνθίοις ἐξ ἀρχῆς, ἕως ἐν αὐτῇ τῇ χώρᾳ τὸ στράτευμα παρῆν ἔχων. ἢ καὶ τότε τοὺς ἀμύνεσθαι κελεύοντας πόλεμον ποιεῖν φήσομεν; οὐκοῦν ὑπόλοιπον δουλεύειν· οὐ γὰρ ἄλλο γε οὐδὲν ἔνι.

you arraign certain persons, and occupy yourselves with bringing them to trial, they by accusing them will secure both advantages, be popular with you.."

ἀμφ... καὶ .. καὶ] 1. 14.

§ 60. αἱ μέν, κ.τ.λ.] "such are the hopes of these men, such the contrivance of their charges that .." Madv. 10.

For πολλὰ Dem. 8. 58 has καὶ ἄλλα πολλὰ Φ., which is Dindorf's reading here.

εἰς Καρδίαν] cf. 9. 35.

μὴ προσποιεῖσθαι] "to pretend that he is not," "assume that he is not." 6. 33, οὐχὶ βουλοίμην. In 8. 58 the emphasis of the last words of the sentence is different. For ἡμῖν ἐκεῖνον, Dem. has αὐτὸν ἡμῖν.

ἀρνῶνται] sc. ἀδικούμενοι. Compare with Schäfer Eur. Alc. 1177, οὐ γὰρ εὐτυχῶν ἀρνήσομαι, where

Monk quotes Orest. 1597. ἀρνεῖ κατακτὰς κἀφ' ὕβρει λέγεις τάδε.

τί ... προσήκει] Reih. understands ὁμολογεῖν from the preceding ἀρνῶνται, as 19. 81, μὴ δὴ ταῦτα λέγειν αὐτὸν ἐᾶτε, ἀλλ' ὅτι οὐκ ἀπολώλασι Φωκεῖς δεικνύναι, sc. κελεύετε. It is not necessary to supply any thing. "what should the perpetrator of the wrong do?"

§ 61.] For ἐφ' ἡμᾶς αὐτοὺς Dem. (8. 59) has ἐπ' αὐτοὺς ἡμᾶς.

μὲν γάρ] cf. 9. 17. On the subject of this section cf. 9. 10 sq. "he of course will protest that he is not making war, as he did to.. as he did to the Ph. before, when he was assaulting their walls, and to the Ol. at first, until he was actually in their territory at the head of his army."

οὐ] i. e. οὐ φήσει π.

π. ποιεῖν] supr. 58; 9. 7.

οὐ γὰρ ἄλλο .... ἔνι] 8. 59. οὐ

ΚΑΤΑ ΦΙΛΙΠΠΟΥ Δ.

62. Καὶ μὴν οὐχ ὑπὲρ τῶν ἴσων ὑμῖν καί τισι τῶν ἄλλων ἀνθρώπων ἔσθ' ὁ κίνδυνος· οὐ γὰρ ἐφ' αὑτῷ ποιήσασθαι τὴν πόλιν βούλεται Φίλιππος ὑμῶν, οὔ, ἀλλ' ὅλως ἀνελεῖν. οἶδε γὰρ ἀκριβῶς ὅτι δουλεύειν μὲν ὑμεῖς οὔτ' ἐθελήσετε οὔτ', ἂν ἐθέλητε, ἐπιστήσεσθε· ἄρχειν γὰρ εἰώθατε· πράγματα δὲ παρασχεῖν αὐτῷ, ἂν καιρὸν λάβητε, πλείω τῶν ἄλλων ἀνθρώπων ἁπάντων δυνήσεσθε. διὰ ταῦτα ὑμῶν οὐχὶ φείσεται, εἴπερ ἐγκρατὴς γενήσεται. 63. ὡς οὖν ὑπὲρ τῶν ἐσχάτων ἐσομένου τοῦ ἀγῶνος ὑμῖν, οὕτω προσήκει γιγνώσκειν, καὶ τοὺς πεπρακότας αὑτοὺς ἐκείνῳ φανερῶς ἀποτυμπανίσαι· οὐ γὰρ ἔστιν, οὐκ ἔστι τῶν ἔξω τῆς πόλεως ἐχθρῶν κρατῆσαι πρὶν ἂν τοὺς ἐν αὐτῇ τῇ πόλει κολάσητε ἐχθρούς, ἀλλ' ἀνάγκη τούτοις ὥσπερ προβόλοις προσπταίσαντας ὑστερίζειν ἐκείνων. 64. πόθεν οἴεσθε νῦν αὐτὸν ὑβρίζειν ὑμᾶς (οὐδὲν γὰρ ἄλλο ἔμοιγε δοκεῖ ποιεῖν ἢ τοῦτο) καὶ τοὺς μὲν ἄλλους εὖ ποιοῦντα, εἰ μηδὲν ἄλλο, ἐξαπατᾶν, ὑμῖν δὲ ἀπειλεῖν ἤδη. οἷον Θετταλοὺς πολλὰ δοὺς ὑπηγάγετο εἰς

γὰρ ἄλλο γ' οὐδέν ἐστι μεταξὺ τοῦ μήτ' ἀμύνεσθαι μήτ' ἄγειν ἡσυχίαν ἐᾶσθαι.

§ 62. ὑπὲρ τῶν ἴσων] "for an equal risk." Thuc. 2. 42, διδασκαλίαν τε ποιούμενος μὴ περὶ ἴσου ὑμῖν εἶναι τὸν ἀγῶνα καὶ οἷς τῶνδε μηδὲν ὑπάρχει ὁμοίως. For τισι τῶν ἄλλων, which is feeble, Dem. has τοῖς ἄλλοις, which is obviously required to give full rhetorical force to the argument.

οὐ γὰρ . . οὔ] (the second οὐ is wanting in 8. 60). Cf. Dem. 21. 112, οὐ μέτεστι τῶν ἴσων, οὐ μέτεστιν, οὔ. Soph. *Aj.* 970.

ἐθελήσετε] "consent to be subject, nor if you did would you know how."

§ 63. ὡς . . . οὕτω] cf. 4. 16. Thuc. 7. 15, ὡς τῶν ἡγεμόνων ὑμῖν μὴ μεμπτῶν γεγνημένων οὕτω τὴν γνώμην ἔχετε. Don. *Gr. Gr.* p. 605. "you ought then to make up your minds that the struggle will be one for life and death." For ἐσομένου 8. 61 has the more forcible ὄντος.

Bekk. had φανερῶς μισεῖν καὶ ἀποτυμπανίσαι. He now omits μισεῖν καί, with S T.

ἀποτυμπανίσαι] 9. 61.

οὐ γὰρ . . ἐχθρούς] taken from 8. 61; 9. 53.

προβόλοις] Pt. Dem. 25. 84, μὴ δὴ πρὸς οὓς αὐτὸς ἔχωσας λιμένας καὶ προβόλων ἀνέπλησας, πρὸς τούτοις προσορμίζειν. On account of προσπταίσαντες we must understand the word here in a metaphorical sense—"stumbling-blocks," "stones in the way."

ὑ. ἐκείνων] "and so be too late for the others," i. e. your foreign enemies.

§ 64. καὶ τοὺς μέν] "and whilst by conferring benefits on them he deceives the rest, if nothing else (19. 98, ἡ ἀπολογία, καὶ εἰ μηδὲν ἄλλο, τοὔνομα γοῦν ἔχει φιλάνθρωπον), has begun (ἤδη) to threaten you."

πολλά] 2. 7; 6. 22.

ὑπήγαγετο] "artfully led them on," "lured them"—the middle of

[ΔΗΜΟΣΘΕΝΟΥΣ] [10. 65

τὴν νῦν παροῦσαν δουλείαν οὐδ' ἂν εἰπεῖν δύναιτο οὐδεὶς ὅσα τοὺς ταλαιπώρους Ὀλυνθίους πρότερον δοὺς Ποτίδαιαν ἐξηπάτησε καὶ πολλὰ ἕτερα· Θηβαίους τὰ νῦν ὑπάγει τὴν Βοιωτίαν αὐτοῖς παραδοὺς καὶ ἀπαλλάξας πολέμου πολλοῦ καὶ χαλεποῦ. 65. ὥστε καρπωσάμενοί τινα ἕκαστοι τούτων πλεονεξίαν οἱ μὲν ἤδη πεπόνθασιν ἃ δὴ πεπόνθασιν, οἱ δ' ὅ τι ἄν ποτε συμβῇ πείσονται. ὑμεῖς δὲ ὧν μὲν ἀπεστέρησθε σιωπῶ· ἀλλ' ἐν αὐτῷ τῷ τὴν εἰρήνην ποιήσασθαι πόσα ἐξηπάτησθε, πόσων ἀπεστέρησθε. οὐχὶ Φωκέας, οὐ Πύλας, οὐχὶ τὰ ἐπὶ Θρᾴκης, Δορίσκον, Σέρριον, τὸν Κερσοβλέπτην αὐτόν; οὐ νῦν Καρδίαν ἔχει καὶ ὁμολογεῖ; 66. τί ποτ' οὖν ἐκείνως τοῖς ἄλλοις καὶ ὑμῖν τοῦτον τὸν τρόπον προσφέρεται; ὅτι ἐν μόνῃ τῶν πασῶν πόλεων τῇ ὑμετέρᾳ ἄδεια ὑπὲρ τῶν ἐχθρῶν λέγειν δέδοται, καὶ λαβόντα χρήματα αὐτὸν ἀσφαλές ἐστι λέγειν παρ' ὑμῖν, κἂν ἀφῃρημένοι τὰ ὑμέτερα αὐτῶν ἦτε. 67. οὐκ ἦν ἀσφαλὲς λέγειν ἐν Ὀλύνθῳ τὰ Φιλίππου μὴ συνευπεπονθότων τῶν πολλῶν Ὀλυνθίων τῷ Ποτίδαιαν καρποῦσθαι· οὐκ ἦν ἀσφαλὲς λέγειν ἐν Θετταλίᾳ τὰ Φιλίππου μὴ συνευπεπονθότος τοῦ πλήθους τοῦ

course expressing that it was with a selfish object. 6. 31.

Ποτίδαιαν] 2. 7; 6. 20.

ὑπάγει] Bekk. st. from S: ὑπάγεται Bekk.

πολλοῦ] "tedious," i. e. the Phocian War. cf. Grote, 11. 520.

§ 65. ὥστε, κ.τ.λ.] "so that these people, after enjoying each of them a certain advantage, have some of them.." cf. 6. 20 sq.

ἃ δὴ π.] Bekk. st. from S. "what we all know." 3. 8, ἐχόντων ὣς ἔχουσι. Dem. 8, 63 has ἃ δὴ πάντες ἴσασιν, and so Bekk. and Dind.

ὅ τι ἂν ... σ.] "whatever may one day befall them." In 8, 69 we have ὅταν πότε σ., "sooner or later."

ἡμεῖς δὲ ... ἀλλ'] "and as to yourselves, to say nothing of.." 9. 35.

ἐν αὐτῷ τῷ] 6. 7; 9. 15 sq.

Φωκέας] depending on ἔχει.

Καρδίαν] cf. 9. 16, 35. In R. 64, τὴν πόλιν τὴν Καρδιανῶν. ὁμολογεῖ, i. e. ἔχειν.

§ 66.] For τοῦτον τὸν τρ. Dem. 8. 64 has οὐ τὸν αὐτὸν τρ. ἡμῖν.

ὅτι ἐν μ.] "because your city is the only one of them all in which liberty is allowed to speak for its enemies—the only one in which a man may safely after taking a bribe himself speak before you." αὐτὸν to bring out the contrast between the hireling speaker and the people ἀφῃρημένοι.

ἄδεια ... λ.] 1. 15, εἰς ἀνάγκην ποιεῖν.

§ 67. οὐκ ἦν] "it was not safe at O. to speak in favour of P. without the people sharing the benefit by enjoying P." 6. 20.

ΚΑΤΑ ΦΙΛΙΠΠΟΥ Δ.

Θετταλῶν τῷ τοὺς τυράννους ἐκβαλεῖν Φίλιππον αὐτοῖς καὶ τὴν πυλαίαν ἀποδοῦναι· οὐκ ἦν ἐν Θήβαις ἀσφαλές, πρὶν τὴν Βοιωτίαν ὑπέδωκε καὶ τοὺς Φωκέας ἀνεῖλεν. 68. ἀλλ' Ἀθήνησιν οὐ μόνον Ἀμφίπολιν καὶ τὴν Καρδιανῶν χώραν ἀπεστερηκότος Φιλίππου, ἀλλὰ καὶ κατασκευάζοντος ἡμῖν ἐπιτείχισμα τὴν Εὔβοιαν καὶ νῦν ἐπὶ Βυζάντιον παριόντος ἀσφαλές ἐστι λέγειν ὑπὲρ Φιλίππου. καὶ γάρ τοι τούτων μὲν ἐκ πτωχῶν ἔνιοι ταχὺ πλούσιοι γίγνονται καὶ ἐξ ἀνωνύμων καὶ ἀδόξων ἔνδοξοι καὶ γνώριμοι, ὑμεῖς δὲ τοὐναντίον ἐκ μὲν ἐνδόξων ἄδοξοι ἐκ δ' εὐπόρων ἄποροι. 69. πόλεως γὰρ ἔγωγε πλοῦτον ἡγοῦμαι συμμάχους πίστιν εὔνοιαν, ὧν πάντων ὑμεῖς ἐστὲ ἄποροι· ἐκ δὲ τοῦ τούτων ὀλιγώρως ὑμᾶς ἔχειν καὶ ἐᾶν τοῦτον τὸν τρόπον τὰ πράγματα φέρεσθαι ὁ μὲν εὐδαίμων καὶ μέγας καὶ φοβερὸς πᾶσιν Ἕλλησι καὶ βαρβάροις, ὑμεῖς δ' ἔρημοι καὶ ταπεινοί, τῇ μὲν κατὰ τὴν ἀγορὰν εὐετηρίᾳ λαμπροί, τῇ δ' ὧν προσῆκε παρασκευῇ καταγέλαστοι.

70. Οὐ τὸν αὐτὸν δὲ τρόπον περί τε ὑμῶν καὶ περὶ αὑτῶν ἐνίους τῶν λεγόντων ὁρῶ βουλενομένους· ὑμᾶς μὲν γὰρ ἡσυχίαν ἄγειν φασὶ δεῖν, κἂν τις ὑμᾶς ἀδικῇ, αὐτοὶ δ' οὐ δύνανται παρ' ὑμῖν ἡσυχίαν ἄγειν οὐδενὸς αὐτοὺς ἀδικοῦντος. καίτοι λοιδορίας χωρίς, εἴ τις ἔροιτο "εἰπέ μοι, τί δὴ γιγνώσκων ἀκριβῶς Ἀριστόμηδες (οὐδεὶς γὰρ τὰ τοιαῦτ'

ἐκβαλεῖν] 1. 12; 6. 20.
πυλαίαν] 6. 20.
Βοιωτίαν ἀπέδωκε] cf. 19. 141.
§ 68. κατασκευάζοντος] "in converting E. into a fortress against us (9. 17), and is now on his march to attack D." (9. 17, 34).
ἐκ πτωχῶν] 3. 29.
§ 69. ἄποροι] "bankrupt."
ὀλ.... ἔχειν] "regarding these things with indifference." Lys. 26. 9, οὐκ ἀξιον τῆς δοκιμασίας ὀλιγώρως ἔχειν. Don. § 453.
φέρεσθαι] In 8. 67 West., &c., read στέρεσθαι, with S and γρ F—a mere error of the copyist. "to take their course."
τῇ μέν] 8. 67, τῇ τῶν ὠνίων ἀφθο-

ρίᾳ λαμπροί, the rest of the sentence being the same as here. cf. supr. 49.
§ 70. λ. χωρίς] "raillery apart." 9. 4, κολακείας χωρίς. Bekk. st. omits καὶ ἀπρόγμονα after ἀσφαλῆ, with S. The words are retained by Dind. "why is it that when you know... why is it that you choose not the quiet and easy life, but the one surrounded by danger?"
Ἀριστόμηδες] According to Plutarch, Reip. gerendae Praec. c. 14, Demosthenes made no attacks of this kind in his Philippics: καίτοι γε καὶ Δημοσθένης ἐν τῷ δικανικῷ τὸ λοίδορον ἔχει μόνῳ, οἱ δὲ Φιλιππικοὶ καθαρεύουσι καὶ σκώμματος καὶ βωμο-

ἀγνοεῖ) τὸν μὲν τῶν ἰδιωτῶν βίον ἀσφαλῆ καὶ ἀκίνδυνον ὄντα, τὸν δὲ τῶν πολιτευομένων φιλαίτιον καὶ σφαλερὸν καὶ καθ' ἑκάστην ἡμέραν ἀγώνων καὶ κακῶν μεστόν, οὐ τὸν ἡσύχιον καὶ ἀπράγμονα ἀλλὰ τὸν ἐν τοῖς κινδύνοις αἱρῇ;" 71. τί ἂν εἴποις ; εἰ γὰρ ὃ βέλτιστον εἰπεῖν ἂν ἔχοις, τοῦτό σοι δοίημεν ἀληθὲς λέγειν, ὡς ὑπὲρ φιλοτιμίας καὶ δόξης ταῦτα πάντα ποιεῖς, θαυμάζω τί δή ποτε σαυτῷ μὲν ὑπὲρ τούτων ἅπαντα ποιητέον εἶναι νομίζεις καὶ πονητέον καὶ κινδυνευτέον, τῇ πόλει δὲ προέσθαι ταῦτα μετὰ ῥᾳθυμίας συμβουλεύεις. οὐ γὰρ ἐκεῖνό γ' ἂν εἴποις, ὡς δὲ μὲν ἐν τῇ πόλει δεῖ τινὰ φαίνεσθαι, τὴν πόλιν δ' ἐν τοῖς Ἕλλησι μηδενὸς ἀξίαν εἶναι. 72. καὶ μὴν οὐδ' ἐκεῖνό γε ὁρῶ, ὡς τῇ μὲν πόλει ἀσφαλὲς τὸ τὰ αὑτῆς πράττειν, σοὶ δὲ ἐπικίνδυνον εἰ μηδὲν τῶν ἄλλων πλέον περιεργάσῃ, ἀλλὰ τοὐναντίον σοὶ μὲν ἐξ ὧν ἐργάζῃ καὶ περιεργάζῃ τοὺς ἐσχάτους ὄντας κινδύνους, τῇ πόλει δὲ ἐκ τῆς ἡσυχίας. 73. ἀλλὰ νὴ Δία παππῷα καὶ πατρῷα δόξα σοι ὑπάρχει, ἣν αἰσχρόν ἐστιν ἐν σοὶ κατα-

λοχίας ἁπάσης. The Schol. explains it by saying that Dem. singled out Aristomedes as ἕνα τινὰ τῶν προδοτῶν, who opposed the alliance with Persia and the war with Philip. We can hardly believe that the orator, if driven to depart from his usual custom of leaving opponents unnamed, would have wasted his strength upon a nobody. Bekk. and Dind. read 'Ἀριστόδημον, by whom some think the tragic actor of that name is meant; respecting him see Grote, 11. 517, 518. But there is no evidence that Aristodemus took any prominent part in politics except during the preliminary negotiations for peace, when his doing so was in a great measure accidental.

φιλαίτιον] "exposed to attack," "to hostile criticism."

§ 71. εἰ γάρ] "for if we should grant that the best answer you could make is true in your mouth, that . . ."

σ. μέν] "you consider yourself bound to use every exertion and undergo toil and danger. ."

μετὰ ῥ.] "with indifference."

τινά] "a person of consequence," "of importance." 21. 213, τὸ δοκεῖν τινες εἶναι. The neuter is used in the same way (Pl. Apol. ad fin.), like "aliquid" in Latin. Juv. 1. 74, "si vis esse aliquid."

§ 72. καὶ μήν] "nor again do I really see that for the state it is safe to mind her own business," attend to her own affairs as recommended by the peace party. 27. 46, ἐπειδὴ δεῖ λόγον αὐτὸν δοῦναι τούτων, τὰ αὐτοῦ πράττειν φησίν.

ἐργάζῃ καὶ π.] "from your meddling and overmeddling." Mr. K.

§ 73. νὴ Δία] "but I suppose," "but you may tell me . ." 6. 13.

σοι ὑπάρχει] supr. 25, τῶν ὑπαρχόντων. "you inherit," "there has descended to you." Isocr. 9. 19, τὰ . . ἐξ ἀρχῆς Εὐαγόρα παρὰ τῶν προγόνων ὑπάρξαντα. Id. 16. 24, δ' ἐπίστησθ' ὅτι πόρρωθεν ἡμῖν ὑπάρχει μέγιστα καὶ κάλλιστα τῶν πολιτῶν,

λῦσαι· τῇ πόλει δ' ὑπῆρξεν ἀνώνυμα καὶ φαῦλα τὰ τῶν προγόνων. ἀλλ' οὐδὲ τοῦθ' οὕτως ἔχει· σοὶ μὲν γὰρ ἦν κλέπτης ὁ πατήρ, εἴπερ ἦν ὅμοιός σοι, τῇ πόλει δ' ἡμῶν, ὡς πάντες ἴσασιν, οἱ Ἕλληνες ἐκ τῶν μεγίστων κινδύνων σεσωσμένοι. 74. ἀλλὰ γὰρ οὐκ ἴσως οὐδὲ πολιτικῶς ἔνιοι τὰ καθ' ἑαυτοὺς καὶ τὰ κατ' αὐτὴν πολιτεύονται· πῶς γάρ ἐστιν ἴσον τούτων μέν τινας ἐκ τοῦ δεσμωτηρίου ἥκοντας ἑαυτοὺς ἀγνοεῖν, τὴν πόλιν δ', ἣ προειστήκει τῶν ἄλλων τέως καὶ τὸ πρωτεῖον εἶχε, νῦν ἐν ἀδοξίᾳ πάσῃ καὶ ταπεινότητι καθεστάναι;

75. Πολλὰ τοίνυν ἔχων ἔτι καὶ περὶ πολλῶν εἰπεῖν παύσομαι· καὶ γὰρ οὐ λόγων ἐνδείᾳ μοι δοκεῖ τὰ πράγματα οὔτε νῦν οὔτ' ἄλλοτε πώποτε φαύλως ἔχειν, ἀλλ' ὅταν πάντ' ἀκούσαντες ὑμεῖς τὰ δέοντα, καὶ ὁμογνώμονες ὡς ὀρθῶς λέγεται γενόμενοι, τῶν λυμαίνεσθαι καὶ διαστρέφειν ταῦτα βουλομένων ἐξ ἴσου κάθησθε ἀκροώμενοι, οὐκ ἀγνοοῦντες αὐτούς (ἴστε γὰρ εὐθὺς ἰδόντες ἀκριβῶς, τίς μισθοῦ λέγει

i. e. that our family is one of the oldest and most distinguished in Athens. Pl. *Charm.* 155 A.
ἐν σοὶ κ.] "which it is, you would say, disgraceful to terminate in your own person." Thuc. 2. 64, ταῦτα γὰρ ἐν ἴθει τῇδε τῇ πόλει πρότερόν τε ἦν νῦν τε μὴ ἐν ὑμῖν παυλυθῇ.
τῇ π.] "while the city inherits from our ancestors only what is ignoble and mean."
τῇ π. . . . ἐκ] Bekk. had οἱ 'Ε. δὶς ἐκ . . κ. ὑπὸ τῶν προγόνων σ. He now omits δὶς and ὑπὸ τῶν πρ. because they are not supported by S. "Lenissime corrigas οὓς πάντες ἴσασιν οἱ 'Ε." (Schäf.), a conj. introduced into the text by Dind. The emendation though plausible seems unnecessary, as such deviations from strict sequence are not uncommon. "your father was a thief, if he was like you, whereas by our city, as all men know, the Greeks were saved .." cf. 2. 24.

πόλει] Madv. 38 g.
σεσωσμένοι] sc. ἦσαν, from ἦν. See note to 3. 25.
§ 74. οὐκ ἴσως] Bekk. formerly read ἀλλὰ γὰρ οὐκ. He now omits the words ἀλλὰ γάρ, as not found in S. They are rightly, I think, retained by Dind. "but some administer their own affairs and those of the city in a way neither equitable nor becoming them as citizens," "neither equitably nor constitutionally."
πολιτεύῃ] cf. 9. 48; 19. 99.
προειστήκει] "once was at the head of the I*f*. and held the foremost place .."
§ 75. ὁμ. . . . , γενόμενοι] "all agreeing that ..."
ἐξ ἴσου] "with equal favour."
εὐθὺς ἰδόντες] "the moment you see them," "at the first glance." Madv. 175 b. Hyperides could say at a later period, οὐ μόνον αὐτοί, ἀλλὰ καὶ οἱ ἄλλοι 'Αθηναῖοι ἴσασι καὶ τὰ παιδία τὰ ἐκ τῶν διδασκαλείων

καὶ ὑπὲρ Φιλίππου πολιτεύεται, καὶ τίς ὡς ἀληθῶς ὑπὲρ τῶν βελτίστων), ἀλλ' ἵν' αἰτιασάμενοι τούτους καὶ τὸ πρᾶγμα εἰς γέλωτα καὶ λοιδορίαν ἐμβαλόντες μηδὲν αὐτοὶ τῶν δεόντων ποιῆτε. 76. ταῦτ' ἐστὶ τἀληθῆ μετὰ πάσης παρρησίας, ἁπλῶς εὐνοίᾳ, τὰ βέλτιστα εἰρημένα, οὐ κολακείας καὶ βλάβης καὶ ἀπάτης λόγος μεστός, ἀργύριον μὲν τῷ λέγοντι ποιήσων, τὰ δὲ πράγματα τῆς πόλεως τοῖς ἐχθροῖς ἐγχειριῶν. ἢ οὖν παυστέον τούτων τῶν ἐθῶν, ἢ μηδένα ἄλλον αἰτιατέον τοῦ πάντα φαύλως ἔχειν ἢ ὑμᾶς αὐτούς.

καὶ τῶν ῥητόρων τοὺς παρ' ἐκείνων μισθαρνοῦντας .... (*Pro Euxenip.* § 22).
μισθοῦ] "for hire."
ὡς ἀληθῶς] "honestly."

εἰς γ... ἐμβ.] "turning the thing into laughter and raillery."
§ 76. ἁπλῶς] "with perfect freedom, simply out of good will, as the best," "for the best."

CATENA CLASSICORUM,

A SERIES OF CLASSICAL AUTHORS,

EDITED BY MEMBERS OF BOTH UNIVERSITIES UNDER
THE DIRECTION OF

THE REV. ARTHUR HOLMES, M.A.

FELLOW AND LECTURER OF CLARE COLLEGE, CAMBRIDGE, LECTURER AND LATE FELLOW
OF ST. JOHN'S COLLEGE,

AND

THE REV. CHARLES BIGG, M.A.

LATE SENIOR STUDENT AND TUTOR OF CHRIST CHURCH, OXFORD, SECOND CLASSICAL
MASTER OF CHELTENHAM COLLEGE.

The following Parts will be published immediately:—

HOMERI ILIAS,
Edited by S. H. REYNOLDS, M.A.
Fellow and Tutor of Brasenose College, Oxford.
[Vol. I. Books I. to XII.

THUCYDIDIS HISTORIA,
Edited by CHARLES BIGG, M.A. late Senior Student and Tutor of Christ Church, Oxford. Second Classical Master of Cheltenham College.
[Vol. I. Books I. and II. with Introductions.

DEMOSTHENIS ORATIONES PUBLICAE,
Edited by G. H. HESLOP, M.A. late Fellow and Assistant Tutor of Queen's College, Oxford. Head Master of St. Bees.
[Part I. The Olynthiacs.
[Part II. The Philippics.

ARISTOPHANIS COMOE-DIAE,
Edited by W. C. GREEN, M.A. late Fellow of King's College, Cambridge. Classical Lecturer at Queen's College.
[Part II. The Clouds.

The following Part will be published before the beginning of the Michaelmas Term:—

ISOCRATIS ORATIONES,
Edited by JOHN EDWIN SANDYS, B.A. Fellow and Lecturer of St. John's College, Cambridge.
[Part I. Ad Demonicum. Panegyricus.

The following Parts are preparing:—

HERODOTI HISTORIA,
Edited by H. G. WOODS, M.A. Fellow and Tutor of Trinity College, Oxford.

DEMOSTHENIS ORATIONES PRIVATAE,
Edited by ARTHUR HOLMES, M.A.

Fellow and Lecturer of Clare College, Cambridge.
[Part I. De Corona.

TERENTI COMOEDIAE,
Edited by T. L. PAPILLON, M.A. Fellow and Classical Lecturer of Merton College, Oxford.

Catena Classicorum.

HORATI OPERA,
Edited by J. M. MARSHALL, M.A. Fellow and late Lecturer of Brasenose College, Oxford. One of the Masters in Clifton College.

MARTIALIS EPIGRAMMATA,
Edited by GEORGE BUTLER, M.A. Principal of Liverpool College. Late Fellow of Exeter College, Oxford.

The following have been already published:—

SOPHOCLIS TRAGOEDIAE,
Edited by R. C. JEBB, M.A. Fellow and Assistant Tutor of Trinity College, Cambridge.
[Part I. The Electra. Price 3s. 6d.
[Part II. The Ajax. Price 3s. 6d.

ARISTOPHANIS COMOEDIAE,
Edited by W. C. GREEN, M.A. late Fellow of King's College, Cambridge. Classical Lecturer at Queen's College.
[Part I. The Acharnians and the Knights. Price 4s.

JUVENALIS SATIRAE,
Edited by G. A. SIMCOX, M.A. Fellow and Classical Lecturer of Queen's College, Oxford.
[Thirteen Satires. Price 3s. 6d.

Opinions of the Press.

Mr. Jebb's "Electra" of Sophocles.

"'The Electra' is all that could be wished, and a better help could not well be found for those who wish to re-commence an acquaintance with almost forgotten Greek authors."—*Clerical Journal, April 18, 1867.*

"Of Mr. Jebb's scholarly edition of the 'Electra' of Sophocles we cannot speak too highly. The whole Play bears evidence of the taste, learning, and fine scholarship of its able editor. Illustrations drawn from the literature of the Continent as well as of England, and the researches of the highest classical authorities are embodied in the notes, which are brief, clear, and always to the point."—*London Review, March 16, 1867.*

"The editorship of the work before us is of a very high order, displaying at once ripe scholarship, sound judgment, and conscientious care. An excellent Introduction gives an account of the various forms assumed in Greek literature by the legend upon which 'The Electra' is founded, and institutes a comparison between it and the 'Choephorae' of Æschylus. The text is mainly that of Dindorf. In the notes, which are admirable in every respect, is to be found exactly what is wanted, and yet they rather suggest and direct further inquiry than supersede exertion on the part of the student."—*Athenæum, March 23, 1867.*

"The Introduction proves that Mr. Jebb is something more than a mere scholar,—a man of real taste and feeling. His criticism upon Schlegel's remarks on the Electra are, we believe, new, and certainly just. As we have often had occasion to say in this Review, it is impossible to pass any reliable criticism upon school-books until they have been tested by experience. The notes, however, in this case appear to be clear and sensible, and direct attention to the points where attention is most needed."—*Westminster Review, April, 1867.*

"We have no hesitation in saying that in style and manner Mr. Jebb's notes are admirably suited for their purpose. The explanations of grammatical points are singularly lucid, the parallel passages generally well chosen, the translations bright and graceful, the analysis of arguments terse and luminous. There is hardly any obscurity, and no cumbrousness or overloading. We think, too, that Mr. Jebb's plan of furnishing complete analyses of the choric metres an admirable one for a school edition; and we like his method of giving parenthetically the dates of the less known ancient authors whom he quotes, a method which, suggesting as it must to an intelligent student the existence of a world of literature with which he is very likely to be unfamiliar, will do much to create or stimulate in him the spirit and habits of research. Mr. Jebb has clearly shown that he possesses some of the qualities most essential for a commentator."—*Spectator, July 6, 1867.*

"The notes appear to us exactly suited to assist boys of the Upper Forms at Schools, and University students; they give sufficient help without over-doing explanations.... His critical remarks show acute and exact scholarship, and a very useful addition to ordinary notes is the scheme of metres in the choruses."—*Guardian, December 16, 1867.*

"If, as we are fain to believe, the editors of the *Catena Classicorum* have got together such a pick of scholars as have no need to play their best card first, there is a bright promise of success to their series in the first sample of it which has come to hand—Mr. Jebb's *Electra*. We have seen it suggested that it is unsafe to pronounce on the merits of a Greek Play edited for educational purposes until it has been tested in the hands of pupils and tutors. But our examination of the instalment of, we hope, a complete 'Sophocles,' which Mr. Jebb has put forth, has assured us that this is a needless suspension of judgment, and prompted us to commit the justifiable rashness of pronouncing upon its contents, and of asserting after due perusal that it is calculated to be admirably serviceable to every class of scholars and learners. And this assertion is based upon the fact that it is a by no means one-sided edition, and that it looks as with the hundred eyes of Argus, here, there, and every where, to keep the reader from straying. In a concise and succinct style of English annotation, forming the best substitute for the time-honoured Latin notes which had so much to do with making good scholars in days of yore, Mr. Jebb keeps a steady eye for all questions of grammar, construction, scholarship, and philology, and handles these as they arise with a helpful and sufficient precision. In matters of grammar and syntax his practice for the most part is to refer his reader to the proper section of Madvig's 'Manual of Greek Syntax;' nor does he ever waste space and time in explaining a construction, unless it be such an one as is not satisfactorily dealt with in the grammars of Madvig or Jelf. Experience as a pupil and a teacher has probably taught him the value of the wholesome task of hunting out a grammar reference for oneself, instead of finding it, handy for slurring over, amidst the hundred and one pieces of information in a voluminous foot-note. But whenever there occurs any peculiarity of construction, which is hard to reconcile to the accepted usage, it is Mr. Jebb's general practice to be ready at hand with manful assistance."—*Contemporary Review, November, 1867.*

Mr. Jebb's "Ajax" of Sophocles.

"Mr. Jebb has produced a work which will be read with interest and profit by the most advanced scholar, as it contains, in a compact form, not only a careful summary of the labours of preceding editors, but also many acute and ingenious original remarks. We do not know whether the matter or the manner of this excellent commentary is deserving of the higher praise: the skill with which Mr. Jebb has avoided, on the one hand, the wearisome prolixity of the Germans, and on the other the jejune brevity of the Porsonian critics, or the versatility which has enabled him in turn to elucidate the plots, to explain the verbal difficulties, and to illustrate the idioms of his author. All this, by a studious economy of space and a remarkable precision of expression, he has done for the 'Ajax' in a volume of some 200 pages."—*Athenæum, March 21, 1868.*

"The Introduction furnishes a great deal of information in a compact form, adapted to give the student a fair conception of his author, and to aid him in mastering its difficulties. We have observed how the brief notes really throw light on obscurity, and give sufficient aid without making the study too easy,—a main point to be observed by one who edits a classic author for the benefit of learners and students."—*Clerical Journal, February 13, 1868.*

"Mr. Jebb's Edition of the Ajax in the *Catena Classicorum* ought to assure those who have hitherto doubted that this is a Series to adopt. Like his edition of the 'Electra' this of the 'Ajax' is ably and usefully handled. The Introduction alone would prove the wide reading, clear views, and acute criticism of its writer."—*Churchman, February 20, 1868.*

"A more scholarly and thoroughly practical Edition of a Greek play has rarely issued from the Press. The explanations are both copious and freely given: and we have not met with a single note wherein conciseness appears to have been gained at the expense of clearness of meaning. The 'Ajax,' however, is by no means a difficult play, and we must therefore infer that Mr. Jebb takes a more liberal view than some of his coadjutors of the amount of help which an ordinary student may fairly be supposed to require...... Compared with the renderings of most other editions, Mr. Jebb's translations have decidedly the advantage in force and elegance of expression."—*Educational Times, March, 1868.*

Opinions of the Press.

Mr. Green's "Acharnians and Knights" of Aristophanes.

"The Editors of this Series have undertaken the task of issuing texts of all the authors commonly read, and illustrating them with an English Commentary, compendious as well as clear. If the future volumes fulfil the promise of the Prospectus as well as those already published, the result will be a very valuable work. The excellence of the print, and the care and pains bestowed upon the general getting up, form a marked contrast to the school-books of our own day. Who does not remember the miserable German editions of classical authors in paper covers, execrably printed on detestable paper, which were thought amply good enough for the schoolboys of the last generation? A greater contrast to these can hardly be imagined than is presented by the *Catena Classicorum*. Nor is the improvement only external: the careful revision of the text, and the notes, not too lengthy and confused, but well and judiciously selected, which are to be found in every page, add considerably to the value of this Edition, which we may safely predict will soon be an established favourite, not only among Schoolmasters, but at the Universities. The volume before us contains the first part of an Edition of Aristophanes, which comprises the Acharnians and the Knights, the one first in order, and the other the most famous of the plays of the great Athenian Satirist."—*Churchman, May 23, 1867.*

"The utmost care has been taken with this Edition of the most sarcastic and clever of the old Greek dramatists, facilitating the means of understanding both the text and intention of that biting sarcasm which will never lose either point or interest, and is as well adapted to the present age as it was to the times when first put forward."—*Bell's Weekly Messenger, June 8, 1867.*

"The advantages conferred on the learner by these compendious aids can only be properly estimated by those who had experience of the mode of study years ago. The translated passages and the notes, while sufficient to assist the willing learner, cannot be regarded in any sense as *a cram*."—*Clerical Journal, June 6, 1867.*

"Mr. Green has discharged his part of the work with uncommon skill and ability. The notes show a thorough study of the two Plays, an independent judgment in the interpretation of the poet, and a wealth of illustration, from which the Editor draws whenever it is necessary."—*Museum, June, 1867.*

"Mr. Green presumes the existence of a fair amount of scholarship in all who read Aristophanes, as a study of his works generally succeeds to some considerable knowledge of the tragic poets. The notes he has appended are therefore brief, perhaps a little too brief. We should say the tendency of most modern editors is rather the other way; but Mr. Green no doubt knows the class for which he writes, and has been careful to supply their wants."—*Spectator, July 27, 1867.*

Mr. Simcox's Juvenal.

"Of Mr. Simcox's 'Juvenal' we can only speak in terms of the highest commendation, as a simple, unpretending work, admirably adapted to the wants of the school-boy or of a college passman. It is clear, concise, and scrupulously honest in shirking no real difficulty. The pointed epigrammatic hits of the satirist are every where well brought out, and the notes really are what they profess to be, explanatory in the best sense of the term."—*London Review, September 28, 1867.*

"This is a link in the *Catena Classicorum* to which the attention of our readers has been more than once directed as a good Series of Classical works for School and College purposes. The Introduction is a very comprehensive and able account of Juvenal, his satires, and the manuscripts."—*Athenæum, October 5, 1867.*

"This is a very original and enjoyable Edition of one of our favourite classics." — *Spectator, November 16, 1867.*

"Every class of readers,—those who use Mr. Simcox as their sole interpreter, and those who supplement larger editions by his concise matter,—will alike find interest and careful research in his able preface. This indeed we should call the great feature of his book. The three facts which sum up Juvenal's history so far as we know it are soon despatched; but the internal evidence both as to the dates of his writing and publishing his Satires, and as to his character as a writer, occupy some fifteen or twenty pages, which will repay methodical study."—*Churchman, December 11, 1867.*

RIVINGTONS,
London, Oxford, and Cambridge.

May, 1868.

New Works

IN COURSE OF PUBLICATION

BY

Messrs. RIVINGTON,

WATERLOO PLACE, LONDON;

HIGH STREET, OXFORD; TRINITY STREET, CAMBRIDGE.

Newman's (J. H.) Parochial and Plain
Sermons.
Edited by the Rev. W. J. Copeland, Rector of Farnham, Essex. From the Text of the last Editions published by Messrs. Rivington.
Crown 8vo. 8 vols. 5s. each. (*Vol. I. just published.*)

A Key to the Knowledge and Use of
the Book of Common Prayer.
By John Henry Blunt, M.A.
Small 8vo. 2s. 6d.

London, Oxford, and Cambridge

The Mysteries of Mount Calvary.
By Antonio de Guevara.

Being the First Volume of the Ascetic Library, a Series of Translations of Spiritual Works for Devotional Reading from Catholic Sources. Edited by the Rev. **Orby Shipley**, M.A.

Square crown 8vo. 3s. 6d.

The Annotated Book of Common
Prayer; being an Historical, Ritual, and Theological Commentary on the Devotional System of the Church of England. Edited by **John Henry Blunt**, M.A.

Third Edition, pp. 760, with three Plates. Imperial 8vo, 36s. Large paper Edition, royal 4to, with large margin for Notes, 3l. 3s.

The Dogmatic Faith: an Inquiry
into the Relation subsisting between Revelation and Dogma. Being the Bampton Lectures for 1867.

By **Edward Garbett**, M.A., Incumbent of Christ Church, Surbiton.

8vo. 10s. 6d.

On Miracles; being the Bampton
Lectures for 1865.

By J. B. **Mozley**, B.D., Vicar of Old Shoreham, late Fellow of Magdalen College, Oxford.

Second Edition. 8vo. 10s. 6d.

London, Oxford, and Cambridge

Vestiarivm Christianvm: the Origin

and Gradual Development of the Dress of the Holy Ministry in the Church, as evidenced by Monuments both of Literature and of Art, from the Apostolic Age to the present time.

By the Rev. **Wharton B. Marriott**, M.A., F.S.A. (sometime Fellow of Exeter College, Oxford, and Assistant-Master at Eton), Select Preacher in the University, and Preacher, by licence from the Bishop, in the Diocese of Oxford.
Royal 8vo. 38s.

The Prayer Book Interleaved;

with Historical Illustrations and Explanatory Notes arranged parallel to the Text, by the Rev. **W. M. Campion**, B.D., Fellow and Tutor of Queens' College and Rector of St. Botolph's, and the Rev. **W. J. Beamont**, M.A., Fellow of Trinity College, Cambridge, and Incumbent of St. Michael's, Cambridge. With a Preface by the Lord Bishop of Ely.
New Edition. Small 8vo. 7s. 6d.

London Ordination, Advent, 1867;

being Seven Addresses to the Candidates for Holy Orders, in December, 1867.

By **Archibald Campbell, Lord Bishop of London**, and his Chaplains.
Together with the Examination Papers.
8vo. 4s.

The London Diocese Book for 1868

(fourth year of issue), under the sanction of the Lord Bishop of London. Crown 8vo. In wrapper, 1s.

Flowers and Festivals; or, Directions

for the Floral Decorations of Churches. With coloured Illustrations.

By **W. A. Barrett**, of S. Paul's Cathedral, late Clerk of Magdalen College, and Commoner of S. Mary Hall, Oxford.
Square crown 8vo. 5s.

London, Oxford, and Cambridge

The Beatitudes of Our Blessed Lord,
considered in Eight Practical Discourses.
By the Rev. John Peat, M.A., of St. Peter's College, Cambridge, Vicar of East Grinstead, Sussex.
Small 8vo. 3s. 6d.

Selections from Aristotle's Organon.
Edited by John R. Magrath, M.A., Fellow and Tutor of Queen's College, Oxford.
Crown 8vo. 3s. 6d.

Warnings of the Holy Week, &c.;
being a Course of Parochial Lectures for the Week before Easter and the Easter Festivals.
By the Rev. W. Adams, M.A., late Vicar of St. Peter's-in-the-East, Oxford, and Fellow of Merton College.
Sixth Edition. Small 8vo. 4s. 6d.

Curious Myths of the Middle Ages.
By S. Baring-Gould, M.A., Author of "Post-Mediæval Preachers," &c. With Illustrations.
First Series. *Second Edition.* Crown 8vo. 7s. 6d.
Second Series. Crown 8vo. 9s. 6d.

Household Theology: a Handbook of
Religious Information respecting the Holy Bible, the Prayer Book, the Church, the Ministry, Divine Worship, the Creeds, &c. &c.
By J. H. Blunt, M.A.
Third Edition. Fcp. 8vo. 3s. 6d.

London, Oxford, and Cambridge

Farewell Counsels of a Pastor to his

Flock, on Topics of the Day: Nine Sermons preached at St. John's, Paddington.

By **Edward Meyrick Goulburn**, D.D., Dean of Norwich.

Second Edition. Small 8vo. 4s.

Sermons.

By the Rev. **R. S. C. Chermside**, M.A., late Rector of Wilton, and Prebendary of Sarum. With a Preface by the Rev. **G. Rawlinson**, M.A., Camden Professor of Ancient History in the University of Oxford.

Small 8vo. 5s.

Consoling Thoughts in Sickness.

Edited by **Henry Bailey**, B.D., Warden of St. Augustine's College, Canterbury.

Small 8vo. Large type. 2s. 6d.

An Illuminated Edition of the Book of

Common Prayer, printed in Red and Black, on fine toned Paper; with Borders and Titles, designed after the manner of the 14th Century, by **R. R. Holmes**, F.S.A., and engraved by **O. Jewitt**. Crown 8vo. White vellum cloth illuminated. 16s.

This Edition of the PRAYER BOOK *may be had in various Bindings for presentation.*

Scripture Acrostics.

By the Author of "The Last Sleep of the Christian Child."

Square 16mo. 1s. 6d. With Key, 2s.

The Key may also be had separately, 6d.

London, Oxford, and Cambridge

The Sacraments and Sacramental Or-
dinances of the Church; being a Plain Exposition of their History, Meaning, and Effects.
By **John Henry Blunt**, M.A.
Small 8vo. 4s. 6d.

Yesterday, To-day, and For Ever: a
Poem in Twelve Books.
By **Edward Henry Bickersteth**, M.A., Incumbent of Christ Church, Hampstead, and Chaplain to the Bishop of Ripon.
Second and Cheaper Edition. Small 8vo. 6s.

Queen Bertha and her Times.
By **E. H. Hudson**.
Small 8vo. 5s.

Sermons preached before the University
of Oxford, chiefly during the years 1863—1865.
By **Henry Parry Liddon**, M.A., Student of Christ Church, Prebendary of Salisbury, Examining Chaplain to the Lord Bishop of Salisbury, and lately Select Preacher.
Second Edition. 8vo. 8s.

The Annual Register: a Review of
Public Events at Home and Abroad, for the Year 1867; being the Fifth Volume of an improved Series.
8vo. (*In the Press.*)
₊ *The Volumes for* 1863, 1864, 1865, *and* 1866 *may be had, price* 18s. *each*.

London, Oxford, and Cambridge

The Holy Bible.
With Notes and Introductions.
By Chr. Wordsworth, D.D., Archdeacon of Westminster.

			£	s.	d.
Vol. I. 38s. {	I.	Genesis and Exodus. *Second Edit.*	1	1	0
	II.	Leviticus, Numbers, Deuteronomy. *Second Edition*	0	18	0
Vol. II. 21s. {	III.	Joshua, Judges, Ruth. *Second Edit.*	0	12	0
	IV.	The Books of Samuel. *Second Edit.*	0	10	0
Vol. III. 21s. {	V.	The Books of Kings, Chronicles, Ezra, Nehemiah, Esther. *Second Edition*	1	1	0
Vol. IV. 34s. {	VI.	The Book of Job	0	9	0
	VII.	The Book of Psalms	0	15	0
	VIII.	Proverbs, Ecclesiastes, Song of Solomon.	0	12	0

The Greek Testament.
With Notes and Introductions.
By Chr. Wordsworth, D.D., Archdeacon of Westminster.
2 Vols. Impl. 8vo. 4*l.*

The Parts may be had separately, as follows :—

The Gospels, 6*th Edition,* 21*s.*
The Acts, 5*th Edition,* 10*s.* 6*d.*
St. Paul's Epistles, 5*th Edition,* 31*s.* 6*d.*
General Epistles, Revelation, and Indexes, 3*rd Edition,* 21*s.*

The Acts of the Deacons; being a
Course of Lectures, Critical and Practical, upon the Notices of St. Stephen and St. Philip the Evangelist, contained in the Acts of the Apostles.
By Edward Mayrick Goulburn, D.D., Dean of Norwich. *Second Edition.* Small 8vo. 6*s.*

London, Oxford, and Cambridge

Sermons for Children; being Twenty-
eight short Readings, addressed to the Children of St. Margaret's Home, East Grinstead.
 By the late Rev. J. M. Neale, D.D., Warden of Sackville College.
    Small 8vo.   3s.

Our Lord Jesus Christ Teaching on
the Lake of Gennesaret: Six Discourses suitable for Family Reading.
 By Charles Baker, M.A., Oxon, Vicar of Appleshaw, Hants.
    Small 8vo.   1s. 6d.

Thomas à Kempis, Of the Imitation of
Christ: a carefully revised translation, elegantly printed with red borders.
    16mo.   2s. 6d.
 Also a cheap Edition, without the red borders, in Wrapper, 6d.

Thoughts on Men and Things: a Series
of Essays.
 By Angelina Gushington.
    Second Edition.   Crown 8vo.   3s. 6d.

The Electra of Sophocles.
 With English Notes by R. C. Jebb, M.A., Fellow and Assistant Tutor of Trinity College, Cambridge.
 Forming the First Part of CATENA CLASSICORUM.
    Crown 8vo.   3s. 6d.

London, Oxford, and Cambridge

The Acharnians and the Knights of Aristophanes.

With English Notes by W. C. Green, M.A., late Fellow of King's College, Cambridge; Classical Lecturer of Queens' College.

Being the Second Part of CATENA CLASSICORUM.

Crown 8vo. 4s.

Thirteen Satires of Juvenal.

With Notes and Introduction by G. A. Simcox, M.A., Fellow and Lecturer of Queen's College, Oxford.

Being the Third Part of CATENA CLASSICORUM.

Crown 8vo. 3s. 6d.

The Ajax of Sophocles.

With English Notes by R. C. Jebb, M.A., Fellow and Assistant Tutor of Trinity College, Cambridge.

Being the Fourth Part of CATENA CLASSICORUM.

Crown 8vo. 3s. 6d.

Thucydides. Books 1 and 2.

Edited by Charles Bigg, M.A., late Senior Student and Tutor of Christ Church, Oxford; Second Classical Master of Cheltenham College.

Crown 8vo. 7s. 6d. (*Just ready.*)

Church Seasons and Present Times:

Sermons preached chiefly at St. Luke's, Torquay.

By the Rev. George Collyer Harris, M.A., Minister of St. Luke's, and Prebendary of Exeter; Author of "Lessons from St. Peter's Life."

Small 8vo. 5s.

London, Oxford, and Cambridge

The Victory of Divine Goodness.

By **Thomas Rawson Birks**, M.A., Incumbent of Holy Trinity, Cambridge.

Crown 8vo. 4s. 6d.

The Greek Testament.

With a Critically revised Text; a Digest of Various Readings; Marginal References to Verbal and Idiomatic Usage; Prolegomena; and a Critical and Exegetical Commentary. For the use of Theological Students and Ministers. By **Henry Alford**, D.D., Dean of Canterbury.

4 Vols. 8vo. 102s.

The Volumes are sold separately as follows:—

Vol. I.—The Four Gospels. *Sixth Edition.* 28s. (*In the Press.*)
Vol. II.—Acts to II. Corinthians. *Fifth Edition.* 24s.
Vol. III.—Galatians to Philemon. *Fourth Edition.* 18s.
Vol. IV.—Hebrews to Revelation. *Third Edition.* 32s.

The New Testament for English

Readers; containing the Authorized Version, with a revised English Text; Marginal References; and a Critical and Explanatory Commentary. By **Henry Alford**, D.D., Dean of Canterbury.

Now complete in 2 Vols. or 4 Parts, price 54s. 6d.

Separately,

Vol. 1, Part I.—The three first Gospels, with a Map. *Second Edition.* 12s.
Vol. 1, Part II.—St. John and the Acts. 10s. 6d.
Vol. 2, Part I.—The Epistles of St. Paul, with a Map. 16s.
Vol. 2, Part II.—Hebrews to Revelation. 8vo. 16s.

Semele; or, The Spirit of Beauty:

a Venetian Tale.

By **J. D. Mereweather**, B.A. Oxon., English Chaplain at Venice.

Small 8vo. 3s. 6d.

London, Oxford, and Cambridge

Thoughts on Personal Religion; being
a Treatise on the Christian Life in its Two Chief Elements, Devotion and Practice.
By **Edward Meyrick Goulburn**, D.D., Dean of Norwich.
New Edition. Small 8vo. 6s. 6d.
An edition for presentation, Two Volumes, small 8vo. 10s. 6d.
Also, a Cheap Edition. 3s. 6d.

Six Short Sermons on Sin. Lent Lectures
at S. Alban the Martyr, Holborn.
By the Rev. **Orby Shipley**, M.A.
Fourth Edition. Small 8vo. 1s.

The Last Words of Our Lord and
Saviour Jesus Christ; being a Course of Seven Sermons preached during Passion Week, 1867, in the Parish Church of St. Mary, Twickenham.
By the Rev. **R. S. Cobbett**, M.A., of Pembroke College, Oxford.
Small 8vo. 3s.

Simple Sermons.
By **William Henry Ranken**, M.A., Fellow of Corpus Christi College, Oxford, and Vicar of Radley, Berks.
Small 8vo. 5s.

Short Devotional Forms, for Morning,
Night, and Midnight, and for the Third, Sixth, Ninth hours, and Eventide, of each Day in the Week. Compiled and adapted from Bishop Andrewes, and other Sources. Arranged to meet the exigencies of a busy life.
By **Edward Meyrick Goulburn**, D.D., Dean of Norwich.
Third Edition. Square 16mo. 1s. 6d.

London, Oxford, and Cambridge

A Christian View of Christian History, from Apostolic to Mediæval Times.
By John Henry Blunt, M.A.
Crown 8vo. 7s.

Faith and Life:
Readings for the greater Holy Days, and the Sundays from Advent to Trinity. Compiled from Ancient Writers. With Notes on Eternal Judgment; and Christ's Sacrifice.
By William Bright, M.A., Fellow and Tutor of University College, Oxford.
Second Edition. Small 8vo. 5s.

Parish Musings; or, Devotional Poems.
By John S. B. Monsell, LL.D., Vicar of Egham, Surrey, and Rural Dean. *Tenth Edition.*
18mo, 1s., or, in limp cloth, 1s. 6d.
A superior Edition may be had, in small 8vo, price 2s. 6d.

Standing and Stumbling.
Part I.—Seven Common Faults.
Part II.—Your Duty and Mine.
Part III.—Things Rarely Met With.
By James Erasmus Philipps, M.A., Vicar of Warminster.
Small 8vo. 2s. 6d.
(*The Parts may be had separately, price 1s. each.*)

An Outline of Logic,
for the use of Teachers and Students.
By Francis Garden, M.A. Trinity College, Cambridge, Sub-Dean of Her Majesty's Chapels Royal; Chaplain to the Household in St. James' Palace; Professor of Mental and Moral Science, Queen's College, London.
Small 8vo. 4s.

London, Oxford, and Cambridge

Arithmetic for the Use of Schools;
with a numerous collection of Examples.
By B. D. Beasley, M.A., Head Master of Grantham Grammar School, and formerly Fellow of St. John's College, Cambridge; Author of "Elements of Plane Trigonometry."

12mo. 3s.

The Examples are also sold separately:—Part I., Elementary Rules 8d. Part II., Higher Rules, 1s. 6d.

The Formation of Tenses in the Greek
Verb; showing the Rules by which every Tense is Formed from the pure stem of the Verb, and the necessary changes before each Termination. By C. S. Jerram, M.A., late Scholar of Trinity College, Oxon.

Crown 8vo. 1s. 6d.

Professor Inman's Nautical Tables,
for the use of British Seamen. *New Edition*, by the Rev. J. W. Inman, late Fellow of St. John's College, Cambridge, and Head Master of Chudleigh Grammar School. Revised, and enlarged by the introduction of Tables of $\frac{1}{2}$ log. haversines, log. differences, &c.; with a more compendious method of Working a Lunar, and a Catalogue of Latitudes and Longitudes of Places on the Seaboard.

Royal 8vo. 21s.

Arithmetic, Theoretical and Practical;
adapted for the use of Colleges and Schools.
By W. H. Girdlestone, M.A., of Christ's College, Cambridge.

Crown 8vo. 6s. 6d.

A Greek Primer for the use of Schools.
By the Rev. Charles H. Hole, M.A., Scholar of Worcester College, Oxford; late Assistant Master at King Edward's School, Bromsgrove.

Crown 8vo. 4s.

London, Oxford, and Cambridge

Sacred Allegories:

The Shadow of the Cross—The Distant Hills—The Old Man's Home—The King's Messengers.

By the Rev. W. Adams, M.A., late Fellow of Merton College, Oxford. With Illustrations.

New Edition. Small 8vo. Price 5s.

The Four Allegories are also published separately in 18mo., price 1s. each in limp cloth.

Sermons, preached in Liverpool.

By Andrew Wilson, B.A., Curate of St. Catharine's, Liverpool.

Small 8vo. 6s.

Priest and Parish.

By the Rev. Harry Jones, M.A., Incumbent of St. Luke's, Berwick Street, Soho; Author of "Life in the World."

Square crown 8vo. 6s. 6d.

Private Devotions for School Boys;

together with some Rules of Conduct given by a Father to his Son, on his going to School.

By William Henry, third Lord Lyttleton; revised and corrected by his Son, fourth Lord Lyttleton.

Fifth Edition. 32mo. 6d.

Daily Devotions; or, Short Morning

and Evening Services for the use of a Churchman's Household.

By the Ven. Charles C. Clarke, Archdeacon of Oxford.

18mo. 1s.

London, Oxford, and Cambridge

A Fourth Series of Parochial Sermons,

preached in a Village Church.

By the Rev. **Charles A. Heartley**, D.D., Rector of Fenny Compton, Warwickshire, Margaret Professor of Divinity, and Canon of Christ Church, Oxford.

Small 8vo. 4s. 6d.

On the Duty and the Discipline of

Extemporary Preaching. By F. **Barham Zincke**, Vicar of Wherstead, Suffolk, and Chaplain in Ordinary to the Queen.

Crown 8vo. 5s.

The Office of the Most Holy Name:

Devotional Help for Young Persons.
By the Editor of "The Churchman's Guide to Faith," &c.

18mo. 2s. 6d.

Hesperidum Susurri.

Sublegerunt **Thomas J. Bellingham Brady**, A.M., **Robertus Yelverton Tyrrell**, A.D., **Maxwell Cormac Cullinan**, A.D., Collegi S.S. et Indiv. Trin. Juxta Dublin Alumni.

Small 8vo. 5s.

Hymns and other Poems.

By **William Bright**, M.A., Fellow and Tutor of University College, Oxford.

Small 8vo. 4s. 6d.

London, Oxford, and Cambridge

Aids to Prayer. Six Lectures delivered
at Holy Trinity Church, Paddington, on the Sunday mornings in Lent, 1868.
By **Daniel Moore**, M.A.
Crown 8vo.   (*Just ready*).

Henry's First Latin Book.
By **Thomas Kerchever Arnold**, M.A., late Rector of Lyndon, and formerly Fellow of Trinity College, Cambridge.
Twentieth Edition.   12mo.   3s.

Hymns and Poems for the Sick and
Suffering; in connexion with the Service for the Visitation of the Sick. Selected from various Authors.
Edited by **T. V. Fosbery**, M.A., Vicar of St. Giles's, Reading.
This Volume contains 233 separate pieces; of which about 90 are by writers who lived prior to the 18th Century; the rest are Modern, and some of these original. Amongst the names of the writers (between 70 and 80 in number) occur those of Sir J. Beaumont, Sir T. Browne, Elizabeth of Bohemia, Phineas Fletcher, George Herbert, Dean Hickes, Bishop Ken, Francis Quarles, George Sandys, Jeremy Taylor, Henry Vaughan, Sir H. Wotton; and of modern writers, Mrs. Barrett Browning, Bishop Wilberforce, Samuel Taylor Coleridge, William Wordsworth, Archbishop Trench, Rev. J. Chandler, Rev. J. Keble, Rev. H. F. Lyte, Rev. J. S. Monsell, Rev. J. Moultrie.
New Edition.   3s. 6d.

Sermons, Doctrinal and Didactic,
bearing on the Religious Topics of the Day. By **Thomas Williamson Peile**, D.D., Incumbent of St. Paul's, Hampstead, late Head Master of Repton School, and sometime Fellow of Trinity College, Cambridge.
Crown 8vo.   6s. 6d.

London, Oxford, and Cambridge

A Practical Introduction to Latin

Prose Composition: Part I.

By **Thomas Kerchever Arnold**, M.A., late Rector of Lyndon, and formerly Fellow of Trinity College, Cambridge.

Fourteenth Edition. 8vo. 6s. 6d.

A Practical Introduction to English

Prose Composition. An English Grammar for Classical Schools; with Questions, and a Course of Exercises.

By **Thomas Kerchever Arnold**, M.A., late Rector of Lyndon, and formerly Fellow of Trinity College, Cambridge.

Eighth Edition. 12mo. 4s. 6d.

A Plain and Short History of England

for Children: in Letters from a Father to his Son. With a Set of Questions at the end of each Letter.

By **George Davys**, D.D., late Bishop of Peterborough.

New Edition. 1s. 6d.

The Life of our Blessed Saviour. An

Epitome of the Gospel Narrative, arranged in order of Time from the latest Harmonies. With Introduction and Notes.

By the Rev. **I. Gregory Smith**, M.A., Rector of Tedstone Delamere, and late Fellow of Brasenose College, Oxford.

Second Edition, revised. Square 8vo. 2s.

A Manual of Confirmation, comprising

—1. A General Account of the Ordinance. 2. The Baptismal Vow, and the English Order of Confirmation, with Short Notes, Critical and Devotional. 3. Meditations and Prayers on Passages of Holy Scripture, in connexion with the Ordinance. With a Pastoral Letter instructing Catechumens how to prepare themselves for their first Communion.

By **Edward Meyrick Goulburn**, D.D., Dean of Norwich.

Seventh Edition. Small 8vo. 1s. 6d.

London, Oxford, and Cambridge

An Introduction to the Devotional
Study of the Holy Scriptures.
By **Edward Meyrick Goulburn**, D.D., Dean of Norwich.
Ninth Edition. Small 8vo. 3s. 6d.

Euchai Idiai Kathemerinai tou Pan-
ierotatou Lagkelotton Andreeos, I.Th.K., Episkopou Ouintonias en Agglia.
Ekdidontos **Phriderikou Merrikou**, T.D.
Small 8vo. 1s.

Preces Privatæ Quotidianæ Lanceloti
Andrewes, Episcopi Wintoniensis.
Edidit **Fredericus Meyrick**, A.M.
Small 8vo. 1s.

Exposicion Histórica y Doctrinal, de
los Treinta y Nueve Artículos de la Iglesia Anglicana.
Por el Illmo. Sr. Dr. D. **Eduardo Harold Browne**, Obispo de Ely. Parte I.
Traducido del Ingles por D. **Juan B. Cabrera**, Presbítero, Ex-individuo de las escuelas pias de españa.
Small 8vo. 1s.

Döderlein's Handbook of Latin Synonymes.
Translated from the German, by **H. H. Arnold**, B.A.
Third Edition. 12mo. 4s.

The Church Builder. A Quarterly
Journal of Church Extension in England and Wales. Published in connexion with "The Incorporated Church Building Society."
Volume for 1867. *With Illustrations.* Crown 8vo. 1s. 6d.

London, Oxford, and Cambridge

Latin via English:

being the Second Part of Spelling turned Etymology.

By **Thomas Kerchever Arnold**, M.A., late Rector of Lyndon, and formerly Fellow of Trinity College, Cambridge.

Third Edition. 12mo. 4s. 6d.

A Collection of English Exercises,

translated from the writings of Cicero, for Schoolboys to re-translate into Latin.

By **William Ellis**, M.A.; re-arranged and adapted to the Rules of the Public School Latin Primer, by **John T. White**, D.D., joint Author of White and Riddle's Latin-English Dictionary.

12mo. 3s. 6d.

A complete Greek and English Lexicon

for the Poems of Homer, and the Homeridæ; illustrating the domestic, religious, political, and military condition of the Heroic Age, and explaining the most difficult passages.

By **G. Ch. Crusius**. Translated from the German, with corrections and additions, by **Henry Smith**, Professor of Languages in Marietta College. Revised and edited by **Thomas Kerchever Arnold**, M.A., late Rector of Lyndon, and formerly Fellow of Trinity College, Cambridge.

Third Edition. 12mo. 9s.

A copious Phraseological English-

Greek Lexicon; founded on a work prepared by **J. W. Fradersdorff**, Ph. Dr., late Professor of Modern Languages, Queen's College, Belfast.

Revised, Enlarged, and Improved by the late **Thomas Kerchever Arnold**, M.A., formerly Fellow of Trinity College, Cambridge, and **Henry Browne**, M.A., Vicar of Pevensey, and Prebendary of Chichester.

Fourth Edition, corrected, with the Appendix incorporated.

8vo. 21s.

London, Oxford, and Cambridge

The Divinity of our Lord and Saviour

Jesus Christ; being the Hampton Lectures for 1866.

By **Henry Parry Liddon**, M.A., Student of Christ Church, Prebendary of Salisbury, and Examining Chaplain to the Bishop of Salisbury.

    Second Edition. Crown 8vo. (*Nearly ready.*)

Annals of the Bodleian Library, Oxford;

from its Foundation to A.D. 1867; containing an Account of the various collections of printed books and MSS. there preserved; with a brief Preliminary Sketch of the earlier Library of the University.

By **W. D. Macray**, M.A., Assistant in the Library, Chaplain of Magdalen and New Colleges.

    8vo. (*Nearly ready.*)

The Olynthiacs and Philippics of Demosthenes.

Edited by **G. H. Heslop**, M.A., late Fellow and Assistant Tutor of Queen's College, Oxford; Head Master of St. Bees.

    Crown 8vo. 4s. 6d. (*Nearly ready.*)

Homeri Ilias.

Edited by **S. H. Reynolds**, M.A., Fellow and Tutor of Brasenose College, Oxford.

    Vol. I. Books I. to XII. (*Nearly ready.*)

Sermons on Unity; with an Essay on

Religious Societies, and a Lecture on the Life and Times of Wesley.

By **F. C. Massingberd**, M.A., Chancellor of Lincoln.

    Crown 8vo. (*Just ready.*)

London, Oxford, and Cambridge

Selections from the Cheltenham College
Prize Poems, 1846—1866.
Edited by C. S. Jerram, M.A., Trinity College, Oxford, and Rev. Theodore W. James, M.A., Pembroke College, Oxford.
Crown 8vo. 9s. (*Just ready.*)

Vox Ecclesiæ Anglicanæ: a Selection
of Extracts from the Chief Divines of the Church of England on the Main Points of Doctrine and Discipline.
By **George G. Perry**, M.A., Prebendary of Lincoln, Rector of Waddington, Rural Dean, and Proctor for the Diocese of Lincoln.
Small 8vo. (*In preparation.*)

A Key to the Knowledge and Use of the Bible.
By **John Henry Blunt**, M.A.
Small 8vo. (*In the Press.*)

Manual of Family Devotions, arranged
from the Book of Common Prayer.
By the Hon. **Augustus Duncombe**, D.D., Dean of York.
Printed in red and black. Crown 8vo. (*Nearly ready.*)

Sketches of the Rites and Customs of
the Greco-Russian Church.
By **H. C. Romanoff.** With an Introductory Notice by the Author of "The Heir of Redclyffe."
Crown 8vo. (*Nearly ready.*)

London, Oxford, and Cambridge

Family Prayers: compiled from various
sources (chiefly from Bishop Hamilton's Manual), and arranged on the Liturgical Principle.
By **Edward Meyrick Goulburn**, D.D., Dean of Norwich.
New Editions. (*In the Press.*)

Poems.
By **Henry Francis Lyte**, M.A., Late Vicar of Lower Brixham, Devon.
New Edition. Small 8vo. (*In the Press.*)

Isocratis Orationes.
With Notes and Introduction by **John Edwin Sandys**, B.A., Fellow and Lecturer of St. John's College, and Lecturer at Jesus College, Cambridge.
Part I. Crown 8vo. (*In the Press.*)

The Life and Times of S. Gregory the
Illuminator, Patron Saint and Founder of the Armenian Church.
By **S. C. Malan**, M.A., Vicar of Broadwindsor.
(*Nearly ready.*)

The Clouds of Aristophanes.
With English Notes by **W. C. Green**, M.A., late Fellow of King's College, Cambridge, Classical Lecturer of Queens' College.
Crown 8vo. 3s. 6d.

London, Oxford, and Cambridge

Liber Precum Publicarum Ecclesiæ

Anglicanæ,
A Gulielmo Bright, A.M., et Petro Goldsmith Medd, A.M., Presbyteris, Collegii Universitatis in Acad. Oxon. Sociis, Latine redditus.

In an elegant pocket volume, with all the Rubrics in red.
New Edition. Small 8vo. (*In the Press.*)

The Greek Testament.

With English Notes, intended for the Upper Forms of Schools, and for Pass-men at the Universities. Abridged from the larger work of the **Dean of Canterbury**.

In one Volume, Crown 8vo. (*In the Press.*)

Eastern Orthodoxy in the Eighteenth

Century; being a Correspondence between the Greek Patriarchs and the Nonjurors.

Edited, with an Introduction, by the Rev. **George Williams**, B.D., Senior Fellow of King's College, Cambridge.

8vo. (*In the Press.*)

Catechetical Notes and Class Questions,

Literal and Mystical; chiefly on the Earlier Books of Holy Scripture.

By the late Rev. **J. M. Neale**, D.D., Warden of Sackville College, East Grinstead.

Crown 8vo. (*In the Press.*)

Stones of the Temple: a familiar

Explanation of the Fabric and Furniture of the Church, with Illustrations, engraved by **O. Jewitt**.

By the Rev. **Walter Field**, M.A., Vicar of Godmersham.

(*In preparation.*)

London, Oxford, and Cambridge

The Voice of the Good Shepherd to His

Lost Sheep; being an Exposition of the former part of the Parable of the Prodigal Son.

By **Robert G. Swayne**, M.A., Rector of St. Edmund's, Salisbury.

Small 8vo. (*In the Press.*)

Selections from Modern French Authors.

With English Notes.

By **Henri Van Laun**, French Master at Cheltenham College.

Part 1.—Honoré de Balzac.
Part 2.—H. Taine.

Crown 8vo. (*In the Press.*)

The Hawaiian Mission.

By the Right Rev. **Thomas N. Staley**, D.D., Missionary Bishop of Honolulu. With Illustrations.

Crown 8vo. (*In the Press.*)

From Morning to Evening:

a Book for Invalids. From the French of M. L'Abbé Henri Perreyve.

Translated and adapted by an Associate of the Sisterhood of S. John Baptist, Clewer.

Small 8vo. (*In the Press.*)

The Virgin's Lamp:

Prayers and Devout Exercises for English Sisters, chiefly composed and selected by the late Rev. **J. M. Neale**, D.D., Founder of St. Margaret's, East Grinstead.

Small 8vo. (*In the Press.*)

A Summary of Theology and Ecclesiastical History:
a Series of Original Works on all the principal subjects of Theology and Ecclesiastical History.
By Various Writers.
In 8 Vols., 8vo. (*In preparation.*)

Counsels upon Holiness of Life.
Translated from the Spanish of "The Sinner's Guide" by **Luis de Granada**; forming the second volume of the "Ascetic Library."
Crown 8vo. (*In the Press.*)

Songs of Joy for the Age of Joy.
By the Rev. John P. Wright, B.A.
18mo. (*In the Press.*)

A Glossary of Ecclesiastical Terms;
containing Explanations of Terms used in Architecture, Ecclesiology, Hymnology, Law, Ritualism, Theology, Heresies, and Miscellaneous Subjects.
By Various Writers. Edited by the Rev. **Orby Shipley**, M.A.
Crown 8vo. (*In preparation.*)

Perranzabuloe, the lost Church found;
or, the Church of England not a new Church, but Ancient, Apostolical, and Independent, and a Protesting Church Nine Hundred Years before the Reformation.
By the Rev. **C. Trelawney Collins**, M.A., Rector of Timsbury, Somerset, and late Fellow of Balliol College.
New Edition. Crown 8vo. (*In preparation.*)

London, Oxford, and Cambridge

NEW PAMPHLETS.

Conference of Bishops of the Anglican Communion,
holden at Lambeth Palace, September 24—27, 1867. I. An Address, delivered at the Opening of the Conference, by Charles Thomas, Lord Archbishop of Canterbury. II. The Resolutions of the Conference. III. Address of the Bishops to the Faithful in Christ Jesus. Published by Authority. 8vo. 1s.

Meeting of Adjourned Conference of Bishops of the
Anglican Communion, holden at Lambeth Palace, December 10, 1867. I. Reports of Committees appointed by the Conference. II. Resolutions of the Adjourned Conference. Published by Authority. 8vo. 1s.

BY THE BISHOP OF OXFORD.

The Resurrections of the Truth. A Sermon
Preached in the Church of S. Mary-the-Virgin, Oxford, on S. Mark's Day, April 25th, 1868, being the day appointed for Laying the First Stone of Keble College. By SAMUEL, Lord Bishop of Oxford. 8vo. 3d.

BY THE BISHOP OF CAPETOWN.

A Statement relating to Facts which have been
misunderstood, and to Questions which have been raised, in connexion with the Consecration, Trial, and Excommunication of the Right Rev. Dr. Colenso. By the Bishop of CAPETOWN, Metropolitan. With an Appendix, relating to the Election of a Bishop, and containing further Replies to the Bishop of S. David's and the Dean of Westminster. *Second Edition.* 8vo. 1s.

Correspondence of the Most Reverend the Lord Arch-
bishop of Canterbury, the Most Reverend the Lord Archbishop of York, the Right Reverend the Lord Bishop of London, with the Bishop of Capetown, concerning the Appointment of an Orthodox Bishop to Natal. 8vo. 1s.

Some Remarks upon the Published Speeches of the
Most Rev. the Lord Archbishop of York and the Very Rev. the Dean of Ripon, delivered in the Convocation of York; also upon a Pamphlet by I. Brunel, Esq., M.A., of Lincoln's Inn, Barrister at Law. By the Bishop of CAPETOWN. 8vo. 1s.

BY ARCHDEACON DENISON.

The Charge of the Archdeacon of Taunton, April 21,
1868. 8vo. 2s.

What is the Government Bill? National Elemen-
tary Education: a Letter to the Right Hon. Gathorne Hardy, M.P., Secretary of State for the Home Department. By GEORGE ANTHONY DENISON, M.A., Archdeacon of Taunton. 8vo. 3d.

New Pamphlets

BY THE REV. H. P. LIDDON.

The Attraction of Jesus Christ Crucified: a Sermon preached in St. Paul's Cathedral, at the Special Evening Service on Good Friday, 1868. By H. P. LIDDON, M.A., Student of Christ Church, and Chaplain to the Lord Bishop of Salisbury. Price 3d., or 2s. 6d. per dozen.

Personal Responsibility for the Gift of Revelation: a Sermon, preached in the Church of St. Mary the Virgin (in the Oxford Lenten Series), on Friday, February 28, 1868. By H. P. LIDDON, M.A., Student of Christ Church, Prebendary of Sarum, and Examining Chaplain to the Lord Bishop of Salisbury. 8vo. 1s.

The Honour of Humanity: a Sermon, preached in the Church of St. Mary the Virgin, Oxford, on the First Sunday in Lent, 1868. By H. P. LIDDON, M.A., Student of Christ Church, Prebendary of Sarum, and Chaplain to the Bishop of Salisbury. 8vo. 1s.

BY THE REV. CANON SEYMOUR.

Diocesan Synods: a Speech delivered in the Jerusalem Chamber, Friday, July 3, 1863; with a Preface on the Present Crisis in the Church. By RICHARD SEYMOUR, M.A., Rector of Kinwarton, Honorary Canon of Worcester, and Proctor for the Clergy of the Diocese of Worcester. *Third Edition.* 8vo. 1s.

BY THE REV. J. R. MAGRATH.

A Plea for the Study of Theology in the University: a Sermon, preached before the University of Oxford on the Second Sunday after the Epiphany, January 19, 1868. By J. R. MAGRATH, M.A., Fellow and Tutor of Queen's College, and Select Preacher. 8vo. 1s.

BY THE REV. A. GARFIT.

The Conscience Clause, and the Extension of Education in the Neglected Districts; practically considered with reference to the present state of the Education Question. By the Rev. ARTHUR GARFIT, M.A. 8vo. 1s.

BY ISAMBARD BRUNEL, ESQ.

Remarks on the Proceedings at Capetown in the matter of the Bishop of Natal. By ISAMBARD BRUNEL, M.A., of Lincoln's Inn, Barrister at Law. *Second Edition.* With Observations upon the Reply of the Lord Bishop of Capetown. 8vo. 1s.

BY CHARLES McCABE, ESQ.

Annual Supplement to the Tithe Commutation Tables payable for the year 1868, according to the average prices of Wheat, Barley, and Oats for the seven preceding years, as published in the "London Gazette" of 7th Jan., 1868. By CHARLES McCABE, Secretary of the University Life Assurance Society. Royal 8vo. 1s.

ON THE IRISH CHURCH QUESTION.

BY THE BISHOP OF OSSORY.

The Case of the Established Church in Ireland. By JAMES THOMAS O'BRIEN, D.D., Bishop of Ossory, Ferns, and Leighlin. *Third Edition.* With Appendix. 8vo.

BY LORD MAYO.

Speech delivered in the House of Commons, 10th March, 1868, upon Mr. Maguire's Motion as to the State of Ireland. By the Earl of MAYO. 8vo. 1s.

BY LORD REDESDALE.

Some of the Arguments by which Mr. Gladstone's Resolutions are Supported Considered. By Lord REDESDALE. 8vo. 6d.

BY JOHN JEBB, D.D.

The Rights of the Irish Branch of the United Church of England and Ireland Considered on Fundamental Principles, Human and Divine. By JOHN JEBB, D.D., Rector of Peterstow, Prebendary and Prælector of Hereford Cathedral, and one of the Proctors for the Clergy of Hereford in the Convocation of Canterbury. 8vo. 1s.

BY THE REV. LORD O'NEILL AND THE REV. DR. LEE.

The Church in Ireland. 1. *The Difficulties of her* Present Position Considered. By the Rev. Lord O'NEILL, of Shane's Castle, formerly Prebendary of S. Michael's, Dublin. II. The Duty of Churchmen in England and Ireland at this Crisis towards Her. By the Rev. ALFRED T. LEE, LL.D., Rector of Ahoghill, and Chaplain to his Excellency the Lord Lieutenant. Two Sermons, lately preached in the Parish Church of Ahoghill, Diocese of Connor. *Second Edition.* 8vo. 6d.

The Irish Difficulty. 1. *The Church Question.* 2. The Land Question. 3. The Education Question. Being a Review of the Debate in the House of Commons on Mr. Maguire's Motion (March 10, 1868). By an OBSERVER. 8vo. 6d.

The Church, the Land, and the Constitution; or, Mr. Gladstone in the newly-reformed Parliament. *Second Edition.* 8vo. 6d.

RIVINGTONS,
London, Oxford, and Cambridge.

CATENA CLASSICORUM,

A SERIES OF CLASSICAL AUTHORS,

EDITED BY MEMBERS OF BOTH UNIVERSITIES UNDER THE DIRECTION OF

THE REV. ARTHUR HOLMES, M.A.

FELLOW AND LECTURER OF CLARE COLLEGE, CAMBRIDGE, LECTURER AND LATE FELLOW OF ST. JOHN'S COLLEGE,

AND

THE REV. CHARLES BIGG, M.A.

LATE SENIOR STUDENT AND TUTOR OF CHRIST CHURCH, OXFORD, SECOND CLASSICAL MASTER OF CHELTENHAM COLLEGE.

The following Parts will be published immediately:—

HOMERI ILIAS,
Edited by S. H. REYNOLDS, M.A. Fellow and Tutor of Brasenose College, Oxford.
[Vol. I. Books I. to XII.

THUCYDIDIS HISTORIA,
Edited by CHARLES BIGG, M.A. late Senior Student and Tutor of Christ Church, Oxford. Second Classical Master of Cheltenham College.
[Vol. I. Books I. and II. with Introductions. Price 7s. 6d.

DEMOSTHENIS ORATIONES PUBLICAE,
Edited by G. H. HESLOP, M.A. late Fellow and Assistant Tutor of Queen's College, Oxford. Head Master of St. Bees.
[Parts I & II. The Olynthiacs and the Philippics. Price 4s. 6d.

ARISTOPHANIS COMOEDIAE,
Edited by W. C. GREEN, M.A. late Fellow of King's College, Cambridge. Classical Lecturer at Queen's College.
[Part II. The Clouds. 3s. 6d.

The following Parts are preparing:—

HERODOTI HISTORIA,
Edited by H. G. WOODS, M.A. Fellow and Tutor of Trinity College, Oxford.

DEMOSTHENIS ORATIONES PRIVATAE,
Edited by ARTHUR HOLMES, M.A. Fellow and Lecturer of Clare College, Cambridge.
[Part I. De Coronâ.

TERENTI COMOEDIAE,
Edited by T. L. PAPILLON, M.A. Fellow and Classical Lecturer of Merton College, Oxford.

ISOCRATIS ORATIONES,
Edited by JOHN EDWIN SANDYS, B.A. Fellow and Lecturer of St. John's College, and Lecturer at Jesus College, Cambridge. [Part I.

HORATI OPERA,
Edited by J. M. MARSHALL, M.A. Fellow and late Lecturer of Brasenose College, Oxford. One of the Masters in Clifton College.

MARTIALIS EPIGRAMMATA,
Edited by GEORGE BUTLER, M.A. Principal of Liverpool College. Late Fellow of Exeter College, Oxford.

The following have been already published:—

SOPHOCLIS TRAGOEDIAE,
Edited by R. C. JEBB, M.A. Fellow and Assistant Tutor of Trinity College, Cambridge.
[Part I. The Electra. Price 3s. 6d.
[Part II. The Ajax. Price 3s. 6d.

ARISTOPHANIS COMOEDIAE,
Edited by W. C. GREEN, M.A. late Fellow of King's College, Cambridge. Classical Lecturer at Queen's College.
[Part I. The Acharnians and the Knights. Price 4s.

JUVENALIS SATIRAE,
Edited by G. A. SIMCOX, M.A. Fellow and Classical Lecturer of Queen's College, Oxford.
[Thirteen Satires. Price 3s. 6d.

Opinions of the Press.

Mr. Jebb's "Electra" of Sophocles.

"'The Electra' is all that could be wished, and a better help could not well be found for those who wish to re-commence an acquaintance with almost forgotten Greek authors."—*Clerical Journal, April 18, 1867.*

"Of Mr. Jebb's scholarly edition of the 'Electra' of Sophocles we cannot speak too highly. The whole Play bears evidence of the taste, learning, and fine scholarship of its able editor. Illustrations drawn from the literature of the Continent as well as of England, and the researches of the highest classical authorities are embodied in the notes, which are brief, clear, and always to the point."—*London Review, March 16, 1867.*

"The editorship of the work before us is of a very high order, displaying at once ripe scholarship, sound judgment, and conscientious care. An excellent Introduction gives an account of the various forms assumed in Greek literature by the legend upon which 'The Electra' is founded, and institutes a comparison between it and the 'Choephorae' of Æschylus. The text is mainly that of Dindorf. In the notes, which are admirable in every respect, is to be found exactly what is wanted, and yet they rather suggest and direct further inquiry than supersede exertion on the part of the student."—*Athenæum, March 23, 1867.*

"The Introduction proves that Mr. Jebb is something more than a mere scholar,—a man of real taste and feeling. His criticism upon Schlegel's remarks on the Electra are, we believe, new, and certainly just. As we have often had occasion to say in this Review, it is impossible to pass any reliable criticism upon school-books until they have been tested by experience. The notes, however, in this case appear to be clear and sensible, and direct attention to the points where attention is most needed."
—*Westminster Review, April, 1867.*

"We have no hesitation in saying that in style and manner Mr. Jebb's notes are admirably suited for their purpose. The explanations of grammatical points are singularly lucid, the parallel passages generally well chosen, the translations bright and graceful, the analysis of arguments terse and luminous. There is hardly any obscurity, and nocumbrousness or overloading. We think, too, that Mr. Jebb's plan of furnishing complete analyses of the choric metres is an admirable one for a school edition; and we like his method of giving parenthetically the dates of the less known ancient authors whom he quotes, a method which, suggesting as it must to an intelligent student the existence of a world of literature with which he is very likely to be unfamiliar, will do much to create or stimulate in him the spirit and habits of research. Mr. Jebb has clearly shown that he possesses some of the qualities most essential for a commentator."—*Spectator, July 6, 1867.*

"The notes appear to us exactly suited to assist boys of the Upper Forms at Schools, and University students; they give sufficient help without over-doing explanations. . . . His critical remarks show acute and exact scholarship, and a very useful addition to ordinary notes is the scheme of metres in the choruses."—*Guardian, December 16, 1867.*

"If, as we are fain to believe, the editors of the *Catena Classicorum* have got together such a pick of scholars as have no need to play their best card first, there is a bright promise of success to their series in the first sample of it which has come to hand—Mr. Jebb's *Electra*. We have seen it suggested that it is unsafe to pronounce on the merits of a Greek Play edited for educational purposes until it has been tested in the hands of pupils and tutors. But our examination of the instalment of, we hope, a complete 'Sophocles,' which Mr. Jebb has put forth, has assured us that this is a needless suspension of judgment, and prompted us to commit the justifiable rashness of pronouncing upon its contents, and of asserting after due perusal that it is calculated to be admirably serviceable to every class of scholars and learners. And this assertion is based upon the fact that it is a by no means one-sided edition, and that it looks as with the hundred eyes of Argus, here, there, and everywhere, to keep the reader from straying. In a concise and succinct style of English annotation, forming the best substitute for the time-honoured Latin notes which had so much to do with making good scholars in days of yore, Mr. Jebb keeps a steady eye for all questions of grammar, construction, scholarship, and philology, and handles these as they arise with a helpful and sufficient precision. In matters of grammar and syntax his practice for the most part is to refer his reader to the proper section of Madvig's 'Manual of Greek Syntax:' nor does he ever waste space and time in explaining a construction, unless it be such an one as is not satisfactorily dealt with in the grammars of Madvig or Jelf. Experience as a pupil and a teacher has probably taught him the value of the wholesome task of hunting out a grammar reference for oneself, instead of finding it, handy for slurring over, amidst the hundred and one pieces of information in a voluminous foot-note. But whenever there occurs any peculiarity of construction, which is hard to reconcile to the accepted usage, it is Mr. Jebb's general practice to be ready at hand with manful assistance."
—*Contemporary Review, November, 1867.*

Mr. Jebb's "Ajax" of Sophocles.

"Mr. Jebb has produced a work which will be read with interest and profit by the most advanced scholar, as it contains, in a compact form, not only a careful summary of the labours of preceding editors, but also many acute and ingenious original remarks. We do not know whether the matter or the manner of this excellent commentary is deserving of the higher praise; the skill with which Mr. Jebb has avoided, on the one hand, the wearisome prolixity of the Germans, and on the other the jejune brevity of the Porsonian critics, or the versatility which has enabled him in turn to elucidate the plots, to explain the verbal difficulties, and to illustrate the idioms of his author. All this, by a studious economy of space and a remarkable precision of expression, he has done for the 'Ajax' in a volume of some 200 pages."—*Athenaeum, March 21, 1868.*

"The Introduction furnishes a great deal of information in a compact form, adapted to give the student a fair conception of his author, and to aid him in mastering its difficulties. We have observed how the brief notes really throw light on obscurity, and give sufficient aid without making the study too easy,—a main point to be observed by one who edits a classic author for the benefit of learners and students."—*Clerical Journal, February 13, 1868.*

"Mr. Jebb's Edition of the Ajax in the *Catena Classicorum* ought to assure those who have hitherto doubted that this is a Series to adopt. Like his edition of the 'Electra' this of the 'Ajax' is ably and usefully handled. The Introduction alone would prove the wide reading, clear views, and acute criticism of its writer."—*Churchman, February 20, 1868.*

"A more scholarly and thoroughly practical Edition of a Greek play has rarely issued from the Press. The explanations are both copious and freely given; and we have not met with a single note wherein conciseness appears to have been gained at the expense of clearness of meaning. The 'Ajax,' however, is by no means a difficult play, and we must therefore infer that Mr. Jebb takes a more liberal view than some of his coadjutors of the amount of help which an ordinary student may fairly be supposed to require. . . . . . . Compared with the renderings of most other editions, Mr. Jebb's translations have decidedly the advantage in force and elegance of expression."—*Educational Times, March, 1868.*

Mr. Green's "Acharnians and Knights" of Aristophanes.

"The Editors of this Series have undertaken the task of issuing texts of all the authors commonly read, and illustrating them with an English Commentary, compendious as well as clear. If the future volumes fulfil the promise of the Prospectus as well as those already published, the result will be a very valuable work. The excellence of the print, and the care and pains bestowed upon the general getting up, form a marked contrast to the schoolbooks of our own day. Who does not remember the miserable German editions of classical authors in paper covers, execrably printed on detestable paper, which were thought amply good enough for the schoolboys of the last generation? A greater contrast to these can hardly be imagined than is presented by the *Catena Classicorum*. Nor is the improvement only external: the careful revision of the text, and the notes, not too lengthy and confused, but well and judiciously selected, which are to be found in every page, add considerably to the value of this Edition, which we may safely predict will soon be an established favourite, not only among Schoolmasters, but at the Universities. The volume before us contains the first part of an Edition of Aristophanes, which comprises the Acharnians and the Knights, the one first in order, and the other the most famous of the plays of the great Athenian Satirist."—*Churchman, May 23, 1867.*

"The utmost care has been taken with this Edition of the most sarcastic and clever of the old Greek dramatists, facilitating the means of understanding both the text and intention of that biting sarcasm which will never lose either point or interest, and is as well adapted to the present age as it was to the times when first put forward."—*Bell's Weekly Messenger, June 8, 1867.*

"The advantages conferred on the learner by these compendious aids can only be properly estimated by those who had experience of the mode of study years ago. The translated passages and the notes, while sufficient to assist the willing learner, cannot be regarded in any sense as *a cram*."—*Clerical Journal, June 6, 1867.*

"Mr. Green has discharged his part of the work with uncommon skill and ability. The notes show a thorough study of the two Plays, an independent judgment in the interpretation of the poet, and a wealth of illustration, from which the Editor draws whenever it is necessary."—*Museum, June, 1867.*

"Mr. Green presumes the existence of a fair amount of scholarship in all who read Aristophanes, as a study of his works generally succeeds to some considerable knowledge of the tragic poets. The notes he has appended are therefore brief, perhaps a little too brief. We should say the tendency of most modern editors is rather the other way; but Mr. Green no doubt knows the class for which he writes, and has been careful to supply their wants."—*Spectator, July 27, 1867.*

Mr. Simcox's Juvenal.

"Of Mr. Simcox's 'Juvenal' we can only speak in terms of the highest commendation, as a simple, unpretending work, admirably adapted to the wants of the school-boy or of a college passman. It is clear, concise, and scrupulously honest in shirking no real difficulty. The pointed epigrammatic hits of the satirist are everywhere well brought out, and the notes really are what they profess to be, explanatory in the best sense of the term."—*London Review, September 28, 1867.*

"This is a link in the *Catena Classicorum* to which the attention of our readers has been more than once directed as a good Series of Classical works for School and College purposes. The Introduction is a very comprehensive and able account of Juvenal, his satires, and the manuscripts."—*Athenæum, October 5, 1867.*

"This is a very original and enjoyable Edition of one of our favourite classics."—*Spectator, November 16, 1867.*

"Every class of readers,—those who use Mr. Simcox as their sole interpreter, and those who supplement larger editions by his concise matter,—will alike find interest and careful research in his able preface. This indeed we should call the great feature of his book. The three facts which sum up Juvenal's history so far as we know it are soon despatched; but the internal evidence both as to the dates of his writing and publishing his Satires, and as to his character as a writer, occupy some fifteen or twenty pages, which will repay methodical study."—*Churchman, ... 11, 1867.*

www.ingramcontent.com/pod-product-compliance
Lightning Source LLC
Chambersburg PA
CBHW030315170426
43202CB00009B/1008